The Civilized Wilderness

The Civilized Wilderness

Backgrounds to American Romantic Literature, 1817–1860

Edward Halsey Foster

THE FREE PRESS
A Division of Macmillan Publishing Co., Inc.
NEW YORK

Collier Macmillan Publishers
LONDON

The Free Press
A Division of Macmillan Publishing Co., Inc.
866 Third Avenue, New York, N.Y. 10022

Collier Macmillan Canada, Ltd.

Library of Congress Catalog Card Number: 74-33091

Printed in the United States of America

printing number
1 2 3 4 5 6 7 8 9 10

Library of Congress Cataloging in Publication Data

Foster, Edward Halsey.
    The civilized wilderness.

    Bibliography: p.
    Includes index.
    1. American literature--19th century--History and
criticism. 2. Romanticism. 3. United States--
Civilization--1783-1865. I. Title.
PS217.R6F6   810'.9'14   74-33091
ISBN 0-02-910350-9

For ELAINE

In the old countries, with which fiction has long been conversant, a certain conventional privilege seems to be awarded to the romancer; his work is not put exactly side by side with nature; and he is allowed a license with regard to every-day probability, in view of the improved effects which he is bound to produce thereby. Among ourselves, on the contrary, there is as yet no such Faery Land, so like the real world, that, in a suitable remoteness, one cannot well tell the difference, but with an atmosphere of strange enchantment, beheld through which the inhabitants have a propriety of their own. This atmosphere is what the American romancer needs. In its absence, the beings of imagination are compelled to show themselves in the same category as actually living mortals; a necessity that generally renders the paint and pasteboard of their composition but too painfully discernible.

Nathaniel Hawthorne, "Preface," *The Blithedale Romance* (1852).

Contents

Preface

THIS BOOK sketches out various backgrounds against which we can profitably view American literature of the years 1817–1860—those years which opened with the publication of William Cullen Bryant's "Thanatopsis" and closed with the publication of *The Marble Faun,* the last of Hawthorne's finished novels. There are good reasons for giving this period individual attention. Except for the less well-known poetry of Philip Freneau, "Thanatopsis" was the first really significant poem to come from the new nation —the first poem, that is, which may be considered of more than national interest. James Fenimore Cooper, the first of whose novels appeared three years after Bryant's poem, was the first indisputably major American novelist. At the other end of this time span lies the Civil War, which was followed by a new generation of writers, including Henry James and Mark Twain, whose literary interests were substantially different from those of their earlier compatriot writers. Vernon Parrington once called the years from 1800 to 1860 an age of American Romanticism, and if we do not insist on too strict a definition of "Romanticism," this distinction is a helpful one. In this book, I have concentrated on the last four decades of that period, because, quite simply, they offer the richest materials for literary exploration.

Definitions of "Romanticism" are quicksand in which many good critics have floundered, and it seems unlikely that anyone will ever provide a truly comprehensive definition of the term. There are, however, aspects of Romanticism which can be identified, isolated, and examined independently. In an essay variously entitled "Nature and the National Ego" and "The Romantic Dilemma in American Nationalism and the Concept of Nature," Perry Miller was able to pin down characteristic aspects of Romanticism in America; in particular, he showed that American identity in the Romantic period depended heavily on the American setting—the wilderness, which was popularly associated with virtue and good. "The sublimity of the natural backdrop," wrote Miller, "not only relieved us of having to apologize for a deficiency of picturesque ruins and hoary legends: it demonstrated how the vast reservoirs of our august temple furnish the guarantee that we shall never be contaminated by artificiality."[1] Although I cannot accept everything that Miller said about America in the Romantic period, the influence of his thinking can be traced in every chapter of this book.

Within the years covered by my study, it is possible to distinguish two generations of writers, the second incomparably more significant—at least to students and critics of American literature—than the first. Included in the first generation are James Fenimore Cooper, William Cullen Bryant, and Washington Irving; in the second are Nathaniel Hawthorne, Herman Melville, Edgar Allan Poe, Ralph Waldo Emerson, Henry David Thoreau, and Walt Whitman. Among the less significant writers—less significant to most present-day critics and readers, but of considerable interest 125 years ago—are William Gilmore Simms, John Pendleton Kennedy, Robert Montgomery Bird, Catharine Maria Sedgwick, Harriet Beecher Stowe, Oliver Wendell Holmes, Henry Wadsworth Longfellow, John Greenleaf Whittier, James Russell Lowell, and Margaret Fuller. Indeed the years 1817–1860 mark out, as clearly as such distinctions ever do, the first major phase of the literature of the United States.

The primary subject of this book, however, is not the literature itself but rather various ways in which it was shaped by and therefore reflected certain extraliterary interests. This book is concerned with, among other things, the significance to Romantic American literature of popularly apprehended symbols, beliefs, and ideas. The first section of the book is concerned with popular attitudes towards landscape and the aesthetic and moral values which wilderness landscapes in particular were supposed to have, and with the use of these values and attitudes in literature. The second section outlines the American Romantic desire to blend, or resolve the tensions between nature and civilization; to create, that is, a "civilized wilderness"—an objective which was partially attained in Thoreau's *Walden*, on the one hand, and in what was considered the ideal home in its ideal, natural setting, on the other hand. The final section of the book is concerned principally with reactions against this ideal world, this "civilized wilderness" which Americans, at least middle-class Americans, created for themselves.

I have dealt selectively, of course, with both the period and its literature and have passed over some works—*Moby-Dick* being the major one—which have been studied elsewhere so closely and so well that it would be, I think, presumptuous and certainly not essential to deal with them at length once again. I have also given comparatively little attention to poetry, in part because the period's better work is, by and large, in prose. The primary reason for my emphasis on prose, however, is that relationships between American civilization and American poetry have already been studied effectively and at sufficient length by Roy Harvey Pearce in *The Continuity of American Poetry*. Although the approach to my subject is necessarily selective, I trust that the following chapters suggest at least the nature of that complex cultural matrix out of which the literature of American Romanticism was shaped.

Much good criticism of nineteenth-century American literature has been concerned with understanding literary works within the historical contexts that produced them, for these works, generally speaking, were intently political. Each was—like all works of art—a response to a historical moment. All literature, as Orwell reminded us, is political, but while the literary work survives, its political context and purpose are frequently obscured. Salvaging that purpose and that context, or at least as much as can be salvaged, is where literary interpretation begins.

Edward Halsey Foster

New York City and
Cummington, Massachusetts

Note

1. Perry Miller, "The Romantic Dilemma in American Nationalism and the Concept of Nature," in *Nature's Nation* (Cambridge, Mass.: Harvard University Press, 1967), p. 203. The same essay, but under the title "Nature and the National Ego," is available in Miller's *Errand into the Wilderness* (Cambridge, Mass.: Harvard University Press, 1956), reprinted as a Harper Torchbook (New York: 1964). The essay was earlier printed in the *Harvard Theological Review*, XLVIII (1955), 239–253.

Acknowledgments

THOSE who are acquainted with the writings of Perry Miller and his successors, Henry Nash Smith, Leo Marx, and Charles Sanford, among others, will recognize how deeply I am indebted to their writings. I am more particularly indebted to Quentin Anderson, not only for the model established by his writings, but also for his wise counsel and criticism of my own work.

Russel Nye read the entire manuscript and provided extensive and valuable criticism from which this book has greatly benefited. I am very deeply indebted to his thoughtful and judicious comments on my work. My colleague Robert Packard not only read much of the manuscript and offered important suggestions but also, while I was writing about the Hawthorne-Melville friendship, loaned me his material on the subject. Sylvia Crane read the pages on *The Marble Faun* and Hawthorne in Rome, and her encouragement and comments are sincerely appreciated. My students in American literature and American studies have contributed to this book more than they may realize, for year after year their questions have forced me to refine my conclusions about American attitudes toward wilderness and civilization. Although it should be obvious, let me add that I alone am responsible for any errors of judgment or fact.

David Goff, Ann White, Sally Packard, Thomas B. Gentry, Gilbert A. Ball, Jan Blair, Walter Creese, Mara Lusis, and Wanda Gifford are among those who provided necessary information and advice. I owe particular thanks to Violet Durgin, Rowena Le-Beau, and Lee Snook of the interlibrary loan department of Forbes Library in Northampton, Mass.; they were able to locate all the obscure and forgotten nineteenth-century books which I requested.

My research on the Stevens family and the Elysian Fields was encouraged by a grant from the New Jersey Historical Commission.

Both my mother, Edith Foster, and my mother-in-law, Elaine Dunphy, worked hard at eliminating misspellings and bad grammar in the manuscript, and Katherine and John, just by being themselves, made it all worthwhile.

Introduction

PARTS of this book were written across the Hudson from New York in Hoboken, N. J., a city justly famed today for urban blight, but once known, oddly enough, as one of the most romantic spots in America. In 1831, the fastidious Frances Trollope came to Hoboken and discovered not docks, tenements, factories, and slums, but, of all unlikely things, "a broad belt of light underwood and flowering shrubs, studded at intervals with lofty forest trees," and she listened as "the gentle waves" broke on the Hudson's "pebbly shore" and ". . . made a music which [mimicked] softly the loud chorus of the ocean."[1] She had discovered Hoboken's River Walk and Elysian Fields, which included what were then some of America's most highly praised landscapes.

Before the Civil War, the then rural village of Hoboken served New Yorkers in much the way Central Park does today. Those who consider the word "Hoboken" faintly obscene need the reminder that this place was once considered delightfully bucolic, the ideal setting for an afternoon's outing. William Cullen Bryant and the Knickerbocker poet Robert Sands had country homes here, and artists of the Hudson River School, including Jasper Cropsey and Robert Weir, used the landscapes of Hoboken in countless paintings. That part of the town known as the Elysian Fields enjoyed such considerable renown that Samuel Lorenzo Knapp in his *Picturesque Beauties of the Hudson* (1835–1836) noted that "some days there are not less than twenty thousand visiters on the grounds, from lisping infancy to decrepitude, all in search of health and pleasure."[2] Sands, commenting on the Elysian Fields, said, "its grove is worthy of being painted by Claude Lorraine [sic],"[3] and Bryant claimed that the route north from Hoboken to Weehawken provided "one of the most beautiful walks in the world."[4] (That walk, by the way, would now take one to the site of docks, factories, and an entrance to the Lincoln Tunnel.) Visitors to Hoboken and the Elysian Fields could also obtain a glimpse of one of the country's most famous homes, Stevens Castle, the property of the family who not only owned the pleasure grounds but also thoughtfully and profitably provided transportation to them.

Hoboken was in large part the property of the Stevens family, the founder of which, John Stevens (1749–1838), wished to develop the land profitably. Even after he had established a ferry service linking Hoboken with New York, however, he found that few people were willing to move permanently across the river. It must have seemed as if the Hudson, flowing between the two communities, would always frustrate Stevens's plans. But then he discovered that while few New Yorkers were willing to make his town their permanent home, many were eager to travel there for outings, and so, together with his sons, Stevens, ever the entrepreneur, improved his landscaped grounds, cut paths through the woods, and established businesses to cater to visitors.*

Most visitors to Stevens's public grounds were as delighted as Mrs. Trollope, but there were occasional complaints. The diarist George Templeton Strong, always the haughty aristocrat, was dismayed to find that people whom he considered social riffraff frequented Stevens's grounds, and Lydia Maria Child wrote discouragingly, "alas, the city intrudes her vices into this beautiful sanctuary of nature. There stands a public house, with its bar room, and bowling alley, a place of resort for the idle and profligate; kept within the bounds of decorum, however, by the constant presence of respectable visitors."[5] What Mrs. Child appar-

---

* Stevens later proposed that the city of New York buy his pleasure grounds and maintain them as a public park. That, of course, would have saved him the cost and trouble of upkeep, but the city fathers wisely declined his offer. A few decades later the city initiated the construction of the much more conveniently situated Central Park.

ently failed to realize was that Hoboken's romantic acres were operated for profit, and the public house was very profitable indeed. To this rural domain, Stevens, his family, and others contributed a primitive kind of ferris wheel, a merry-go-round, a race track, various taverns, and several other features, including America's first railroad, which traveled round and round a 640-foot circle. In Hoboken, Romanticism, or at least the cult of nature, was a business. Technology and romantic landscapes worked together to enrich Hoboken's entrepreneurs. Ultimately, however, New Yorkers became interested, as John Stevens had hoped, in living in Hoboken, and rural landscapes proved less profitable than real estate development. A gridiron plan was imposed on the woods and fields, and the Hudson's "pebbly shore" vanished, replaced by an almost unbroken line of docks. In the 1860s, the historian Benson J. Lossing wrote that he remembered the Elysian Fields "as a delightful retreat at 'high noon,' or by moonlight, for those who loved Nature in her quiet and simple forms." But rural beauty had fled. "All is now changed; the trips of Charon to the Elysian Fields are suspended, and the grounds, stripped of many of the noble trees, have become 'private,' and subjected to the manipulations of the 'real estate agent.'"[6]

It is in general fair to say that American Romanticism existed as long as someone profited from it financially—and it was increasingly and substantially less profitable after the Civil War taught Americans to be more concerned with actualities than with the idealities of Romanticism. Romanticism survived as long as it helped the publisher, art dealer, housebuilder—or, for that matter, the landowner like John Stevens—turn a profit. These people were businessmen and to get their profits, they, of course, had to provide their customers with what the customers wanted. One wonders what Melville, say, could have written, and how well he would have written it, if he had never had to concern himself with the interests and demands of his publishers and his readers. In fact, his books and the books of those major American writers who were his contemporaries, are in a measure, as the following chapters suggest, dialogues with a specific audience. "What I feel most moved to write," said Melville, "that is banned, —it will not pay. Yet, altogether, write the *other* way I cannot. So the product is a final hash, and all my books are botches." The author simply *had* to attend (in some way, at some level) to the interests of publisher and prospective reader. Otherwise, he spoke to a void: "Though I wrote the Gospels in this century," wrote Melville, "I should die in the gutter."[7] Surely the businessmen and the customers were, and of course still are, of such massive importance to literature that until we understand them, their prejudices and points of view, we will never know why the literature of American Romanticism took the directions it did.

Notes

1. Frances Trollope, *Domestic Manners of the Americans,* Donald Smalley, ed. (New York: Vintage Books, 1960), p. 343. In many instances, I have cited in the footnotes modern editions of nineteenth-century texts. Although this practice is not common, it should obviously benefit those readers—and I assume they are a majority—who do not have easy access to large libraries and rare book collections.

2. Samuel Lorenzo Knapp, *Picturesque Beauties of the Hudson River and Its Vicinity* (New York: J. Disturnell, 1835), p. 21.

3. Robert C. Sands, "Hoboken," *The New-York Mirror,* X (1832), 1.

4. William Cullen Bryant, ed., *The American Landscape* (New York: Elam Bliss, 1830), p. 7.

5. Lydia Maria Child, *Letters from New York* (New York: C. S. Francis & Co., 1845), p. 28.

6. Benson J. Lossing, *The Hudson, from the Wilderness to the Sea* (Troy, N.Y.: H. B. Nims & Co., 1866), p. 449.

7. Julian Hawthorne, *Nathaniel Hawthorne and His Wife* (Boston: James R. Osgood and Company, 1884), vol. I, pp. 402, 403.

part one

The Wilderness

The Importance of the Wilderness
in Romantic American Literature

Chapter One

The Greatest Traveling Nation in the World

[The Hudson] . . . *is the greatest thoroughfare of the Union. Its scenery throughout is magnificent, and in this particular region [the Highlands] sublime. Health and happiness dwell among its hills, and every luxury that the earth can yield is wafted by its waters. It is within a few hours' journey to New York, and the facilities of access are unexampled in convenience, economy, and opportunity. The day is not distant, when the entire banks of the Hudson will be dotted with villas of the refined and elegant.* . . .

Freeman Hunt, *Letters about the Hudson River* (1836).[1]

DeWitt Clinton, speaking before the American Academy of the Fine Arts in October 1816, claimed that in this country "Nature has conducted her operations on a magnificent scale. . . ." "The imagination of the artist," he said, "must derive its power and receive its complexion [sic] from the country in which he was born, and in which he resides," and therefore, Americans, surrounded by "wild, romantic, and awful scenery," might create works of an imaginative power that could not be expected from artists bred in more cultivated, civilized landscapes.[2]

Clinton's remarks are of special interest since the group which he was addressing, and of which he was president, was generally unsympathetic to the development of a truly native American art. The American Academy, founded and maintained by members of New York's aristocracy, promoted an American art based on classical precedent, and while it is true that much of Clinton's address was spent summarizing the achievements of classical art, the remarks quoted above suggested the possibility of an American art owing more to native landscape than to the heritage of Greece and Rome.

One could hardly have found a person more appropriate than Clinton to speak of a truly American art, for although he could not have been aware of the fact, it was to be he—through, oddly enough, his Erie Canal—who would make possible the popular reception and consequent growth of the Hudson River School, devoted to portraying American, not foreign, landscapes. The Erie Canal, which owed its existence to Clinton and his political influence, initiated the transformation of New York from a place which was the property and rule of old colonial and Federalist families into that diversified and complex city which we know today. Quite literally, the Erie made New York the economic gateway to the West, but what is of greater interest to us here is that the canal, by improving westward transportation, made accessible to travelers much of the American landscape which had previously been known to few except settlers and pioneers. Before the Erie was completed, a journey from Albany to Niagara could take as long as six weeks—and in conveyances far from elegant. Even a journey up the Hudson, provided with steamboats, took twenty-four hours. But the Erie changed all this; as soon as the canal route was established as the official way west, entrepeneurs searched for improved means of transportation. Finally New York and the Great Lakes were connected by the railroad, and by 1864 Henry T. Tuckerman was able to report in *America and Her Commentators* that the traveler could leave "New York in the morning, to sleep at night under the roar of Niagara."[3] The transformation brought about by Clinton's Erie Canal had an effect on more than the nation's economy; Americans could now easily embark on an exploration of their country's landscapes. Correspondingly, there followed a substantial public interest in paintings which portrayed the landscapes up the Hudson and along the route of the canal. It is not entirely a coincidence that the Hudson River School—devoted to portraying that "wild, romantic, and awful scenery" which the travelers discovered—can be dated from 1825, the same year that the Erie was completed.

American landscapes, especially those of the Hudson River and Niagara Falls, had been subjects for artists long before 1825, but there was a considerable difference between what those earlier artists and their later compatriots were trying to accomplish. Early American landscape paintings, as James Thomas Flexner reminds us in *That Wilder Image,* were often "topographical," where "the fundamental objective was the literal representation of the maximum amount of detail."[4] Furthermore, these earlier artists, or at least the better educated among them, often adapted the scenery they saw to patterns and colors found in the paintings of such European landscapists as Salvator Rosa and Claude Lorrain. It was with reason that the writer John Neal in 1829 attacked American paintings as minor and derivative. Referring to an exhibition in which paintings by the European masters had been hung near paintings by Americans, Neal wrote, "Do you remember the Ruysdael, just over the head of the stair-case, the leafing of which, and the very tone have passed over into a couple of [Thomas] Doughty's on the side of the hall?" Americans' chauvinistic acceptance of their country's landscapists was plain: "Did you see anybody stop to look at this picture [Ruysdael's], where you saw a thousand gathered before Doughty's or [Alvan] Fisher's?"[5]

By 1829, however, America already had in the person of Thomas Cole an artist far superior to either Doughty or Fisher. Cole, like his American predecessors, at times applied the formulas of European landscapists to his paintings, and yet whatever these paintings owe to European influence, they are specifically and undeniably American. Samuel F. B. Morse's "View from Apple Hill" (1829) is an example of an American painting so thoroughly under European influence that one well might wonder if the scene portrayed were in Italy rather than, as the artist claimed, in the vicinity of Cooperstown, N.Y. On the other hand, Cole's "The Clove, Catskills," painted in 1827, offers a landscape immediately recognizable as one this side of the Atlantic. Cole could transfer to canvas the coloring and outlines of American scenery better than any of his predecessors could.

Cole, who was born in England and lived there until 1818 when he was seventeen, spent the years from 1829 until 1832 and again from 1841 until 1842 in England and on the Continent, and the results of these trips were not only paintings of specifically European scenery but also narrative paintings such as "The Past" and "The Present" which in both theme and treatment owe little to American materials. Cole, English by birth and American by adoption, owed allegiance to both sides of the Atlantic.

Early in 1825 Cole moved to New York from Philadelphia, where he had studied at the Pennsylvania Academy of Fine Arts, and that summer he took a tour up the Hudson and through the Catskills. The products of this tour were three landscape paintings which were sold to, respectively, Colonel John Trumbull, William Dunlap, and Asher B. Durand—three of the most influencial figures in American art at the time. As Dunlap later reported, "From that time forward, Mr. Cole," who previously had been almost unknown as an artist, "received commissions to paint landscapes from all quarters; was enabled to increase his prices and his facility of handling, as well as his truth of drawing and power of colouring."[6]

NEW YORK, in the years following 1825, rapidly became the nation's largest metropolis—by 1860 the city had over a million inhabitants—and fittingly, it was from New York, north to Albany and westward to Niagara, that the first national school of landscape painting grew. American landscapes had long been acclaimed by Americans, especially American writers and artists, but never to such a degree as during the years after 1825. With the completion of Clinton's project, the Hudson River–Erie Canal route became the nation's major thoroughfare, attracting artists, writers, and travelers inland to discover for themselves the sublimity of the American landscape. The Erie, wrote Henry T. Tuckerman,

> . . . was the foundation of all that makes the city and state of
> New York preëminent; and when, a few years since, a thousand
> American citizens sailed up the Mississippi to commemorate its
> alliance with the Atlantic, the ease and rapidity of the transit,
> and the spectacle of virgin civilization thus created, were but a
> new act in the grand drama of national development, whose

opening scene occurred twenty-seven years before, when the waters of Lake Erie blended with those of the Hudson.[7]

AMERICAN ARTISTS AND WRITERS who chose landscapes located along the Hudson–Erie route as subjects and settings for their work could depend on a sympathetic response from much of their American audience. During the three and a half decades before the Civil War, Clinton's westward route became, not surprisingly, the route most traveled by Americans in search of landscapes, specifically those natural landscapes untouched by civilization. In an era in which transportation was highly limited, the Hudson–Erie route was simply better equipped to carry large numbers of travelers from one destination to another, and Pine Orchard, the great Catskill resort hotel, as well as Trenton Falls and other resorts of once substantial renown owed much of their popularity to Clinton's achievement. But it is safe to assume that even if the Erie had not been built, and even if the Hudson had not become part of *the* major national thoroughfare, Americans would have developed resorts like Trenton Falls, far from cities and urban life. Clinton's act determined that the future of the country rested with the Hudson—rather than, let us say, with the Susquehanna or the Rappahannock—but this does not explain the most significant difference between travel in America and travel in Europe. After all, on the other side of the Atlantic, a nineteenth-century tourist might have defined his travels as much by visits to Paris, Florence, and Rome as by visits to the Alps or journeys down the Rhine. It is true that American cities, especially Washington and New York, were as amply supplied with tourists as one could reasonably expect, but the fact is that the most popular routes of travel led away from these cities, not to them. And the most popular route of travel, along the Hudson and the Erie, took one through what was as yet very much unsettled countryside and ended at what Cole titled "that wonder of the world," Niagara Falls.[8] Evidently enough, the objectives of European and American travel could be very different things. Nor should this surprise us: compared with the great metropolitan centers of Europe, American cities were insignificant indeed. New York could not begin to offer the traveler the wealth of culture and tradition found in London or

Rome, and yet, on the other hand, the American wilderness offered the traveler certain things which even Europe could not match.

Among the Southern landscapes most visited by American tourists were the Natural Bridge and Harper's Ferry in Virginia. Harper's Ferry was well known to tourists long before its association with John Brown.* Among the landscapes offered by the Middle Atlantic states were the Susquehanna River and the valley of the Wyoming, the Delaware Water Gap and Passaic Falls. Farther north, in New England, the sites explored by tourists included the White Mountains, the Berkshire Hills, the Connecticut River Valley, and the coastal area in and around Newport, R.I. Most important of all, the Hudson–Erie route made accessible such relatively primitive landscapes as Lake George and the Catskill Mountains, the valley of the Mohawk River, the Finger Lakes region and the falls of the Genesee, and the visitor to the sublime majesty of Niagara might also stop to view the picturesque beauties of Trenton Falls. Those who went to "take the waters" might also explore the scenic walks and drives around Lebanon, Ballston Spa, and Saratoga Springs, three of New York State's most popular health resorts.

Although, in general, the traveler sought primitive landscapes, not cities, he was virtually always assured of comfortable hotel accommodations at his destinations. Searching through the East, and particularly the state of New York, for wilderness landscapes had advantages over tours of the prairies and the far West in that one seldom needed to fear being ill-accommodated,

---

* One of the earliest and most enthusiastic visitors to the Natural Bridge and Harper's Ferry was Thomas Jefferson. In 1774, Jefferson became in fact the owner of the Natural Bridge, which he called in 1781–1782 "the most sublime of Nature's works." "It is impossible for the emotions arising from the sublime, to be felt beyond what they are here: so beautiful an arch, so elevated, so light, and springing, as it were, up to Heaven, the rapture of the Spectator is really indiscribable!" Jefferson also noted that "the passage of the Patowmac [sic] through the Blue ridge [where Harper's Ferry is now located] is perhaps one of the most stupendous scenes in nature." "This scene," wrote Jefferson, "is worth a voyage across the Atlantic." [Thomas Jefferson, *Notes on Virginia* (Boston: Lilly and Wait, 1832), pp. 21, 22, 17, 18.]

overtaxing one's health, or violating one's standards of decorum —serious matters indeed for the professed gentleman or lady. The average traveler in mid-nineteenth-century America was no pioneer; rather he, like one of the characters in James Fenimore Cooper's *Home as Found,* looked forward to leaving the city or town "in order to breathe the pure air, and enjoy the tranquil pleasures of the country."[9]

Traveling through the American countryside—at least the easily accessible countryside—had become so popular by 1850 that the essayist Henry T. Tuckerman wrote that "our times might not inaptly be designated as the age of travelling."[10] Some years before, in 1834, Theodore Dwight, member of a family much given to publishing reports of their back-country tours, remarked that he was "a traveller, periodically, like all my countrymen." America, he said, was "the greatest travelling nation in the world."[11] Yet on the other hand, Mrs. E. F. Ellet— a nineteenth-century authority on who, socially, was who—complained that "this land abounds with scenes of beauty, which have seldom been noticed by tourists,"[12] and Dwight called attention to the fact that "the rapidity of our steamboats and railroad cars deprive us of a great many interesting sights and agreeable reflections. . . ."[13] Furthermore, Washington Irving argued that "we have some main routes for the fashionable traveller, along which he is hurried in steamboats and railroad cars; while on every side extend regions of beauty, about which he hears and knows nothing."[14] Freeman Hunt, whose *Letters about the Hudson River* was published in 1836, claimed, "I have passed up and down [the Hudson] a hundred times; I have repeatedly wandered along its shores for miles, and every time I find some new prospect to admire, or some new incident to interest."[15] But Hunt was certainly an exception; fashionable travelers—and they were the majority—preferred the recommended routes of travel and the landscapes which could be seen from the decks of a steamboat or from the verandas of a hotel. In short, while it is in one sense true that the traveling American was attracted to the primitive and the wild, it is also true that he brought with him much of the baggage of civilization.

On the surface, then, it would seem that there was a world of difference between the interests of the nineteenth-century American traveler and the concerns of, for example, Cole's landscape paintings and Cooper's Leather-Stocking Tales, and yet there are a considerable number of similarities which are far more than incidental. As we will discover, travelers sought in their native landscapes essentially the same interpretations as those offered by Cole in his paintings and Cooper in his fiction.

JOEL TYLER HEADLEY, minister and historian, explored the wilderness regions of the Adirondack Mountains in New York State and described the area extensively in *The Adirondack, or Life in the Woods* (1849), but as Roland Van Zandt, the historian of *The Catskill Mountain House,* has written, "As late as 1850 when hundreds of visitors were frequenting the area of the Mountain House during the summer months, the Adirondacks were known only to a few lumbermen, hunters or trappers."[16] Headley explicitly wished to avoid civilization and all the formal rules of nineteenth-century social life.[17] But his choice was an unusual one; most travelers liked the social atmosphere of traveling, and besides, the Catskills were provided with conveniences simply not available in the more primitive Adirondacks. The Catskills had steamboat service and, in the later years of the Romantic period, train service as well as truly gigantic resort hotels. Thoreau could explore the Maine woods, but for every person who undertook a journey like his, there were thousands who contented themselves with the better-known, and fashionable, routes of travel. Such volumes as Washington Irving's *A Tour on the Prairies* (1835) and Francis Parkman's *The Oregon Trail* (1847) described scenery which few Americans saw until the transcontinental railroad was completed in 1869; most Americans, after all, lived east of the Mississippi and so, necessarily, confined their travels to the eastern half of the continent. A book about the Rockies dealt with a subject virtually as exotic as the Tropics; the "American scenery" which Americans knew first hand was, in general, in the East.

The American traveler's concentration on Eastern scenery is acutely evident in the writings of Nathaniel Parker Willis, who sought to popularize the Hudson-Erie route. A man of good social credentials, Willis was, as his biographer Henry Beers notes, at mid-point in his career, "beyond a doubt, the most successful magazinist that America had yet seen."[18] It is true that nineteenth-century America was occasionally shocked by rumors of Willis's alleged extramarital affairs, but such rumors did little to hurt the sales of his books, for they remained among the most widely read of the day, and his magazine columns, many of which dealt with his travels, had large audiences.

To be sure, Willis was not the sort of man to join Thoreau in an exploration of the Maine woods. Willis had a decided preference for steamboats and trains, and the hotels in which he stayed were generally the very best. He did record that once in an attempt to explore some relatively inaccessible countryside around the Hudson, he had "seen the world from the seat of a farmer's wagon, for two or three weeks," but episodes like this were very much exceptions, and they seldom, if ever, occurred when more comfortable transportation was available.[19] A ride through the backwoods of Kentucky was "interesting," he said, ". . . for one never tires of the primitive with its fragmented sublimities and splendid accidents of beauty," but "the site of the more civilized looking fence, which betokened an approach to the place of our destination, was a considerable relief."[20] Like his fellow travelers, Willis was no pioneer, and he was most comfortable with scenery located near the amenities of civilized life.

American Scenery (1840), lavishly illustrated by the English artist William Henry Bartlett, is now perhaps the best known of Willis's travel books. Probably the book is better known today for Bartlett's illustrations than for Willis's text, yet the text is still worth examining as an index to what Willis and his countless readers thought worth special attention in a discussion of American scenery. The book's format involves a Bartlett illustration for each of Willis's chapters, and of the various landscapes illustrated and described, nearly all are in the Northeast—and furthermore, with few exceptions they are landscapes which were well known to travelers of Willis's day. None of the 119 illustrated landscapes were located in the West, and there were none south of the Old Dominion. Virginia did receive at least passing attention: two of the illustrations showed Harper's Ferry, two showed Mount Vernon—if for present purposes we may call them "landscapes"—and there was one each of the Valley of the Shenandoah and the Natural Bridge. At the same time, though the West was entirely ignored and the South given only nominal attention, there were no fewer than twenty-six engravings of the Hudson River and its vicinity, thirty-two if the engravings of the Catskills are included. There were six engravings of Lake George—as many as there were of the entire South—and others portrayed scenes on or near the Erie Canal. Two engravings pictured scenes at Trenton Falls, three at Saratoga, and fourteen at Niagara Falls and its environs. By the 1830s, when Bartlett made his illustrations and Willis wrote his text, the Hudson–Erie route had achieved a central importance for Americans, and the concentration of *American Scenery* on the landscapes along that route would not have seemed as surprising then as it may seem to some people today. Willis, in other books, described scenery that had not yet become "fashionable," but he always returned to the Hudson, the Catskills, Trenton Falls, and the New York resorts with particular interest.

Southern and Western landscapes had more adherents than Willis's very cursory treatment suggests. Fourteen years after his book was published, T. Addison Richards, an artist and writer from Charleston, published a volume also entitled *American Scenery*, in which the Hudson-Erie route received the cursory treatment, but Richards' text was poor, and his illustrations few. Charles A. Dana's *The United States Illustrated* appeared shortly after Richards' book. The second of its two volumes dealt with "The West; or, The States of the Mississippi Valley, and the Pacific," but Dana's book, like Willis's, demonstrated a decided lack of interest in scenery south of the Potomac—there were only two illustrations of this section of the country—and if *The United States Illustrated* did provide a full volume on the West, purchasers of the work were informed in a prefatory note that purchase of the first volume did not necessarily entail purchase of the second. Finally, the illustrations in Dana's book were very poor, considerably inferior to those in Willis's. In fact, although most of the illustrations in the first volume carry the legend "Drawn after nature for the Proprietor: Herrmann J. Meyer," many are nothing more than rather crude copies of the engravings for Willis's *American Scenery*. It was to be many years before any book on American scenery would give as adequate attention to the South and the West as Willis and Bartlett gave to the Northeast.

Before the Civil War, other illustrated landscape books— William Cullen Bryant's *The American Landscape* (1830) and the anonymously edited *Home Book of the Picturesque* (1852), among others—also emphasized the Northeast. Not until the two volumes of William Cullen Bryant's *Picturesque America* appeared in the 1870s did Willis's *American Scenery* have a serious competitor among books concerned with this country's landscapes. Although there were illustrators working in the South and West long before the Civil War began, their work never appeared in any book as professionally organized as Willis's, and the two books—Dana's and Richards'—which might have offered Willis's *American Scenery* serious competition did not provide their purchasers with illustrations that equaled Bartlett's in number, originality, or quality. Only Bryant's *Picturesque America,* which covered South, East, and West—and not in separate volumes—really gave a satisfactory demonstration of how limited was the sense of American scenery outlined by Willis and his compatriot travelers. It must be remembered, however, that by the 1870s the transcontinental railroad had been completed, and it was far more possible for the adventurous traveler to discover the number and variety of American landscapes than it had been forty years before.

THE NINETEENTH-CENTURY AMERICAN TRAVELER classified the scenery of his country according to aesthetic categories derived from the writings of various eighteenth- and early nineteenth-century British and continental theorists. The three categories most frequently encountered in nineteenth-century descriptions of American scenery are the beautiful, the picturesque, and the sublime. None of the three readily lends itself to a precise definition, for, often enough, different writers meant very different things by these categories. (The Englishmen Uvedale Price and Richard Payne Knight, for example, carried on an extensive debate over the meaning of "picturesque."[21]) Nonetheless, it is possible to develop at least a general sense of what Americans meant when they used the terms "beautiful," "picturesque," and "sublime." The very fact that most American writers did not feel called upon to append definitions of these terms when they were used suggests that there was some common agreement over their meanings.

"Beautiful" was often used by nineteenth-century American travelers and writers to describe pastoral landscapes—low rolling hills, smooth plains, and so forth—while "picturesque" was used for landscapes which were varied, rough, rocky, irregular in outline. However, some American theorists such as the landscape gardener Andrew Jackson Downing gave these categories more than a pictorial significance; to state it briefly, Downing believed that the beautiful suggested tranquillity and the picturesque suggested power.[22] We are at times confronted, therefore, with the problem, when dealing with a nineteenth-century American text, of determining whether the writer was using "beautiful" or "picturesque" solely to describe pictorial qualities —or whether, as in Downing's writings, he wished to say much more.

The problem of determining whether more than a pictorial significance is implied is also encountered in dealing with the word "sublime." On the one hand, the sublime could be employed in the essentially pictorial sense used by Uvedale Price. If a picturesque scene is expanded in scale, "so that the whole may impress an idea of awe and grandeur," that scene, wrote Price, becomes sublime.[23] The difference between the picturesque and the sublime was basically then a matter of scale, and this particular use of the term—a largely descriptive use—is to be found in countless nineteenth-century discussions of Niagara Falls, the Natural Bridge, and the Rocky Mountains. In his "Essay on American Scenery," however, Thomas Cole implied a much larger definition in his use of "sublime." In his discussion of Niagara Falls in that essay, he was speaking of much more than size, "awe," and "grandeur," when he referred to "sublimity." He wrote:

> In gazing on [Niagara Falls], we feel as though a great void had been filled in our minds—our conceptions expand—we become a part of what we behold! At our feet the floods of a thousand rivers are poured out—the contents of vast inland seas. In its volume we conceive immensity; in its course, everlasting duration;

in its impetuosity, uncontrollable power. These are the elements
of its sublimity.[24]

Space, time, and dynamics, as Paul Weiss has written, are "the
essential dimensions of existence," those things which limit and
define man's place in the universe.[25] In the sublime experience
described by Cole, however, the viewer of Niagara is able to
transcend these limitations and "become a part of what" he be-
holds: "immensity," "everlasting duration," and "uncontrollable
power." The sublime here involves a transcendental union of
temporal man with the eternal. Little wonder that Cole was
horrified by the "civilized" destruction of wilderness landscapes,
for as he wrote, "Amid them the consequent associations are of
God the creator—they are his undefiled works, and the mind is
cast into the contemplation of eternal things," and he also noted
that ". . . with the improvements of cultivation the sublimity of
the wilderness [will] pass away."[26]

As with "picturesque" and "beautiful," it is impossible to advance any single definition of "sublime" which holds true
throughout the literature of the period. The text in which the
word is found may prove the best guide for ascertaining just
what a writer meant when he called, for example, the falls of
Niagara "sublime." There are, however, numerous instances in
which it is impossible to determine just what meaning the writer
intended to convey. Even literary archeology, alas, has its limits.

GEORGE WILLIAM CURTIS, a thoroughly experienced traveler,
was one of the harshest mid-nineteenth-century critics of American scenery. His *Nile Notes of a Howadji* (1851) and *The
Howadji in Syria* (1852) concern travel on the other side of the
Atlantic. *Lotus-Eating* (1852), a book that is far from being as
exotic as its title, recounts his experiences along the fashionable
routes of American travel. His subjects include the Hudson, the
Catskills, Trenton Falls, Niagara, Saratoga, Lake George, Na-
hant, and Newport. Although these locations were among those
most frequently praised by tourists, Curtis was pleased by little
of the scenery he encountered, and he concluded that "One
would be loth to exhort a European to visit America for other
reasons than social and political observation, or buffalo hunt-

ing." Unlike Cole, he did not seek out the sublime in wilderness landscapes, was in fact more interested in the picturesque, a term which he employed in its pictorial sense. Furthermore, he thought that "water, woods, and sky" require ". . . the human impress of Art upon them, to satisfy the sense that craves the picturesque." The art of landscape gardening should be employed to improve landscapes when, as he believed was often the case in America, ". . . Nature gives no landscape material, when the forms of hill and shore are monotonous or unimportant of themselves, yet suggest a latent possibility of picturesque effects." "This is not irreverent meddling with Nature," he concluded, "it is only following her lead." Meanwhile, traveling through the unimproved American countryside, he ". . . opened [his] eyes upon the placid picturesqueness of the actual landscape, and anon closed them to behold, instantly, the enchanted scenery of sleep."[27]

If Cole had been living—he died in 1849, three years before *Lotus-Eating* was published—he might have argued with Curtis that American scenery, if subjected to art, would lose much of its sublimity. However, there was another of Curtis's charges which would have been far more difficult to answer. Imbued with the thinking of various Scottish philosophers who held that objects were interesting because of their associations rather than because of any intrinsic element, Curtis demanded that landscapes, to be interesting, possess associations with literature, legend, or history—and this was indeed a difficult prescription for Americans to fill. For Curtis, the Rhine was a more interesting river than the Hudson simply because the former possessed more of the desired associations. Unlike European landscapes, few of those in America had associations with art, literature, legend, or history, and none possessed even the vestiges of castellated ruins or deserted abbeys. As even Curtis was willing to admit, the Hudson did have associations with works of Washington Irving and with Joseph Rodman Drake's then very popular poem, "The Culprit Fay," and yet the Rhine possessed "genuine delights . . . of romantic association and suggestion . . . which are only possible in an old and storied country."[28] Nor was Curtis alone in noting an American inferiority in this respect. Even Irving had noted in *The Sketch Book* (1819) that while "on no country have the charms of nature been more prodigally lavished" than on America, it was Europe which "held forth the charms of storied and poetical associations."[29] And Mrs. Sarah Josepha Hale, editor and refined poet (author of "Mary Had a Little Lamb"), wrote that although this country offered much to its citizens in the way of tourist delights, ". . . European travellers, accustomed to a land where every place and object has its real or romantic legend, would pronounce a tour of the United States insufferably dull, and its inhabitants destitute of taste."[30] The worship of "storied" Europe, that respect for things European at the expense of things American, finally angered Theodore Dwight so much that he condemned it as "that foreign disease."[31]

Seldom have Americans willingly admitted their inferiority in any respect, and it should hardly surprise us that many felt called on to prove that at least some American landscapes did provide a wealth of associations. Lydia Howard Huntley Sigourney, a phenomenally popular poetess known as the "Sweet Singer of Hartford," reminded her readers that "Though of comparatively recent date, many of [our country's] associations are as lofty and spirit-stirring as those which strike more deeply into the dimness of antiquity."[32] The Knickerbocker poet Robert Sands claimed that in America ". . . the local associations are many, and of deep interest. Some of them, too, are beginning to assume the rust of antiquity."[33] Cole noted that ". . . the great struggle for freedom has sanctified many a spot, and many a mountain, stream, and rock, has its legend, worthy of the poet's pen or the painter's pencil."[34]

Historical novelists, including James Fenimore Cooper, Catharine Maria Sedgwick, William Gilmore Simms, and John Pendleton Kennedy, discovered materials for their works in episodes of the Revolutionary War and in colonial conflicts with the Indians, and these two aspects of American history were firmly associated with various American landscapes. It is often remembered that Hawthorne described his country as one "where there is no shadow, no antiquity, no mystery, no picturesque and gloomy wrong, nor anything but a commonplace prosperity, in broad and simple daylight," and yet of course, that description possessed something less than literal truth as its author's own "May-Pole of Merry Mount" and *The Scarlet Letter* suggest.[35]

There was, however, one difficulty for the observer who wished to find associations with the American landscape: visually, at least, America was very much a country without a past. Excepting a few abandoned forts, there were no vine-clad ruins to remind one of the Revolution, and aside from geographical locations, there were few physical reminders of the Indian wars. The author and editor Lydia Maria Child noted that "an Indian encampment," if not picturesque in itself, might lead one to the discovery of a picturesque scene. With what is surely a curious sense of Indian psychology, she wrote that "These children of the forest, like the monks of olden time, always had a fine eye for the picturesque." "Whenever you find a ruined monastery, or the remains of an Indian encampment," she concluded, "you may be sure you have discovered the loveliest site in all the surrounding landscape."[36]

No matter how effectively one argued that American landscapes could indeed be associated with the past and with legend or literature, the fact was that Europe simply offered more of these associations. However, it was always possible to argue that American associations were with the future rather than the past —an idea which could be used to reinforce the concept of "Manifest Destiny." This concept was evident in America long before 1845, when it received its name. "Where the wolf roams," wrote Cole, "the plough shall glisten; on the gray crag shall rise temple and tower—mighty deeds shall be done in the now pathless wilderness; and poets yet unborn shall sanctify the soil."[37] N. P. Willis, futhermore, declared that in America, "He who journeys here, if he would not have the eternal succession of lovely natural objects—'Lie like a load upon the weary eye,' must feed his imagination on the *future*. The American does so. His mind, as he tracks the broad rivers of his own country, is perpetually reaching forward."[38] And to select another example, the essayist Elihu G. Holland in somewhat heightened rhetoric, characteristic of many who took the American landscape as their theme, claimed that ". . . though the genius of the past does not hover over [American] scenes as in the hoary ruins of the European world, the Angel of the Future spreads his white wings over them, whilst all things intimate that nature awaits a coming history. Europe is Memory, America is Hope."[39]

Holland's statements reach out to suggest a vast future that, free from the constrictions of the past, involves only hope, not memory—but the rhetoric Holland employed was no more his invention than were the ideas he sought to express. Writings of the time, whether the work of a politician or a Whitman, whether they concerned American politics or landscape painting, railroads or literature, industry or religion, were often caught by a need to express a commonly felt, enthusiastic hope for the future, and the language chosen was usually like Holland's, intensely passionate, electric.

THE BEAUTIFUL, the sublime, the picturesque, historical and literary associations, promises for the future—these are the central terms and ideas which crowd the rhetoric of most nineteenth-century descriptions of the American landscape. Perhaps no section of the country received as full attention from travelers as did the Hudson-Erie route and especially the Hudson itself, so obviously inviting comparison with the great rivers of Europe: the Rhine, the Danube, the Seine, the Thames, and so forth. An examination of writings about the Hudson reveals that in such comparisons more than aesthetic issues were resolved. Indeed the intensity with which Americans defended the Hudson strongly suggests that political (in the broadest sense of that term) as well as aesthetic questions were being answered.

"The Hudson for natural magnificence is unsurpassed," wrote Thomas Cole,[40] and his friend William Cullen Bryant claimed that "The western shore . . . is as worthy of a pilgrimage across the Atlantic as the Alps themselves."[41] In James Fenimore Cooper's *Home as Found*—a novel decidedly not noted for patriotic sentiment—Edward Effingham states that ". . . few rivers, perhaps no river, offers so great and so pleasing a variety in so short a distance . . .,"[42] and Washington Irving, who spent much of his adult life exploring the great landscapes and cities of Europe, wrote that "The Hudson is, in a manner my first and last love; and after all my wanderings, and seeming infidelities, I return to it with a heartfelt preference over all the other rivers in the world."[43] The essayist Elihu G. Holland, a man of no less enthusiasm, if somewhat less renown, concluded that "The Hudson . . . is in its whole course decidedly sacred to the imagination."[44]

According to Holland, neither the Seine nor the Rhine could "stand a moment's comparison with the Hudson."[45] Cooper was willing to admit that ". . . Europe offers to the senses sublimer views and certainly grander, than are to be found within our own borders, unless we resort to the Rocky Mountains, and the ranges in California and New Mexico." Nontheless, he did not think the Rhine was "in its best parts, equal to the Hudson in its whole length, though," he added, "the character of these two rivers are so very different as scarcely to admit of a fair comparison."[46] The anonymous author of *The Hudson River, by Pen and Pencil* had no reservations, however, when he claimed that the Rhine "is monotonous compared with the Hudson," which indeed "no river in Europe [can equal] in varied, picturesque charm."[47] Freeman Hunt, who had explored the river more thoroughly than most people had, added that even "the Danube or Rhine, does not furnish more beautiful or picturesque views than our own beautiful Hudson."[48]

Those who thought with George William Curtis that the Hudson suffered from a lack of ruined castles needed the reminder of the Knickerbocker writer Frederick William Shelton that although no Rhinish castles lined the banks, yet ". . . in all their towering and natural grandeur the cliffs shoot up where the castles ought to be;—and whether the fogs wreathe their summits, or they stand clear and well-defined in an amber atmosphere, the eye never tires of enjoyment."[49] Furthermore, Thomas Cole foresaw "the time when the amber waters shall reflect temple, and tower, and dome, in every variety of picturesqueness and magnificence"[50]—a prophecy very nearly fulfilled by the end of the century when the architectural styles along the river included, for example, Persian, Palladian, and Greek. The Swedish novelist Fredrika Bremer was happy with the lack of ruins along the river's bank: "We have . . . enough in the Old World,"[51] she wrote, but those travelers who could not satisfy themselves with her conclusion could seek out the ruins of Fort Putnam near West Point—reminiscent, said one commentator, "of the romantic ruined towers of defense in the gorges of the Pyrenees."[52] Furthermore, later in the century, picturesquely arranged ruins were to be found on the Clews and Cruger estates up in Dutchess County—artificial ruins, to be sure, which their proprietors had erected for "romantick" effects.

Of the various landscapes along the Hudson, perhaps none received such high praise as those in the Highlands and those in the Catskills—both of which, not so incidentally, were also provided with the river's best resort hotels. Willis was the particular spokesman for the Highlands, in the northern reaches of which he built his home, Idlewild. According to Willis, this area was "the most celebrated spot in the world for picturesque beauty."[53] In another work, he described it as "a complex wilderness, of romantic picturesqueness and beauty."[54] If the special attribute of the Highlands was the picturesque, that of the Catskills was the sublime. Remembering the landscape seen from the porch of the Catskill Mountain House—the most popular of all Catskill resort hotels and quite possibly the most popular in the country—the editor Willis Gaylord Clark wrote:

> Good reader! expect me not to describe the indescribable. I feel now, while memory is busy in my brain, calling up that vision to my mind, much as I did when I leaned upon my staff before that omnipotent picture, and looked upon its GOD-written magnitude. It was a vast and changeful, a majestic, an *interminable* landscape. . . .[55]

This same view, exclaimed Cooper's Natty Bumppo, who had presumably arrived several generations before the tourists, encompassed "all creation," recommendation enough for any journey into the wilderness.[56]

FOR ONLY $2, the American traveler of 1844 could travel by steamboat from New York to Albany. The price may seem a small one, considering the rewards promised by Willis and Clark, but it should be remembered that the average laborer was then earning only $1 a day. Laborers, furthermore, had little time for the extensive investigations of their country's landscapes, and what the immigrant workingman sought from the country was certainly not the sublime view from a resort hotel.

It is necessary to keep the matter in perspective by remembering that the average traveler would have been a lady or gentleman pleased to discover Samuel Lorenzo Knapp's comment in *Pictur-esque Beauties of the Hudson* that "the scenery at West Point is picturesque, the air is fresh, and the accommodations for the traveller, of the highest order."[57] It took Fulton's steamboat and Clinton's canal to entice American travelers into the wilderness; comfort was essential. The Englishwoman Harriet Martineau noted that when she traveled up the Hudson, most of the ladies on board the steamboat remained inside the cabin rather than on deck where they could view the passing scenery.[58] Men like Cole, Bryant, and Holland wrote extensively defending Ameri-can landscapes, yet after all, most travelers, however much they wanted to see the sunrise from Catskill Mountain House, also looked upon explorations of the "wilderness" as very much social enterprises. The discussions which went on within the cabin on Miss Martineau's boat were as much a part of the itinerary for many, perhaps most, travelers as were the recommended views. When the nineteenth-century American traveler set off to ex-plore his country's wilderness, he took his social identification with him.

WHEN DeWITT CLINTON, in November of 1825 signified the opening of the Hudson-Erie route by pouring a keg of water from the Great Lakes into the bay of New York, he did more than open the Western lands to settlement and trade and far more than initiate New York's growth as the nation's financial center. In fact he opened a wilderness to men less interested in pioneering and settlement than in discovering a landscape which, read emblematically, might explain the seemingly vast difference between Europe and America—a landscape, further-more, which could also provide a decidedly American backdrop for literature. If on the one hand the travelers, as a group, can be distinguished by their sterling mediocrity, on the other hand they composed the largest group of Americans seeking a sym-pathetic understanding of American landscapes, and the concerns of these travelers were much the same as the concerns out of which authors as disparate as Bryant and Melville were able to carve an American literature.

Notes

1. Freeman Hunt, *Letters about the Hudson River* (New York: Freeman Hunt and Co., 1836), p. 109.
2. DeWitt Clinton, *A Discourse, Delivered before the American Academy of the Arts* (New York: T. and W. Mercein, 1816), p. 16.
3. Henry T. Tuckerman, *America and Her Commentators* (New York: Charles Scribner, 1864), p. 405.
4. James Thomas Flexner, *That Wilder Image* (Boston: Little, Brown and Company, 1962), p. 17.
5. John Neal, "Landscape and Portrait Painting," *Yankee and Boston Literary Gazette*, N.S. I (1829), 121.
6. William Dunlap, *History of the Rise and Progress of the Arts of Design in the United States* (New York: George P. Scott and Company, 1834) vol. II, p. 11.
7. Tuckerman, *op. cit.*, p. 408.
8. Thomas Cole, "Essay on American Scenery," *American Monthly Magazine*, N.S. I (1836), p. 8.
9. James Fenimore Cooper, *Home as Found* (Boston: Houghton, Mifflin and Company, n.d.), p. 111.
10. Henry T. Tuckerman, *The Optimist* (New York: George P. Putnam, 1850), p. 31.
11. Theodore Dwight, *Things as They Are* (New York: Harper and Brothers, 1934), p. 192.
12. Elizabeth F. Ellet, *Rambles about the Country* (New York: Harper and Brothers, 1834), p. vi.
13. Dwight, *op. cit.*, p. 62.
14. Pierre Irving, *The Life and Letters of Washington Irving* (New York: G. P. Putnam, 1864), vol. III, p. 170.
15. Hunt, *op. cit.*, p. 157.
16. Roland Van Zandt, *The Catskill Mountain House* (New Brunswick, N.J.: Rutgers University Press, 1966), p. 12.
17. Joel Tyler Headley, *The Adirondack* (New York: Charles Scribner, 1849). See Preface, pp. i–iv.
18. Henry A. Beers, *Nathaniel Parker Willis* (Boston: Houghton, Mifflin and Company, 1885), p. 262.

19. Nathaniel Parker Willis, *Hurry-Graphs* (New York: Charles Scribner, 1851), p. 146.

20. Nathaniel Parker Willis, *Health Trip to the Tropics* (New York: Charles Scribner, 1854), p. 149.

21. The debate over the meaning of the word "picturesque" is documented in Christopher Hussey's *The Picturesque* (London: G. P. Putnam's Sons, 1927) and in Walter John Hipple's *The Beautiful, the Sublime, and the Picturesque in Eighteenth-Century British Aesthetic Theory* (Carbondale, Ill.: The Southern Illinois University Press, 1957).

22. Downing's definitions of the picturesque and the beautiful are discussed in Chapter Three.

23. Sir Uvedale Price, *On the Picturesque* (Edinburgh: Caldwell, Lloyd, and Company, 1842), p. 98.

24. Cole, *op. cit.*, p. 8.

25. Paul Weiss, *Nine Basic Arts* (Carbondale, Ill.: The Southern Illinois University Press, 1966), p. 8.

26. Cole, *op. cit.*, p. 5.

27. George William Curtis, *Lotus-Eating* (New York: Dix, Edwards and Company, 1856), pp. 138, 140–141, 136, 60–61.

28. *Ibid.*, p. 21.

29. Washington Irving, *The Sketch Book* (New York: G. P. Putnam, n.d.), pp. 16, 17.

30. Sarah Josepha Hale, *Traits of American Life* (Philadelphia: E. L. Carey and A. Hart, 1835), p. 190.

31. Dwight, *op. cit.*, p. 192.

32. Lydia Howard Huntley Sigourney, *Scenes in My Native Land* (Boston: James Munroe and Company, 1845), p. 31.

33. Robert C. Sands, "Domestic Literature," *Atlantic Magazine,* I (1824), 130.

34. Cole, *op. cit.*, p. 11.

35. Nathaniel Hawthorne, *The Marble Faun* (Columbus, Ohio: Ohio State University Press, 1968), p. 3.

36. Lydia Maria Child, *Letters from New York* (New York: C. S. Francis and Company, 1845), p. 28.

37. Cole, *op. cit.*, p. 12.

38. Nathaniel Parker Willis, *American Scenery* (London: George Virtue, 1840), vol. I, p. 2.

39. Elihu G. Holland, *Essay: and a Drama in Five Acts* (Boston: Phillips, Sampson, and Company, 1852), p. 30.

40. Cole, *op. cit.*, p. 8.

41. Parke Godwin, *A Biography of William Cullen Bryant* (New York: D. Appleton and Company, 1883), vol. I, p. 367.

42. Cooper, *op. cit.*, p. 112.

43. Washington Irving, *Biographies and Miscellanies* (New York: G. P. Putnam's Sons, n.d.), p. 503.

44. Holland, *op. cit.*, p. 50.

45. *Ibid.*, pp. 74–75.

46. James Fenimore Cooper, "American and European Scenery Compared," *The Home Book of the Picturesque* [George P. Putnam, ed.?], (New York: George P. Putnam, 1852), pp. 52, 62–63.

47. Anonymous, *The Hudson River by Pen and Pencil* (New York: D. Appleton and Company, 1875), p. 4.

48. Hunt, *op. cit.*, p. 70.

49. Frederick William Shelton, *Up the River* (New York: Charles Scribner, 1853), p. xi.

50. Cole, *op. cit.*, p. 9.

51. Fredrika Bremer, *The Homes of the New World* (New York: Harper and Brothers, 1853), vol. I, p. 34.

52. William Cullen Bryant, ed., *The American Landscape* (New York: Elam Bliss, 1830), p. 11.

53. Nathaniel Parker Willis, *The Convalescent* (New York: Charles Scribner, 1859), p. 39.

54. Willis, *Out-Doors at Idlewild* (New York: Charles Scribner, 1855), p. 18.

55. Charles Rockwell, *The Catskill Mountains* (New York: Tainter Brothers and Company, 1867), p. 212.

56. James Fenimore Cooper, *The Pioneers* (Boston: Houghton Mifflin and Company, 1898), p. 303.

57. Samuel Lorenzo Knapp, *Picturesque Beauties of the Hudson River and Its Vicinity* (New York: J. Disturnell, 1835), p. 8.

58. Harriet Martineau, *Retrospect of Western Travel* (London: Saunders and Otley, 1838), vol. I, p. 55.

Chapter Two

Landscapes, Real and Imagined

It is difficult to form a correct idea of a country from any description that can be given. Men are apt to expect too much—to draw their pictures too fair; they look to those wild and distant regions [of the West] for something surpassing nature, and they are disappointed. The world contains now no Garden of Eden. There is no particular portion of the habitable globe that possesses advantages greatly superior to the rest. If one has a better climate, the other has a better soil; if one has a better commercial situation, the other has some counterbalancing advantage, sufficient to make them nearly or quite equal.

Overton Johnson and William H. Winter,
Route across the Rocky Mountains
(1865).[1]

The Yosemite! As well interpret God in thirty-nine articles as portray it to you by word of mouth or pen. As well reproduce castle or cathedral by a stolen frieze, or broken column, as this assemblage of natural wonder and beauty by photograph or painting. The overwhelming sense of the sublime, of awful desolation, of transcending marvelousness and unexpectedness, that swept over us, as we reined our horses sharply out of green forests, and stood upon high jutting rock that overlooked this rolling, heaving sea of granite mountains, holding far down its rough lap this vale of beauty of meadow and grove and river, —such tide of feeling, such stoppage of ordinary emotions comes at rare intervals in any life. It was the confrontal of God face to face, as in great danger, in solemn sudden death. It was Niagara magnified. All that was mortal shrank back, all that was immortal swept to the front and bent down in awe. We sat till the rich elements of beauty came out of the majesty and desolation, and then, eager to get nearer, pressed tired horses down the steep, rough path into the Valley.

And here we have wandered and worshipped for four days.

Samuel Bowles, *Across the Continent*
(1865).[2]

THESE TWO PASSAGES, one the work of the prosperous editor of a New England newspaper and the other the work of two Western settlers, offer antipodal impressions of the West. The passage by Johnson and Winter is from *Route Across the Rocky Mountains,* a guide for people moving west. The authors are essentially practical men; they have found no Garden of Eden in the West, and they remind their readers, particularly those who think that the better life is on the Pacific side of the continent, that no part of the world is altogether a paradise. Whatever advantages one region has, they conclude, are balanced equally by defects. On the other hand, in *Across the Continent* Bowles celebrates the West as a land of milk and honey, and the Yosemite Valley seems virtually the cathedral of this paradise: here was "the confrontal of God face to face." But while Bowles was one of the West's great boosters, his home was in Massachusetts, not California. He knew the West not as a settler but as a tourist; he could ignore the realities of frontier life and concern himself with spiritual and aesthetic matters instead of the realities of making a living in what was still largely a wilderness. Bowles warmly recommended Americans to seek their fortunes in the West, but he stayed at home and made his own fortune in Springfield, Mass.

The works we will be considering in this chapter were in no instance written by people who shared Johnson and Winter's economic commitment to the land. None of them, that is, were forced to view the land primarily in economic terms. Like Bowles, they could give primary attention to aesthetic and spiritual matters, to the contemplation of the picturesque, the beautiful, the sublime, to historical associations with landscapes, and so forth. It should be added, however, that even men like Johnson and Winter—once economic problems had been resolved—could turn their attention to the interests of the tourist. "The scenery in Oregon," they wrote, "is varied, romantic, picturesque, and grand . . . although much has been said of the beauty and grandeur of the scenery of Switzerland, we doubt if anything can be there found to equal it. . . ."[3] Similarly, Bowles, in his more polished and cultivated diction, claimed that "All my many and various wanderings in the European Switzerland, three summers ago, spread before my eye no panorama of mountain beauty surpassing, nay none equalling, that which burst upon my sight at sunrise upon the Plains, when fifty miles away from Denver. . . ."[4] Both settler and tourist, however different their economic relation to the land, attributed to American landscapes the highest aesthetic value—particularly when those landscapes were compared with their counterparts in Europe. Even men as practical as Johnson and Winter could insist, although they had no proof, that landscapes in America were superior to those in Europe. National identity was clearly linked to the nature and quality of landscapes; the interests of the American tourist, therefore, should be of much value to the interpretation of both American identity and American literature during the Romantic period.

COOPER'S THE LAST OF THE MOHICANS (1826) suggests one way in which American landscapes were of service to American literature. Many of the landscapes in this novel are pointedly among those which were well known to travelers in America. As the author's footnotes insistently remind his readers, many of the adventures in this novel occur at locations well known to many of his contemporary Americans, particularly those who had the time and the money to explore the conveniently available segments of the wilderness and the countryside. Glens Falls, "this picturesque and remarkable little cataract" not far from Saratoga Springs, is the site of the island and caverns where Natty Bumppo and his comrades attempt to protect Cora and Alice Munro—a site, says the author, "well known to every traveller." In a later episode, Natty and his friends stop for a drink at a spring, "around which, and its sister fountains," Cooper writes, "within fifty years, the wealth, beauty, and talents of a hemisphere were to assemble in throngs, in pursuit of health and pleasure." The site is identified as Ballston Spa, one of the best-known resorts in the country. Still later, while Natty and others are traveling up Lake George in pursuit of the Indians who have captured Cora and Alice, Cooper stops the action to add, in a footnote, that "the beauties of Lake George are well known to every American tourist," and he then compares this body of water with "the finest of the Swiss and Italian lakes."[5]

Today Cooper's footnotes may amuse us because of their seeming irrelevance or may appear merely unwarranted distractions, and yet they were certainly of particular interest to nineteenth-century readers. After all, Cooper's novel gave the various locations historical or at least literary associations; in effect he was narrowing, however slightly, the margin of interest between European and American landscapes. Travelers in America were now provided with landscapes of an interest similar to the interest of landscapes in Europe; here in America were landscapes which could now be appreciated according to a European scale of values—and those landscapes were already, of course, part of the itinerary of travelers in America.

Since the Hudson was of such great importance to American travelers, it eventually became, as one would expect, particularly important to American literature. The Hudson is central to many historical novels, novels of manners, poems, and sketches. Irving's "Legend of Sleepy Hollow" and "Rip Van Winkle," originally published in *The Sketch Book* (1819–1820), are certainly the best-known sketches with a Hudson geography, but Irving wrote a number of other works which introduce the river as a setting, and he had his imitators who introduced the Hudson into their works also. One of his better-known imitators was Joseph Holt Ingraham, the author of numerous sensational and best-selling romances as well as a number of Irvingesque sketches, including one which he set in the Hudson Highlands. Entitled "The Kelpie Rock, or Undercliff" and published in *The American Lounger* (1839), this sketch contained the same basic materials as "Rip Van Winkle"—that is, mythology and picturesque descriptions of the Hudson. Others who wrote similar pieces set in this region included N. P. Willis and Andrew Jackson Downing.

What Washington Irving did in the sketch, Joseph Rodman Drake did in the poem. "The Culprit Fay" (which was not published until 1835, fifteen years after its author's death) is set in the Hudson Highlands and involves the love of a fay, or elf, for a human. At one time, Drake's poem was quite well known, but it had few imitators. Other poets, such as Bryant and Halleck, who wrote about the Hudson were more concerned with its landscapes and its history.

Among novelists, both Cooper (in *The Spy*, 1821) and Miss Sedgwick (in *The Linwoods*, 1835) made literary use of episodes of the Revolutionary War at West Point and along the shores of the Hudson. Cooper also made use of the Hudson in his novel of manners, *Home as Found* (1838), which devotes a full chapter to a journey up this "American Rhine." Cooper's travelers include American aristocrats who comment on the river's scenery, not always in favorable terms. Cooper offers qualified praise for the Palisades: ". . . though wanting in the terrific grandeur of an Alpine nature, and perhaps disproportioned to the scenery they [adorne]," they are, he concludes, "bold and peculiar." However, one of his travelers decides that the entrance to the Highlands "is hardly grand scenery."[6] Cooper's novel is, of course, the exception, for few American writers of the time dared or desired to criticize American scenery.

In contrast to Cooper's travelers is Gerty, the heroine of Maria Cummins's *The Lamplighter*. This best seller of the 1850s devotes nearly a hundred pages to an account of an excursion up the Hudson to Saratoga Springs and back again—an excursion dramatically interrupted when the boat takes fire and burns in the river, while the passengers, including the heroine, escape for their lives. During the journey up the river and especially at West Point, the novel's heroine shows herself to be sensitive to the beauties of nature, while less agreeable women appear more interested in gossip and flirtation. At West Point, Gerty has "one solitary moonlight evening" to view

   . . . the beauties of the place. She [has] no opportunity to view it in detail; she [sees] it only as a whole; but, thus presented to her vision in all the dreamy loveliness of a summer's night, it [leaves] on her fresh and impressive mind a vague sentiment of wonder and delight at the surpassing sweetness of what [seems] rather a glimpse of Paradise than an actual show of earth, so harmonious [is] the scene, so calm, so still, so peaceful.[7]

Literary associations with the Hudson were noted with much respect by tourists, and guidebooks to the region usually made reference to "Rip Van Winkle," "The Culprit Fay," and so forth. Among the more erudite visitors to Glens Falls was the historian Francis Parkman, who carefully noted its associations with *The Last of the Mohicans*. (Parkman, incidentally, spent much time traveling around the country and was the author of a guidebook to upper New York State.) In one of Charles Lanman's popular travel books, he recorded the spot where Rip Van Winkle was said to have slept for twenty years, and when Lanman needed the right language to describe the Catskills, he quoted a passage from Cooper's *The Pioneers* (1823)—the passage in which Natty Bumppo claims that from one spot high in the mountains he is able to see "all creation."[8]

Lewis Gaylord Clark, editor of the *Knickerbocker Magazine*, reminded his readers that "the wizzard region" of Sleepy Hollow, near Tarrytown, N.Y., had been the home of Baltus Van Tassel and his daughter Katrina in "The Legend of Sleepy Hollow."[9] In *Letters about the Hudson River*, Freeman Hunt noted that Irving was building a new home near Tarrytown and that "His elegant and graphic pen, and his chastened and classic imagination, will add new charms to the noble, the majestic, the exquisite scenery of the Hudson.[10] The river was so fully endowed with literary associations that in "The Four Rivers" N. P. Willis wrote, "The passage of the Hudson is doomed to be rewritten, and we will not again swell its great multitude of describers."[11]

TOURIST LANDSCAPES OTHER THAN THOSE ALONG THE HUDSON also made their way into American literature. Hawthorne told his readers about the trip west along the Erie Canal to Niagara, and his works about the White Mountains include "The Great Stone Face" and "The Ambitious Guest." Lesser writers such as Willis wrote at much length about Trenton Falls, Lake George, and the White Mountains. Lebanon Springs, Trenton Falls, and

Mount Holyoke all made their way into the once popular novels of Catharine Maria Sedgwick. The best of these novels is *Hope Leslie* (1827), set in Puritan Massachusetts but clearly written with the interests of nineteenth-century Americans in mind. One episode, for example, is set on Mount Holyoke on the banks of the Connecticut River to the east of present-day Northampton, Mass. In 1827, Mount Holyoke was among the favored tourist spots, for its summit provided a full panorama of the Connecticut River Valley and its pastoral surroundings. (Thomas Cole's "The Ox-Bow" (1836) is a view of the landscape seen from this mountain.) From the summit, Miss Sedgwick's heroine Hope Leslie and her companions view this landscape, and their reactions make them sound more like nineteenth-century pantheists than the seventeenth-century Puritans they are supposed to be. Hope says that "He must have a torpid imagination, and a cold heart, I think, who does not fancy these forests filled with invisible intelligences"—"the spirits," suggests a friend, "of those who have died for liberty and religion." The landscape, furthermore, makes her "pious companions raise their eyes in silent devotion."[12] It was, of course, typically the nineteenth-century tourist, not his seventeenth-century ancestor, who approached landscapes with such reverence. To the Puritan, the wilderness seen by Hope and her companions would probably have seemed threatening. (Incidentally, one of Hope's companions is a figure borrowed from history, Elizur Holioke [sic], the man for whom the mountain was named. According to the novel, in fact, the mountain was given its name on the day Holioke visited it with Hope Leslie. But the visit, of course, is fictional, and so we have here a curious instance of fiction supplying the "facts" for history.)*

---

* Miss Sedgwick was not the only American writer to provide colonial figures with nineteenth-century interests and ideas. In Cooper's *The Deerslayer*, published in 1841 but set in the upper New York State of a century earlier, Natty Bumppo, although a largely untutored woodsman, appears to know as much about the sublime and the picturesque as nineteenth-century American travelers.

The heroes, heroines, and noble savages of American novels written during the Romantic period can often be identified by their ability to sense nature's aesthetic and moral values. William Gilmore Simm's

AMERICAN INTEREST IN LANDSCAPES AND TRAVEL may explain
why parts of some nineteenth-century American novels read
more like guidebooks than fiction. This is the case, for example,
in the opening pages of Daniel Pierce Thompson's novel of the
American Revolution, *The Green Mountain Boys* (1839). Thompson begins:

---

best-known novel, *The Yemassee* (1835), is set in the early eighteenth
century, and yet the heroine of this novel feels "all the poetry, all
the truth of [a particular wilderness landscape]—its passion, its
inspiration; and, with a holy sympathy for all of nature's beautiful
works, the associated feelings of admiration for all that [is] noble,
also [awakens] in her mind a sentiment, and in her heart an emotion,
that [leads] her, not less to the most cheerful forbearance to tread
upon the humblest flower, than to a feeling little short of reverence
in the contemplation of the gigantic trees." To be sure, there were
people in the eighteenth century who reacted in this way to natural
landscapes—but generally not in America, and seldom, if ever, in the
wilderness. The wilderness, after all, was far more a threat to one's
well-being than a source of pleasure.

A wilderness such as that seen by his heroine, explains Simms,
divests "the mind of its associations of every-day and busy life, throws
it back upon its early and sophisticated nature . . . ," but later he, or
at least his narrative, suggests that this seemingly benevolent or
benign wilderness can also deceive and threaten. In the forest, his
heroine encounters a rattlesnake, "lying coiled at the bottom of a
beautiful shrub, with which, to her dreaming eye, many of its
glorious hues [have] become associated." In the wilderness, the snake—
and presumably the evil of which it is an emblem—is disguised or
cloaked by its surroundings. The wilderness, it would seem, is far
from being altogether the paradise which Simm's heroine has imagined it to be. But if this interpretation is the one which the author
intended (and it appears to be the only likely one) he does not press
the point very far; his audience after all expected to find innocence
and goodness, not deception or evil, associated with the wilderness.
In a last-minute rescue, an Indian arrives and kills the snake, but this
does not mitigate the impression which has been conveyed—namely,
that nature can be deceptive, maliciously so. The episode is so unusual in nineteenth-century American literature that Simms had to
justify it by claiming that it was based on an actual incident. [William
Gilmore Simms, *The Yemasee* (Boston: Houghton Mifflin Company,
1961), pp. 139, 142–143.]

Those who have wandered along the banks of the Otter Creek in search of the beautiful and the picturesque may have extended their rambles, perhaps, to Lake Dunmore, which lies embosomed among the hills a few miles to the eastward of that quiet stream. If so, their taste for the natural scenery had doubtless been amply gratified; for there is no spot in the whole range of the Green Mountains [of Vermont] that combines more of the requisites for a perfect landscape than this romantic sheet of water and its surrounding shores.[13]

Thompson describes this landscape explicitly and then uses it as the opening setting of his novel. In effect, Thompson addresses his reader as a traveler; by attaching the historical narrative to a specific landscape, the author provides the sort of historical associations which travelers of that day wished to find in natural landscapes.

A more extended example of the reader addressed as a traveler is found in *Horse-Shoe Robinson* (1835) by the Southern novelist John Pendleton Kennedy. Like William Gilmore Simms, William Alexander Caruthers, and others, Kennedy wrote novels which were intended to show the South advantageously, and in *Horse-Shoe Robinson,* he described western Virginia, an area which he apparently considered to be as rich in historical associations and picturesque scenery as the Valley of the Hudson River.*

Kennedy's book opens with a topographical description of this mountainous region and then notes that it is a welcome spot for travelers "who yearly migrate in quest of health"—since ap-

---

* Kennedy was not the only novelist who found the scenery of western Virginia, including what today is West Virginia, to be worthy material for fiction. The best-selling novelist Mrs. E. D. E. N. Southworth used this region in her novels, including one of her most popular works, *The Hidden Hand* (1859). The region's picturesque scenery, often embellished by thunderstorms, makes its appearance frequently in this book. In the opening paragraphs Mrs. Southworth, famed for abilities with melodrama, informs us that "when storms and floods were high, the loud roaring of the wild mountain gorges, and the terrific raging of the torrent over its rocky course, gave to this savage locality ["in one of the loneliest and wildest of the mountain regions of Virginia"] its ill-omened names of Devil's Hoof, Devil's Run, and Hurricane Hall." [Mrs. E. D. E. N. Southworth, *The Hidden Hand* (New York: Robert Bonner, 1889), p. 9.]

parently both the climate and the "waters" in this region may be considered healthful—as well as for travelers who wish "a refuge from the heats of summer, or who, perchance, wander in pursuit of those associations of hill and dale which are supposed to repair a jaded imagination, and render it romantic and fruitful." Kennedy recommends that travelers stop in Charlottesville, for in this area, he says, are not only the homes of three presidents, including Jefferson, but also the University of Virginia with "its gorgeous and fantastic piles of massive and motley architecture." (This is, incidentally, a highly inappropriate way to describe the miniature, often delicate temples which were the main buildings at the University; but then, Kennedy was no architect or student of architecture.) If Charlottesville provides travelers with patriotic associations and noteworthy architecture, the mountains to the west provide spectacular, romantic scenery. The streams to be found in this region, he says,

> . . . have worn deep channels through the hills, and constantly seem to solicit the road into narrow passes and romantic dells, where fearful crags are seen toppling over the head of the traveller, and sparkling waters tinkle at his feet; and where the richest and rarest trees of the forest seem to have chosen their several stations, on mossy bank or cloven rock, in obedience to some master mind intent upon the most tasteful and striking combinations of these natural elements.[14]

Only after Kennedy has guided his tourist-reader through the landscapes of this region, does the story itself begin. Kennedy's novel is about the Revolutionary War, and since the story is placed in the region he has described, the book, like *The Green Mountain Boys,* serves the function of providing its readers with historical and literary associations for particular landscapes.

Another and more famous novel of the Revolution, Herman Melville's *Israel Potter* (1855), opens in much the same way as *Horse-Shoe Robinson* and *The Green Mountain Boys.* Melville, like Thompson and Kennedy, places the reader in the position of a traveler:

> The traveller who at the present day is content to travel in the good old Asiatic style, neither rushed along by locomotive, nor dragged by a stage-coach; who is willing to enjoy hospitalities at far-scattered farmhouses, instead of paying his bill at an inn; who is not to be frightened by any amount of loneliness, or to be

deterred by the roughest roads or highest hills; such a traveller in the eastern part of Berkshire, Massachusetts, will find ample food for poetic reflection in the singular scenery of a country, which, owing to the ruggedness of its soil and its lying out of the track of all public conveyances, remains almost as unknown to the general tourist as the interior of Bohemia.[15]

The paragraphs which follow this passage describe the Berkshires as they appear along the ridge from Otis to Windsor, Mass., during the different seasons of the year. Melville offers his readers the seemingly obligatory historical associations as well as picturesque descriptions. He refers, for example, to the original settlers and their descendants who have since deserted the region; signs of their former lives here remain in abandoned farmhouses ("these ancient buildings") and stone walls ("the tokens of ancient industry"). In order to be "ancient," of course, nothing here would have to be more than a hundred years old; before that time there was little but wilderness in this region. By referring to "ancient buildings" and "ancient industry," however, Melville is suggesting a vast reach of time commensurate with the vast space, the panoramas seen from the mountains: "Unless by a sudden precipitation of the road you find yourself plunging into some gorge, you pass on, and on, and on, upon the crests or slopes of pastoral mountains, while far below, mapped out in its beauty, the valley of the Housatonic lies endlessly at your feet." In its vastness, the landscape seems sublime —a landscape which in summer leaves the traveler with the desire for "no company but Nature" but which in winter presents "wild, unfrequented roads," "inaccessible and impassable." In winter, "as if an ocean rolled between man and man, intercommunication is often suspended for weeks and weeks." The landscape is also sublimely powerful in its ability to absorb and destroy the few remaining emblems of civilization: "Spotted gray and green with the weather-stain, [the timbers of the farmhouses] seem to have lapsed back into their woodland original, forming now part of the general picturesqueness of the natural scene."[16]

Melville knew well the region he was describing, for Arrowhead, his home in Pittsfield, Mass., was situated only a few miles to the west. He did more, however, than merely provide descriptions of the region, for he also tried to make his reader react to the region in the way a traveler would. Melville was not simply telling his reader about the region but was trying to make him sense it in a more personal or intimate way.*

MOST OF THE WEST REMAINED WILDERNESS AS LATE AS 1860, and the lack of efficient transcontinental transportation until 1869, when the Union Pacific and Central Pacific Railroads were completed, kept travelers, especially fashionable travelers, in the East.† Nonetheless, there was a popular interest in the West, and from time to time, travel books and fictional works about this region were made available to the public. In addition, a

---

* Melville's interest in traveling extended far beyond *Israel Potter*, of course. Indeed Melville was addicted to the fashionable terminology of landscape description and to traveling itself. In *Typee* (1846), he reported that he had explored the Pacific and discovered in the Marquesas Islands "a scene so enchanting" that he "experienced a pang of regret that [it] should be hidden from the world in these remote seas, and seldom meet the eyes of devoted lovers of nature." All of Melville's major fiction makes extensive use of picturesque, sublime, and beautiful landscapes, and in *Moby-Dick*, Ishmael demonstrates a good knowledge of locations well known to American tourists: the Hudson Highlands, the Catskills, the Erie Canal, and the Natural Bridge, among others. Not only does Ishmael know well American landscapes which were appreciated by American tourists, however; he also shares with many nineteenth-century travelers the ability to see the physical world as an emblem of larger, spiritual truth. Ishmael discusses landscape with the same philosophical equipment that Cole, Bryant, and countless others used when they dealt with American landscapes. [Herman Melville, *Typee* (Evanston and Chicago: Northwestern University Press and The Newberry Library, 1968), p. 24.]

† For our purpose, the West in 1817 may be described as everything between the Alleghenies and the Pacific, but by 1860, so many communities had been firmly established west of the Alleghenies that the boundary of the West may be said to have shifted to the Mississippi. During the intervening years, the increasing number of settlements established by New Englanders in the Midwestern section of the country, east of the Mississippi, deprived that area of the frontier character that is usually associated with the West. Culturally, the prairie region seems to have become by 1860 very nearly a duplicate of the pastoral or agricultural Northeast.

number of guidebooks intended largely or solely for emigrants were published. Since there were very few professional writers living in the West (Timothy Flint was perhaps the most famous of those who lived there) this region received less literary attention than the East. Nonetheless, there were some highly significant literary works about the West, and in turn, these reflected the preoccupation of Americans in general and American tourists in particular with the nation's wilderness landscapes.

Occasionally writings about the West were indebted more to imagination than to experience—Cooper's *The Prairie*, for example, made use of an area which the author had never seen—but most books which dealt with the West attempted to deal with the area accurately. On the other hand, the terminology which was used to describe landscapes in the West was the same as that which was used to describe landscapes along the Hudson. No attempt was made to develop descriptive terms appropriate to this new area, an area which in many ways was visually quite different from anything in the East. The terms "sublime," "picturesque," and "beautiful" were as freely used to describe the Rockies as they were used to describe the Catskills.

In *From West to East: Studies in the Literature of the American West*, Robert Edson Lee argues that Eastern diction in literature contributed to a distorted image of the West. He believes that Irving's journals, the raw material out of which *A Tour on the Prairies* (1835) was formed, are superior in certain respects to the finished book; they are more Western, he thinks, because their literary style is more plain and direct (in effect, less literary) than is the book which Irving fashioned from them.[17] It is true that Irving conscientiously "improved" his journal notes by using literary English in his book and, incidentally, by giving increased attention to picturesque scenery. It is *A Tour on the Prairies*, not the journals, however, which may be considered characteristic of travel literature in pre–Civil War America. In fact, it can be argued that Irving did the West a service, for he praised it in terms which Easterners, who made up, in turn, the largest segment of American readers, could readily understand. Lengthy romantic descriptions of scenery were welcome in the East, and readers might have been more confused than pleased if the polished gentleman who created *The Sketch Book* and

Bracebridge Hall had written his Western book in that pithy, direct, occasionally colloquial English which Lee finds so admirable.

Like a traveler along the Hudson, Irving in *A Tour on the Prairies* engages in "rural repose," notes the picturesqueness of a human figure "in unison with the wild scenery around him," and points out how much a particular "crest of broken rocks" resembles "a ruined fortress," "the ruin of some Moorish castle, crowning a height in the midst of a lonely Spanish landscape." Here in the wilderness of the West, Irving discovers associations with, of all things, the great cathedrals of Europe:

> We were overshadowed by lofty trees, with straight, smooth trunks, like stately columns; and as the glancing rays of the sun shone through the transparent leaves, tinted with the many-colored hues of autumn, I was reminded of the effect of sunshine among the stained windows and clustering columns of a Gothic cathedral. Indeed there is a grandeur and solemnity in our spacious forests of the West, that awaken in me the same feeling I have experienced in those vast and venerable piles, and the sound of the wind sweeping through them, supplies occasionally the deep breathings of the organ.[18]

Elsewhere in the book, Irving claims that a particular landscape has "the golden tone of one of the landscapes of Claude Lorrain"—no small praise since these paintings were widely considered ideal landscapes. Even the absence of human life in much of the West visited by Irving is turned to purposes of which an educated traveler could only approve:

> The weather was in its perfection, temperate, genial and enlivening; a deep blue sky with a few light feathery clouds, an atmosphere of perfect transparency, air pure and bland, and a glorious country spreading out far and wide in the golden sunshine of an autumn day; but all silent, lifeless, without a habitation, and apparently without an inhabitant! It was as if a ban hung over this fair but fated region. The very Indians dared not abide here, but made it a mere scene of perilous enterprise, to hunt for a few days and then away.[19]

Irving, it seems, had found in the American West an excellent setting for a romance by Scott or Bulwer-Lytton—a landscape "fair but fated," the setting for "perilous enterprise."

Irving's *The Adventures of Captain Bonneville, U.S.A.* (1837), based on the adventures of one of the first men to explore the Rocky Mountains, also describes Western landscapes in ways which Americans used to describe landscapes in the East. For example, the reader is told that certain "high and beetling cliffs" in the West bear "the semblance of towers, castles, churches, and fortified cities."[20] One is reminded of the traveler who, disappointed that the Hudson had no castles, found consolation in the fact that the Palisades "in all their towering and natural grandeur . . . shoot up where the castles ought to be."[21] Incidentally, Irving had never seen the landscapes which he described in *Bonneville*. He had available Bonneville's personal notes, together with the knowledge of the established ways of describing landscapes, and with these aids, he was able to create descriptions which must have been as thoroughly convincing to his contemporaries as were his descriptions of the prairies and the Hudson River Valley.

Irving wrote a third Western book, *Astoria* (1836). John Jacob Astor had personally commissioned the work, and it made Astor's fur trading in the West seem a truly heroic venture. But it was an economic venture that Astor engaged in, and appropriately, the book gave comparatively little attention to landscape except in topographical descriptions.

Incidentally, in 1840 Poe silently borrowed information from *Astoria* and the journals of Lewis and Clark for a work entitled *The Journal of Julius Rodman*, a book which was never completed but parts of which were published in *Burton's Gentleman's Magazine*. The journal was offered as fact, not fiction— "an account of the first passage across the Rocky Mountains . . . ever achieved by civilized man." Its hero, no ordinary traveler, is a misanthrope, a Byronic figure who avoids civilization and seeks "in the bosom of the wilderness, that peace which his peculiar disposition [will] not suffer him to enjoy among men." Rodman, the hero, is "possessed with a burning love of nature; and [worships] her, perhaps, more in her dreary and savage aspects, than in her manifestations of placidity and joy."[22] Rodman is the antithesis of the typical American traveler, journeying from resort to resort, and Poe could have created in his book an imaginary realm which in its complex interest for Rodman would have implied the imaginative barrenness of the American land-scape appreciated by travelers. But the Rockies in Poe's work are no more interesting than the Catskills in Irving's, and the characterization of Rodman is left in outline. Poe lost interest in his project, and the *Journal* was never completed.

In the spring of 1846, Francis Parkman, the Harvard-educated son of a Unitarian minister, traveled west with his cousin Quincy Adams Shaw to explore the Sante Fe and Oregon Trails. He used his experiences along these trails and in parts of what are now Wyoming and Colorado as the primary substance of *The Oregon Trail,* which he began publishing in installments in the *Knickerbocker Magazine* less than six months after he re-turned from his journey. The book is one of the major documents about the West, and for present purposes, it is significant for what it tells about the inadequacies of the usual aesthetic cate-gories in attempts to describe the vast wilderness landscapes west of the Mississippi.

Except for the chapters on Indian life, *The Oregon Trail* is in effect about traveling in the West. The book is held together by Parkman's progress from one place or adventure to another— from Westport (now part of Kansas City, Missouri) to Fort Laramie, Wyo., and then, after living for a while with the Sioux, down to the Sante Fe Trail in what is now southeastern Colo-rado, and finally back to Westport. Parkman, in his own words, completed "a tour of curiosity and amusement"—the travels, in short, of a gentleman.[23] His frequent criticisms of Western emi-grants, Indian life, and Western landscapes reflect the standards of his native Boston; the reader is always aware that Parkman was an outsider, a visitor who brought with him a Harvard edu-cation and the manners of Boston. Much as he claimed to love the wilderness, it is clear that Parkman could never have been comfortable spending his life outside the civilized world.

He was accustomed, of course, to the scenery of the East— the Adirondacks, the White Mountains, and so forth—and in contrast, the Western landscapes which he saw seemed to offer little. He could appreciate landscape which met his criteria for, say, the beautiful or the picturesque, but generally he found the parched, arid landscapes of the Great Plains unpleasant or dis-agreeable. Indeed when he contrasted these Western landscapes

with those in his native New England, the apparent superiority
of the latter was simply reinforced. Under a scorching sun, he
was reminded of "the pine-clad mountains of New-England"
and of water "poured in such wasteful profusion from our thousand hills."[24]

Parkman's sense of New England's superiority is explicit in
the "train of associations" awakened in his mind by the sight of
a meadow of wildflowers in the West. "A throng of fair and well-
remembered faces rose, vividly as life, before me. 'There are
good things,' thought I, 'in the savage life, but what can it offer
to replace those powerful and ennobling influences that can
reach unimpaired over more than three thousand miles of mountains, forests, and deserts?"[25] As long as Parkman valued "those
powerful and ennobling influences" from the civilized East, it
was clear that he could be at best only partially sympathetic to
what, in 1846, was a primitive culture set in the midst of a vast
bleak landscape.

The prairies, sections of which were under cultivation by
settlers from the East, pleased him visually at least, for they
conformed to his sense of the beautiful or the pastoral. The
landscape of the prairie region, he thought, ". . . though tame, is
graceful and pleasing. Here are level plains too wide for the eye
to measure; green undulations, like motionless swells of the
ocean; abundance of streams, followed through all their wind-
ings by lines of woods and scattered groves." In contrast, the
journey through the landscape of the plains was monotonous.
One day he and his companions traveled for many hours and in
that time saw neither a bush nor a tree. The plains seemed to
be "a barren, trackless waste, extending for hundreds of miles
to the Arkansas on the one side and Missouri on the other."
Furthermore, in one mountainous section just to the west of
the Great Plains, he found "nothing . . . either grand or picturesque, though [one setting was] . . . desolate to the last degree,"
while elsewhere the landscape was "a sublime waste, a wilderness of mountains and pine-forests, over which the spirit of lone-
liness and silence seemed brooding."[26]

Although the Western landscapes he encountered seemed
monotonous and desolate, Parkman found something imaginatively interesting in some of them. Consider, for example, his
description of the valley of the Platte:

We all drew rein, and sat joyfully looking down upon the prospect. It was right welcome,—strange, too, and striking to the imagination; and yet it had not one picturesque or beautiful feature; nor had it any of the features of grandeur, other than its vast extent, its solitude, and its wildness. For league after league, a plain as level as a lake was outspread beneath us; here and there the Platte, divided into a dozen thread-like sluices, was traversing it, and an occasional clump of wood, rising in the midst like a shadowy island, relieved the monotony of the waste. No living thing was moving throughout the vast landscape, except the lizards that darted over the sand and through the rank grass and prickly pears at our feet.

Although this landscape has little aesthetic value, it is, says Parkman, rich in moral associations.

And yet stern and wild associations gave a singular interest to the view: for here each man lives by the strength of his arm and the valor of his heart. Here the feeble succumb to the brave, with nothing to sustain them in their weakness. Here society is reduced to its original elements, the whole fabric of art and conventionality is struck rudely to pieces, and men find themselves suddenly brought back to the wants and resources of their natures.[27]

In the context of American literature, it is appropriate that this landscape seems morally primitive; similar vast but desolate landscapes have become common in popular Western movies and novels in which men do in fact "find themselves brought back to the wants and resources of their original natures." Landscapes such as that described by Parkman can be found in novels by Owen Wister, Max Brand, Ernest Haycox, Zane Grey, and others. Also, Frank Norris's *McTeague* (1899) ends in Death Valley, another vast, desolate Western landscape, which suggested to Norris the same moral primitiveness that Parkman associated with the valley of the Platte. More recently, the novels of Larry McMurtry have employed morally primitive landscapes similar to the one Parkman described. Certainly the literary possibilities of such Western landscapes have not yet been exhausted.

Although there is certainly good reason to accuse Parkman of Bostonian snobbishness in his treatment of the West, his attempt to deal truthfully with Western landscapes is more rewarding than Irving's traditional and gentlemanly approach. On the one hand, Irving was able to make the landscapes he encountered

seem less individual to his readers since he insisted on emphasizing picturesqueness and similar qualities. On the other hand,
Parkman looked for qualities which seemed indigenous to Western landscapes. His Boston training was not the best preparation
for a sympathetic tour of the Great Plains and the foothills of
the Rockies, but at least his honesty prevented him from invariably portraying the West as if it were aesthetically an extension of New England or upstate New York.

IN 1832, WILLIAM CULLEN BRYANT TRAVELED WEST to visit
members of his family who had settled in Illinois, and his experiences there provided him with materials for his poem "The
Prairies." Bryant in this poem offers his reader a series of associations with the prairies, still largely uncultivated wilderness. The
vast prairies form the floor of God's temple:

> Man hath no power in all this glorious work:
> The hand that built the firmament hath heaved
> And smoothed these verdant swells, and sown their slopes
> With herbage, planted them with island groves,
> And hedged them round with forests.

Within this temple are monuments to human achievement,
monuments as ancient as the buildings of Greece; for the mound-
builders created their works

> . . . while yet the Greek
> Was hewing the Pentilicus to forms
> Of symmetry, and rearing on its rock
> The glittering Parthenon.

But the associations of the prairies with the past are then forgotten and replaced by a vision of a pastoral civilization which
will someday occupy the landscape.

> I listen long
> To [the bee's] domestic hum, and think I hear
> The sound of that advancing multitude
> Which soon shall fill these deserts. From the ground
> Comes up the laugh of children, the soft voice
> Of maidens, and the sweet and solemn hymn
> Of sabbath worshippers. The low of herds
> Blends with the rustling of the heavy grain
> Over the dark brown furrows.

Bryant's vision of civilization subduing a wilderness is an expression of Manifest Destiny, and this vision—encountered in works as different as Bryant's poem and Whitman's "Passage to India" (1868)—is central to American literature. Although Americans idealized the wilderness, they welcomed the idea that civilization would ultimately spread over the continent. Associations with the landscape, as we have seen, frequently involved the future; "Europe," went one claim previously noted, "is Memory, America is Hope." But it was, obviously, paradoxical to idealize the wilderness as God's temple and at the same time to welcome the advance of civilization.

In "Passage to India," Whitman welcomes such material achievements as the railroad, linking one society with another and thus providing a means for human brotherhood; the moral life in this instance is obtained, not lost, through material progress and the disappearance of the wilderness. Thomas Cole, on the other hand, was among those who wished to preserve the wilderness and yet, paradoxically, looked forward to a time when "on the gray crag shall rise temple and tower—mighty deeds shall be done in the now pathless wilderness."[28] According to Johnson and Winter, the Western emigrants quoted at the beginning of this chapter, one of the greatest delights of their new home in the West was the spectacular landscape, more beautiful and grand, they said, than anything in Europe; however, looking across the valley of the Willamette and "peering far into the future," they beheld, with evident pleasure,

. . . enthroned upon an hundred heights, the lordly mansions of the opulent, surrounded with gardens, teeming with fruits and flowers; with parks, and pools, and groves of ornamental trees; and far up the sides of the surrounding mountains, the herdsmen's and the shepherd's humble cottages repose, in sweet and solitary quiet, deep buried amid the mountain pines.[29]

Similarly, Samuel Bowles, who, as we have seen, wrote enthusiastically about the Western wilderness, was among the nation's leading advocates of Western railroads.

At times it seems as if nineteenth-century Americans envisioned for their country a future in which little or no sublime or picturesque wilderness remained. Bryant's vision of a pastoral civilization advancing over the continent may be disagreeable to those who today wish to protect what little remains of the American wilderness, but in the nineteenth century, progress of civilization across the continent seemed in balance far more important than the preservation of the wilderness. There were few indeed who would have agreed with such thinkers as Thoreau and Theodore Winthrop that American landscapes needed protection from American civilization.

But while wilderness disappeared with the advance of civilization, thousands set out to explore American landscapes—either those along such popular routes as the Hudson Valley route or the less accessible wilderness landscapes which attracted men like Parkman and Thoreau. More significantly, perhaps, there was a widely expressed American desire to incorporate, somehow, the wilderness within civilization—to resolve the paradox and create a "civilized wilderness." This resolution, or attempted resolution, was ultimately, as the following chapters suggest, of enormous significance to American literature.

Notes

1. Overton Johnson and William H. Winter, *Route across the Rocky Mountains,* new ed. (Princeton, N.J.: Princeton University Press, 1932), pp. xiv–xv.
2. Samuel Bowles, *Across the Continent* (Springfield, Mass.: Samuel Bowles and Company, 1865), pp. 223–224.
3. Johnson and Winter, *op. cit.,* p. 78.
4. Bowles, *op. cit.,* pp. 31–32.
5. James Fenimore Cooper, *The Last of the Mohicans* (Boston: Houghton, Mifflin and Company, 1898), pp. 56, 139, 241.
6. James Fenimore Cooper, *Home as Found* (Boston: Houghton, Mifflin and Company, n.d.), pp. 112, 115.
7. Maria Cummins, *The Lamplighter* (Boston: John P. Jewett and Company, 1854), p. 332.
8. Charles Lanman, *A Tour to the River Saguenay in Lower Canada* (Philadelphia: Carey and Hart, 1848), pp. 2, 29–30, 31. Lanman, *Letters from a Landscape Painter* (Boston: James Munroe and Company, 1844), pp. 8–9, 11.

9. L. Gaylord Clark, *Knick-Knacks from an Editor's Table* (New York: D. Appleton and Company, 1852), p. 36.

10. Freeman Hunt, *Letters about the Hudson River* (New York: Freeman Hunt and Co., 1836), p. 29.

11. Nathaniel Parker Willis, "The Four Rivers," in *Rural Letters* (New York: Baker and Scribner, 1849), p. 201.

12. Catharine Maria Sedgwick, *Hope Leslie* (New York: White, Gallaher, and White, 1827), vol. I, pp. 167, 166.

13. Daniel Pierce Thompson, *The Green Mountain Boys* (New York: Grosset and Dunlap, n.d.), p. 1.

14. John Pendleton Kennedy, *Horse-Shoe Robinson* (New York: Hafner Publishing Company, 1962), pp. 13, 14.

15. Herman Melville, *Israel Potter* (New York: G. P. Putnam and Company, 1855), p. 9.

16. *Ibid.*, pp. 11, 10, 12, 14.

17. Robert Edson Lee, *From West to East: Studies in the Literature of the American West* (Urbana, Ill.: University of Illinois Press, 1966), pp. 58–69, *passim.*

18. Washington Irving, *A Tour on the Prairies* (Norman, Okla.: University of Oklahoma Press, 1956), pp. 85, 20, 106, 41.

19. *Ibid.*, pp. 73, 84.

20. Washington Irving, *The Adventures of Captain Bonneville, U.S.A.* (New York: G. P. Putnam's Sons, n.d.), p. 60.

21. Frederick William Shelton, *Up the River* (New York: Charles Scribner, 1853), p. xi.

22. Edgar Allan Poe, *The Journal of Julius Rodman, Complete Works* (New York: Crowell, 1902), vol. IV, pp. 9, 11, 13.

23. Francis Parkman, *The Oregon Trail* (Madison, Wisc.: The University of Wisconsin Press, 1969), pp. 1–2.

24. *Ibid.*, p. 183.

25. *Ibid.*, p. 501.

26. *Ibid.*, pp. 35, 42, 66, 290, 293.

27. *Ibid.*, pp. 65, 401–402.

28. Thomas Cole, "Essay on American Scenery," *American Monthly Magazine*, I (1836), p. 9.

29. Johnson and Winter, *op. cit.*, p. 80.

part two

Smiling Lawns and Tasteful Cottages

The Importance of Rural Ideals
to American Life and Literature

Chapter Three

Smiling Lawns

So long as men are forced to dwell in log huts and follow a hunter's life, we must not be surprised at lynch law and the use of the bowie knife. But, when smiling lawns and tasteful cottages begin to embellish a country, we know that order and culture are established.

> Andrew Jackson Downing, *The Architecture of Country Houses* (1850).[1]

It is as clear to me as sunshine . . . that the greatest possible stumbling-blocks in the path of human happiness and improvement are these heaps of bricks and stones, consolidated with mortar, or hewn timber, fastened together with spike-nails, which men painfully contrive for their own torment, and call them house and home. The soul needs air; a wide sweep and frequent change of it. Morbid influences, in a thousand-fold variety, gather about hearths, and pollute the life of households. There is no such unwholesome atmosphere as that of an old home, rendered poisonous by one's defunct forefathers and relatives.

> Clifford Pyncheon in Nathaniel Hawthorne, *The House of the Seven Gables* (1851).[2]

SOMETIME IN THE EARLY 1850s, SAMUEL H. HAMMOND, the editor of an upstate New York newspaper, left on a journey, or "ramble" as he called it, through some of the back country of his native state. His travels took him to the Finger Lakes region, where he stayed in Canandaigua, one of few towns in what was still a fairly unexplored or at least undeveloped area. While there, he was the guest at "one of the most splendid dwellings in the village," a villa topped with an observatory from which he was able to obtain an excellent view of the surrounding countryside. He wrote:

> The glass was slightly stained, of the windows through which I looked, and it gave a mellowness to the picture that was exceeding [sic] beautiful. I have never been in Italy; I know about an Italian sunset only from descriptions by tourists and from paintings by masters of the art, but if an Italian sunset exceeds in beauty the prospect that was before me, as I looked from that observatory, it is then beautiful indeed. The lake, the farms and avenues lined with trees in the distance, the village residences, the gardens and grounds near by, and the delightful walks and trees, and rich fruits and flowers immediately beneath and around me, formed a landscape which, seen in the mellow light afforded by the stained glass of the windows through which I looked, no painter could transfer to canvas, or Italy excel.[3]

On the one hand, Hammond's description of this landscape is political in that it involves a favorable image of the New World at the expense of the Old, but on the other hand, a close examination of the passage reveals that there is really nothing *particularly* American about this view at all. The context of the description tells us, of course, that it is an American landscape with which Hammond is dealing, but if we isolate the details of that landscape—"the lake, the farms and avenues lined with trees in the distance," and so forth—the scene appears to be in no way characteristically American. Indeed the special quality of this landscape, its coloring, derives not from the fact that it is located on this side of the Atlantic but from the fact that it is perceived through the "slightly stained" windows of the observatory. Hammond is provided with a primitive "Claude glass," a device used to give landscapes the golden coloring found in the paintings of Claude Lorrain. Seen through the golden-tinted "Claude glass," landscape owes much to "art" as well as to nature. Hammond's landscape may be one which "no painter

could transfer to canvas," but it is also one which owes much
to a painterly way of viewing things. Wilderness, the one characteristically American element of landscapes, is obviously lacking in Hammond's description, and so he is left with something
which could as well be in England as in upstate New York.

There were some, like N. P. Willis, who enthusiastically greeted
American landscapes which showed few traces of their wilderness origins. To be sure, Willis could be wholly enthusiastic
about wilderness scenery—providing that it could be seen from
one of his favored resorts—but he was even more enthusiastic
about scenery which reminded him of England and Europe. He
noted that the views from James Fenimore Cooper's library in
Cooperstown, N.Y., "are such as you get upon park-grounds from
the most secluded country-house in England," that a drive in
the environs of Springfield, Mass., had certain likenesses to one
"through Richmond, the prettiest suburban town in England,"
and that a resort hotel in Kentucky "was surrounded by what
might be a nobleman's park, the walks apparently endless and
yet carefully and neatly kept, and the natural advantages of the
undulating woodlands charmingly understood and improved."[4]
He was pleased to note that the area around his own estate,
Idlewild, was "quite rid of the angularity and well-known un-
gracefulness of a newly settled country," and he wrote with
enthusiasm that the town of Walton, N.Y., "looks hardly American. . . . The [Delaware] river and its mountains are like the
Rhine, and the fields have an *old country look*, free from the
rawness of most of our rural scenery."[5] Yet Willis could also be
triumphantly American in his descriptions of wilderness landscapes and could praise the wilderness about the resort at Trenton Falls as well as that "hardly American" scenery at Walton.
Indeed it was wilderness scenery as well as park grounds which
one saw from the windows at Idlewild.

The essentially English or European landscapes which one
could find in this country may have satisfied the patriotism of
those who wished to believe that landscapes here were in no
way inferior to, because they were not different from, the often
idealized landscapes on the other side of the Atlantic. On the
other hand, while patriotism might be satisfied, there remained
a considerable pride in essentially American or wilderness land-

scapes generally associated with the sublime or with God. This problem underlies an ambiguity in the "Essay on American Scenery" (mentioned in the preceding chapter), where Thomas Cole both foresees a great civilization in the American future and at the same time condemns the destruction of the wilderness. Thoreau could seem as marvelously ambiguous about the wilderness as Cole. On the one hand, he believed, as he wrote in "Walking," that "in Wildness is the preservation of the World," and yet he said with equal force in *The Maine Woods* that "A civilized man, using the word in the ordinary sense, with his ideas and associations, must at length pine there [in the wilderness], like a cultivated plant, which clasps its fibres about a crude and undissolved mass of peat." Further, "the wilderness is simple, almost to barrenness." It was "the partially cultivated country . . . which chiefly has inspired, and will continue to inspire, the strains of poets, such as compose the mass of any literature."[6] Whatever the value of wilderness, it was in the pastoral realm that Thoreau pitched his tent. For Cole and Thoreau—and for Willis, too, in fact—it was essential both to preserve the wilderness and to have landscapes which showed the impress of civilization. In short, "exceeding beautiful" landscapes like Hammond's were at least as significant to mid-nineteenth-century Americans as were the sublime and picturesque landscapes of the wilderness.

In the creation of national, state, and local parks and forest reserves, Americans have shown themselves no less concerned with a preservation of wilderness than were Cole, Willis, and Thoreau. But the desire to preserve wilderness has not been evident only in the creation of parks and reserves; it has also shown itself in American attempts to reattain and preserve wilderness as part of an immediate environment. Parks and reserves are not after all the best solution. They are distinct and separate from the environments of everyday life. How much better, therefore, to create or discover landscapes which owe as much to wilderness as to civilization. In few ways did Romantic America reveal itself so clearly as in its attempts to achieve landscapes which were indeed a combination of civilization and wilderness.

IN WILDERNESS AND THE AMERICAN MIND, Roderick Nash demonstrated that Thomas Cole's painting "The Ox-Bow" (1836)

offers a conjunction of these apparently opposed realms: civilization and wilderness. The painting is divided diagonally: to the
left is wilderness, represented by Mount Holyoke with storm
clouds overhead, and to the right are cultivated, pastoral farms
of the Connecticut River Valley. Nash concludes his discussion
of the painting with the observation that "Cole's divided canvas
implied the idea Henry David Thoreau accepted as axiomatic:
man's optimum environment is a blend of wildness and civilization."[7]

As observers of American civilization have long recognized,
this "optimum environment" was an ideal for far more Americans
than a few nineteenth-century artists and writers. It was in fact
a ruling ideal of the age and contributed heavily to the reform
of American architecture, influenced patterns of collective and
individual behavior, and made possible some of the finest literature and art of the period. "The Ox-Bow" and *Walden* were exceptional only in their particulars, not in their general expressions of this "optimum environment."

I have mentioned already that Romantic America attempted
to provide landscapes which combined civilization with wilderness. That is, rather than set aside certain lands for the purposes
of civilization and leave other lands in their wilderness condition, attempts were made to represent civilization and wilderness simultaneously in the same environment—notably *in a
sympathetic linking of architecture with wilderness landscapes*.
Both architecture and wilderness landscapes were modified in
such ways that together house and setting formed an emblem, a
visual statement of the "optimum environment," a civilized wilderness; and this emblem is at the center of some of the period's
greatest literature, of which Thoreau's *Walden* and Melville's
Pierre are among the most noteworthy examples.

The emblem of which I am speaking had its immediate origins
not in New England or on the frontier but rather on, of all
things, the great estates of the English aristocracy. Tracing the
matter back further, it is possible to find origins in the landscape
paintings of Claude Lorrain and Salvator Rosa, and without
stretching credibility too far, one could find origins in the classical world—at Delphi, for example, and in other locations where
temples were constructed in wilderness settings. To be sure,

different ages have employed and interpreted this emblem in different ways; our problem is to understand how it was interpreted in Romantic America.

In America, the first major expression of this emblem occurred at Thomas Jefferson's Monticello, his estate near Charlottesville, Va. At Monticello, the two halves of the emblem, civilization and wilderness, represented by the mansion and the Blue Ridge, confronted each other and, in the middle distance, were visually linked by the landscape garden which surrounded the house. Still, however, Monticello established no civilization-wilderness continuum such as Thoreau sought at Walden. At Jefferson's estate, the two halves, though visually linked, remained suspended in perpetual opposition to each other. To find these halves not only linked but sympathetically blended together, we must move forward several decades to the creation of Glen Ellen, the Baltimore estate of the merchant-gentleman Robert Gilmor, Jr.

IN THE MID-1830s, a visitor to Gilmor's truly princely domain would have had good reason to wonder whether he were still on the American side of the Atlantic. Gilmor's estate, located outside Baltimore, was largely the work of the architect Alexander Jackson Davis, who had landscaped the property according to the theories of such English gardeners as Humphrey Repton. Situated on Glen Ellen's picturesquely landscaped grounds were not only the great mansion itself, an elaborate Gothic composition, but also various Gothic ruins and miniature Greek temples, essential complements of many English landscape gardens.

At Glen Ellen, Davis achieved a *visual* union of architecture and landscape by making both conform to the aesthetics of the beautiful and the picturesque. Of course, the picturesque landscapes at Glen Ellen were no more reminiscent of wilderness than were the landscapes at Stowe, Blenheim, and other great English estates, but while Glen Ellen was more the product of art than nature, it still employed a visual technique to suggest a compatibility between architecture and landscape, notably, picturesque landscape. There had been nothing quite like it in America before. As long as American buildings were designed with strict attention to geometry and symmetry, as long as they were formed in the neoclassical traditions, it was impossible to accommodate them visually to the picturesque complexity of the wilderness. There was consequently a visual tension between architecture and natural landscape. Although one can argue that Gilmor's estate was indistinguishable in kind from numerous country properties in England, it is more important to note how much better suited picturesque gardening and architecture were to this country. In England, the creation of a picturesque landscape garden could involve an entire reorganization of land— sometimes the removal of formal gardens or, quite literally, the building of lakes and hills. In at least one instance, it was necessary to remove an entire village. But in much of America there were neither farms nor formal gardens to interfere with the development of picturesque landscape gardens. Furthermore, the wilderness—rough, uncultivated nature—was obviously rich in picturesqueness, a fact which Downing was eager to exploit.

LANDSCAPE GARDENING originated in a desire to approximate in natural landscape such scenes as those found in the paintings of the Italian artists Claude Lorrain (1600–1682), who was born French but became Italian by adoption, and Salvator Rosa (1615–1673). Elizabeth Manwaring in *Italian Landscape in Eighteenth-Century England* has summarized the differences between landscapes by Claude, as the English informally called him, and those by Salvator:

> An extended rolling plain, or wide valley opening to the south, traversed by a winding stream, and encircled, ampitheatre-like, by wooded hills; a foreground of plants and trees, richly leaved; a middle distance of plain and hill, adorned with groves, villas, bridges, castles, temples of antique pattern, vinehung ruins; a far distance of faint blue hills, and often the sea, all this overspread with golden light, preferably of sunrise or sunset; such was the familiar Claudian landscape. The Salvatorial showed precipices and great rock masses of fantastic form, cascades, torrents, desolate ruins, caves, trees dense of growth, or blasted trunks, and shattered boughs.[8]

Generally in landscape gardening a smooth, graceful, and pastoral landscape was considered Claudian, while one which was wild, rough, irregular, and jagged was thought to be Salvatorial. Both types were originally called picturesque, but later the word "picturesque" took on a more specialized meaning. In nineteenth-century America, Andrew Jackson Downing, seeking a way to distinguish between the beautiful and the picturesque, wrote that "to the lover of the fine arts, the name of Claude Lorraine [sic] cannot fail to suggest examples of beauty in some of its purest and most simple forms," but "on the other hand, where shall we find all the elements of the picturesque more graphically combined than in the vigorous landscapes of Salvator Rosa!"[9]

The paintings of Claude were especially popular among advocates of landscape gardening in eighteenth-century England, and the most famous of these gardens—Blenheim, Stowe, Stourhead, Rousham, and so forth—reflect the Virgilian pastoralism of his works. Even today a visitor to some of these estates may find it necessary to wend his way through flocks of sheep or herds of cows, grazing there not because the owner has been reduced to farming but because animals like these are as much a part of Claudian landscapes as are valleys and streams.

The landscape gardens at Stowe, which were the first and in many ways remain among the best of their kind, will serve as examples of gardening which were obviously modeled on paintings by Claude. It should hardly be surprising to anyone who has been to this estate that William Kent, the man who was responsible for much of its early development, believed that a garden should be "a sequence of three-dimensional landscape paintings, replacing oils on canvas by leaf and stone." The Elysian Fields, Kent's principal contribution to Stowe, is exactly that: "a sequence of three-dimensional landscape paintings."[10]

The development of Stowe's landscape began around 1725 when the central portion of the estate was surrounded by a "ha-ha," as it is usually called, a type of sunken fence which both prevented entry to the grounds by unwelcome visitors and yet allowed views of the surrounding countryside. As Horace Walpole wrote,

> At that moment appeared Kent, painter enough to taste the charms of landscape, bold and opinionative enough to dare and to dictate, and born with a genius to strike out a great system from the twilight of imperfect essays. He leaped the fence, and saw that all nature was a garden. He felt the delicious contrast of hill and valley changing imperceptively into each other, tasted

the beauty of the gentle swell, or concave scoop, and remarked how loose groves crowned an easy eminence with happy ornament, and, while they called in the distant view between their graceful stems, removed and extended the perspective by delusive comparison.[11]

But it would be a mistake, of course, to assume that when Kent "leaped the fence, and saw that all nature was a garden," he correspondingly determined that all nature should be left as it was, either as farmlands, for example, or in a more primitive state. It was idealized landscape such as that found in Claude's paintings which Kent's Englishmen would soon discover in their countryside. Walpole had indeed selected his words well when he described Kent as "painter enough to taste the charms of landscape."

The Elysian Fields at Stowe is a complex of framed views, generally composed with Claudian elements, especially in the use of softened lines and classical structures. Basically, the Elysian Fields consists of a small wood through which flows a stream broken by a dam in the middle. Monuments, temples, and statuary are arranged around the stream, which serves as the middle distance for some of Kent's pictures. The landscape theories applied in the creation of the Elysian Fields were used also in the creation of much of the rest of the estate, which in summary is far more an homage to the genius of Claude Lorrain than to nature itself.

The landscapes at Stowe and other similar English estates are no more "natural" than are the severely pleached, formal avenues of trees and the *tapis vert* at Versailles. Although the two kinds of landscapes are very different, both are idealized versions of nature. The English poet William Shenstone wrote that "the landskip [sic] painter is the gardiner's [sic] best designer,"[12] and as long as this dictum remained undisputed—which it did throughout much of the eighteenth century—English gardening had more to do with an aesthetic appreciation of painting than with any real interest in nature itself.

By the 1830s when Davis created Glen Ellen, landscape gardening had not progressed very far beyond its origins. The English were still forming landscapes into artificial patterns.

Some gardeners, Capability Brown and Humphrey Repton among the best, had originated new kinds of ideal pastoral landscapes. For example, Brown built vast lakes and great expanses of lawn dotted with small clumps of trees, but he was no more willing to enjoy landscape as he found it than Kent had been. Repton even went as far as to oppose the use of painting as a guide to gardening. At least he realized the difference between the constricted, framed views of paintings and the panoramic, ever-changing views which are possible in landscape gardening. (Nonetheless, he used paintings, his own, to show prospective clients how gardening could be used to improve their estates.) But Repton was as enamoured of artifical, ideal landscapes as his predecessors had been.

There had been at least one important addition to the English gardening movement, however, and that was the introduction of picturesque Gothic architecture to landscape gardens. A continuing affection for classical geometry in architecture had ensured a tension between house and setting. Together the informal lines of picturesque Gothic architecture and landscape gardens could resolve that tension. "Opinions might differ as to the exact definition of the word 'picturesque,'" Kenneth Clark has written, "but all agreed that nothing was so undeniably picturesque as Gothic architecture."[13]

In America as in England, landscape gardens were combined with classical buildings long before the Gothic Revival made its initial appearance. We have already noted the relation of mansion to site at Monticello. This was certainly the most interesting use of landscape gardening in the early years of this country, but it was not alone in its use of the English method. Jefferson had visited Stowe, Blenheim, and other English estates and so had a better knowledge of the English approach to landscape than did many of his compatriots, and these visits were undoubtedly of value in designing the garden surrounding his mansion. However, visits to the environs of many American cities during the early years of the Republic would have shown that in matters of gardening at least, Americans had lost little of their affection for British things; throughout the country were examples of informal gardens combined with classical structures.

Indeed Washington's classical Mount Vernon was surrounded by a landscape much of which was patterned on the English plan.

As early as 1799, the Gothic had been used in the design of an American house. In that year, Benjamin Latrobe created a Gothic villa near Philadelphia for William Crammond. The house was surrounded by a picturesque landscape garden, but Gothic though the details on the house were, the house showed all the symmetry of a Georgian mansion. The same must be said of Gelston Castle near Richfield Springs, N.Y. This castle—and in fact there is little "castle" about it—dates from 1832, the same years as Glen Ellen. Although the Gothic does make occasional appearances throughout Gelston, it is otherwise very much unlike Glen Ellen. Gelston Castle preserves a nearly perfect symmetry, and situated on the crest of a hill, lords over a landscape which in 1832 was still largely a wilderness. Gelstone Castle and Glen Ellen are both Gothic, although in very different ways, and both were surrounded by picturesque landscapes, but the similarities are entirely superficial. Not only is the castle beautifully symmetrical, or very nearly so, but nothing seems to have been done to bring house and grounds into a visually sympathetic relationship with each other. From the crest of its hill, it oversees a magnificent landscape but is not part of it.

In all respects, Glen Ellen involved a reshaping of natural American scenery to conform to certain ideal patterns, and the patterns were borrowed directly from England. Furthermore, Glen Ellen offered associations with art and literature. Included at the estate were pastoral landscapes of low rolling hills and gentle contours, and these landscapes, complemented by classical temples and Gilmor's ubiquitous sheep, may have reminded visitors of Claude's paintings. At the same time, the mansion and the Gothic ruins provided associations with medieval life, especially as described by Sir Walter Scott. Over all, Glen Ellen was little more than an exercise in fashionable Anglicisms, and yet an especially American attitude toward architecture and landscape eventually grew out of it.

Davis himself helped to popularize the Glen Ellen scheme by creating many such estates throughout the country, and in these later efforts, he seems to have more of a purist, seldom mixing the beautiful and the picturesque as he had when he included the classical with the medieval, the beautiful with the picturesque, at Glen Ellen. As the partner of the great Greek Revival architect Ithiel Town, Davis had begun his career in a classical tradition; he was at first a designer of columns and temples. In the 1830s when Glen Ellen was built, the Greek Revival still provided the major American architectural vocabulary, but in the following decade the Greek increasingly lost favor to the Gothic. Davis was far more the descriptive artist than the engineer, and the Gothic provided more freedom for him to exercise his abilities. Moreover, he remained involved with pictorial matters and was apparently more concerned with the way his landscapes and buildings looked than with the moral or social ideas they might suggest. Indeed he designed a number of castles and occasionally provided one with a drawbridge— although as his critics realized, medieval fortifications were rather out of place in democratic America. Meanwhile, Davis's friend Andrew Jackson Downing did his best to justify the picturesque in irrefutably American terms. If Davis's castles were somehow out of place in American landscapes, still, as Downing argued, picturesque architecture had real visual value, given the type of wild scenery with which America was provided.

ANDREW JACKSON DOWNING was the proprietor of a successful gardening and nursery business, inherited from his father and located on the Hudson at Newburgh, N.Y. He personally landscaped several estates and at the time of his death was working out a plan for landscaping parts of Washington, D.C. Nothing remains of the nursery, however, and of his projects for landscaping, few are sufficiently intact to reveal his intentions. Little of the Washington project was ever carried out. What we know of Downing's ideas we know primarily through his books, *A Treatise on the Theory and Practice of Landscape Gardening, Adapted to North America* (originally published in 1841, but considerably revised and expanded in later editions), *Cottage Residences* (1842), *The Architecture of Country Houses* (1850), and *Rural Essays,* a collection of essays which first appeared in his magazine, *The Horticulturist and Journal of Rural Art and Rural Taste. Rural Essays* was published in 1853, the year after

Downing's death, but did not mark an end to his work. This was carried on by a number of his disciples, among them Calvert Vaux, the author of *Villas and Cottages* (1857), and Henry Winthrop Sargent, who was responsible for additions to those editions of the *Treatise* which were published after Downing's death.

Catharine Maria Sedgwick claimed that no one in America, "whether he be rich or poor, builds a house or lays out a garden without consulting Downing's works," and while this was surely an exaggeration, it is nearly matched by some of the claims for Downing's influence which more recent commentators have made.[14] John A. Kouwenhoven has said that "no one in the mid-century had a greater influence on American taste in architecture and decoration . . . ,"[15] and according to Russell Lynes, "no one had a greater influence on the taste of Americans a century ago than he, and no one had a more profound impact on the looks of the countryside."[16] If we are to believe Joel E. Spingarn, Downing's influence caused "the whole face of rural America [to be] transformed."[17] Extravagant though these claims may seem, it remains true that Downing's vision of an America visually and morally defined through a union of picturesque landscape and architecture did have a truly extraordinary effect. As the incredibly large number of surviving picturesque homes and gardens attest, he was exceptionally successful in impressing the picturesque on the American countryside.

For Downing, landscape gardening and domestic architecture were by no means of minor significance; these were in fact creative enterprises through which a country of wilderness and recent settlements could be transformed into what he considered a highly cultured and civilized nation. His ideals were those of the middle class: "the love of order, the obedience to law, the security and repose of society, the love of home, and the partiality to localities endeared by birth or association," and he clearly expected to find these ideals shared by the owners of his cottages and villas.[18] The conquest of the wilderness, the advancement of a nation though Manifest Destiny were problems that had little immediate concern for him. More important for him were "smiling lawns and tasteful cottages," for it was his belief that when these "begin to embellish a country, we know that order and culture are established."[19] America's achievement was to be measured not so much by its conquest of the Western territories as by the advancement of its rural life.

The fourth (1849) and subsequent editions of the *Treatise* include Downing's fullest attempts to define the value and methods of landscape gardening. Downing had read both the works of Uvedale Price on the picturesque and the writings of Humphrey Repton and John Claudius Loudon, respectively, on English landscape gardening. As the initial chapter of the *Treatise* suggests, he also knew much about the progress of gardening in the United States. His background and training emphasized the English tradition of landscape gardening begun by William Kent and continued and developed by Capability Brown and Repton, but he did not simply preach the ideas of his predecessors. He was as attracted to ideal landscapes as they, but he also believed that in America nature had already provided landscapes which were largely ideal. Here the gardener aimed at "improvements"; he did not always have to start as in England virtually from the beginning.

The picturesque, wrote Downing, "aims at the production of outlines of a certain spirited irregularity, surfaces comparatively abrupt and broken, and growth of a somewhat wild and bold character." The beautiful, on the other hand, "is produced by outlines whose curves are flowing and gradual, surfaces of softness, and growth of richness and luxuriance." The picturesque and the beautiful were not simply visual categories, however; according to Downing, they had their foundations in a realm of spiritual reality. Both were expressions of "Beauty," which ". . . in all natural objects . . . arises from their expression of those attributes of the Creator—infinity, unity, symmetry, proportion, etc.—which he had stamped more or less visibly on all his works." The beautiful, he believed, ". . . is nature or art obeying the universal laws of perfect existence (i.e., Beauty), easily, freely, harmoniously, and without the *display* of power." The picturesque, on the other hand, "is nature or art obeying the same laws rudely, violently, irregularly, and often displaying power only."[20]

The gardener's problem was to identify the picturesque or the beautiful in a landscape and then heighten its effect. According to Downing,

When we discover the *picturesque* indicated in the grounds of the residence to be treated, let us take advantage of it; and while all harshness incompatible with scenery near the house is removed, the original expression may in most cases be heightened, in all rendered more elegant and appropriate, without lowering it in force or spirit.

Downing would have found pure wilderness no more interesting than did his English predecessors. Nor did he feel the gardener had any business merely reproducing natural landscape or giving "a fac-simile of nature, that could not be distinguished from a wild scene." It was the gardener's business to make landscapes conform to the picturesque or the beautiful.* Downing retained a measured respect for what nature had done already, but with truly sublime confidence, he believed that the landscape gardener could generally do better. Ideally, of course, the gardener would be presented with suitable materials for his picturesque or beautiful landscape. Downing remarked, for example, that

> Within the last five years, we think the Picturesque is beginning to be preferred. It has, when a suitable locality offers, great advantages for us. The raw materials of wood, water, and surface, by the margin of many of our rivers and brooks, are at once appropriated with so much effect, and so little art, in the picturesque mode; the annual tax on the purse too is so comparatively little, and the charm so great![21]

Downing's ideal landscape gardener was, in effect, both artist and priest. As an artist, he provided aesthetically satisfying landscape pictures, and as a priest, he gave expression in his landscapes to certain divine attributes. Downing insisted above

---

* "We must not be supposed to find in nature only the Beautiful and the Picturesque. Grandeur and Sublimity are also expressions strongly marked in many of the noblest portions of natural landscape. But, except in very rare instances, they are wholly beyond the powers of the landscape gardener, at least in the comparatively limited scale of his operations in this country. All that he has to do, is to respect them where they exist in natural landscape which forms part of his work of art, and so treat the latter, as to make it accord with, or at least not violate, the higher and predominant expression of the whole." [Andrew Jackson Downing, *A Treatise on the Theory and Practice of Landscape Gardening*, 6th ed. (New York: A. O. Moore and Co., 1859), pp. 56–57.]

all on the reality of a relationship or interface between the spiritual realm and the material world.

TRUE WILDERNESS had no place in Downing's scheme; only if the wild landscape were made to conform to ideal patterns was it acceptable as a human environment. Unlike Thoreau and Emerson, Downing was unwilling to take nature on its own terms, nor did even the more restricted concerns of ecology (fundamental interests to Cooper and Thoreau) have much interest for Downing. His rural America was to be inhabited almost totally by the middle class, for although he gave much attention to laborers in his outline of rural life, he seemed to feel that sooner or later all America would average out toward the middle. As for an hereditary, moneyed aristocracy, he believed that this, in a country without primogeniture, was an impossibility.[22] Therefore, he offered a vision of a middle-class, rural America— a vision of American landscapes conforming to ideal patterns of both aesthetic and spiritual significance.

Whether Americans ever comprehended the totality of Downing's scheme is, of course, an unanswerable question, but there can be no doubt that the scheme, at least in its physical outlines, had an effect across the continent. A mania for Downing's ideal landscapes, as well as the villas and cottages which he believed should accompany them, affected Americans of all classes, and by the time of the Civil War, Downing's version of the picturesque had left its mark from New York to Oregon. To cite only one of the most famous examples in the West, the Surgeon's Quarters at The Dalles in Oregon was a Downing villa set in an undeniably picturesque landscape—although to be sure that landscape owed its picturesqueness as much to nature as to man. Italian villas, Swiss chalets, board and batten cottages, and Gothic residences were all considered good visual complements for landscape gardens—whether those gardens consisted of many acres or front yards—and while the greater number have probably been destroyed, they are still to be found in places as diverse as San Francisco; New Harmony, Ind; Lexington, Ky; and Portland, Me. Landscape gardens vanish more easily than buildings do, of course, and there are many more picturesque villas surviving today than there are picturesque gardens. In the last hundred years, many landscape gardens have reverted to a more or less wilderness state, while others have vanished entirely, victims of the subdivider or urban renewal.

ROBERT GILMOR, JR., was no typical American: in any age he would have been an exceptional man, but in Jacksonian America he was very nearly without peer. The scion of a family long accutomed to wealth, he had the advantages of a good education, extensive travel, and a socially influencial position. In pre–Civil War America, there were surely few Americans, even among the most rabid of Anglophiles, who were as well acquainted with English aesthetic theories as he, and even fewer possessed the means to create domains as extensive as Glen Ellen. Gilmor was also among the country's most generous patrons, and it was largely his money which financed Thomas Cole's voyage to Europe to study the works of the great landscape painters. Thomas Doughty, Horatio Greenough, and William Sidney Mount were among other well-known American artists who benefited from Gilmor's generosity. Cole had reason to listen to Gilmor's advice, for not only might the dutiful student receive a larger share of the patronage; Gilmor also had a large reputation as a critic of art—a reputation to which William Dunlap gave much attention in *A History of the Rise and Progress of the Arts of Design in the United States* (1834). However, on the question of ideal versus real landscapes, Cole could not bring himself to agree with even so generous a patron as Gilmor. In one of his letters to Cole, Gilmor wrote, "I prefer real American scenes to compositions, leaving the distribution of light, choice of atmosphere and clouds, and in short all that is to render its natural effect as pleasing and spirited as the artist can feel permitted to do, without violation of its truth."[23] Cole disagreed, for although he obtained his reputation largely because of the "real American scenes" he had painted early in his career, he also believed that an artist must render an idealization of his subject, not merely a literal imitation of it.[24] As readers of Neil Harris's *The Artist in American Society* know, the disagreement between Gilmor and Cole is typical of its time, the patron arguing for literal representation and the artist arguing for idealization. But it is curious to find Gilmor arguing for "real American scenes" in painting, while at the same time allowing Davis to create at Glen Ellen a landscape garden, a series of

"compositions" which were in their own way as much idealiza-
tions of natural scenery as were Cole's painted landscapes. It
would seem that as long as "real American scenes" were surrounded by gilded frames—or, one might add, were seen from
the deck of a steamer or the porch of a hotel—they could be
incorporated into experience; however, unlike Thoreau, Gilmor
had no desire to find any wilderness growing up to his front
door; even reality had its limits. It was not until after the Civil
War that Americans in numbers opted for wilderness, not landscaped settings, for even vacation retreats.

JOHN BANVARD is an especially interesting example of the
American differentiating between the type of landscape in which
to live, when the choice was financially possible, and the type of
landscape preferable for art, literature, and travel. In his day,
Banvard was perhaps the most popular, although surely not the
most talented, of American artists. His popularity was no doubt
in part the result of his abilities as a businessman. He was an
entrepeneur in a class with P. T. Barnum, and while he claimed
that his paintings were of "patriotic" value, their primary significance for him appears to have been economic.[25]
A New Yorker by birth, Banvard traveled west when he was
fifteen, and after a short period as a clerk in a drugstore, he
determined that his ambition in life was to be an artist. Apparently
no modest gentleman, he confessed in a third-person narrative of
his life that he ". . . was a self-taught, artist—no—he had a
teacher. He went not to Rome indeed, to study the works of hands
long since passed away; but he studied the works of the One
Great Living Master!—Nature was his teacher." Initiative and
Nature combined to aid him in painting a panoramic view of
Venice, a remarkable accomplishment, since Banvard had never
crossed the Atlantic. But views of the Old World were not his
main objective: his most ambitious project, which occupied him
from 1840 to 1846, was the creation of a "Panorama of the
Mississippi River, Painted on Three Miles of Canvas: Exhibiting
a View of Country 1200 Miles in Length, Extending from the
Mouth of the Missouri River to the City of New Orleans; Being
by far the Largest Picture ever Executed by Man." Whether
Banvard's panorama was in fact "the Largest Picture ever Executed by Man" is still a disputed point, but it was surely much

smaller, by at least two miles, than its artist claimed. Nonetheless, it was sufficiently impressive to reap a substantial fortune; during the first seven months that it was shown in Boston, it earned, Banvard claimed, no less than $50,000. The Mississippi wilderness even made its way to England, where the Queen "commanded" a showing at Windsor Castle, and in this country, Congress, reflecting American sentiment toward the painting, unanimously pronounced the work "herculean," "a truly wonderful and magnificent production."[26] Perhaps of less importance to the artist, although of much greater interest to us, Longfellow used the painting as the basis for descriptive passages in *Evangeline*. "The river comes to me instead of my going to the river," he wrote, "and as it is to flow through the pages of the poem, I look upon this as a special benediction."[27]

Popular enthusiasm for the panorama may have had less to do with Banvard's technical abilities as an artist than with the painting's very size. He admitted that his ambition had been "to paint a picture of the beautiful scenery of the Mississippi, which should be superior to all others, in point of *size*, as that prodigious river is superior to the streamlets of Europe,—a gigantic idea!—which seems truly kindred to the illimitable forests and vast extent of [my] native land."[28] In brief, the vastness of American wilderness was to be expressed in art, but the size of such a landscape required a larger canvas than had ever been used before. He stated also that "The idea of gain never entered [my] mind when [I] commenced the undertaking"—a statement which is perhaps best taken at less than its face value—"but [I] was actuated by a patriotic and honorable ambition, that America should produce the *largest painting* in the world."[29] In point of quality, of course, Americans would have to wait for Frederick Church.

Considering Banvard's professed devotion to panoramic art as well as to "the illimitable forests and vast extent of [my] native land," one might have expected an even larger painting to follow that of the Mississippi—or at the very least a Thoreauvian project of a gigantic sort conducted somewhere in the wilderness in the West. Instead, six years after the panorama's initial success, he was to be found out on the North Shore of Long Island, already a choice spot for the homes of affluent New

Yorkers. Here in the village of Cold Spring Harbor, he designed and built Glenada, a crenellated Gothic villa, which he surrounded with a picturesque landscape garden. Glenada was in every way the impressive equal of Glen Ellen. Domestic life, not the wilderness, marked the years of Banvard's greatest fame. It is worth noting, however, that he may have experienced a change of heart (or fortunes), for he sold his estate eleven years after he built it. He then traveled west and spent his last days in South Dakota.

GLEN ELLEN AND GLENADA have long since vanished. Gilmor's castle was gutted by fire, and more than a generation ago, all that remained of house and landscape garden was leveled and graded over. In their place rose the Loch Raven Dam. Glenada, minus a wing, became a hotel in the 1880s. Considerable additions were made to the building, so that finally it barely suggested the rural retreat Banvard created. Then in 1906 the entire structure was demolished. Unfortunately, the huge panoramic painting, like the house and garden it financed, has been destroyed, and today we can know it only through descriptions by Banvard and his contemporaries—and through *Evangeline*. Only engravings and photographs survive to suggest the princely glories constructed by the Baltimore merchant and the artist of the Mississippi.

James Fenimore Cooper was also attracted by the Gothic and the picturesque, and while his Leather-Stocking novels glorified the wilderness, he chose to redesign his family mansion according to the Gothic style. He added a crenellated roof, and then proceeded to lay out a landscape garden in the picturesque style. In its day, Cooper's estate was surely the most striking place in the vicinity of Cooperstown, but like so many other essays in the picturesque, the mansion later burned and today it also is known to us only through pictures.

Although Cooper's mansion, Glen Ellen, and Glenada are gone, there are relatively few pre–Civil War cities and towns without some vestige of the architecture and landscapes preferred by Gilmor and Banvard. Lyndhurst, in Tarrytown, N.Y., is often considered the apogee of the picturesque in mid-nineteenth-century American architecture, while Central Park in New York City may have been the period's finest expression of the picturesque in landscape gardening. Lyndhurst was certainly the most ambitious of Davis's many villas, and the engineering feats which were required in creating the picturesque landscapes of Central Park were in their day nothing short of astonishing. My personal favorites among examples of picturesque architecture and landscaping include few works as spectacular as Central Park and Lyndhurst, however; rather I prefer such smaller places as Cottage Lawn in the upstate New York village of Oneida. The houses and grounds at these estates can tell us at least as much, and probably more, about the general quality of life in the mid-nineteenth-century as can the more monumental works. As impressive a monument to the picturesque as Lyndhurst is, it tells us only about life among a very special and very rich group of people, but Cottage Lawn and its kind belong to a much larger world, a solidly middle-class world, the world which Downing was most eager to reach.

Cottage Lawn is no Glen Ellen, Glenada, or Lyndhurst. Compared with these, it is indeed a modest villa or large cottage, and its grounds, unlike the extensive acreage of those other estates, is limited to a corner lot on the main street of the village. Its architect was, however, Alexander Jackson Davis, and he provided his client with what must have seemed a most sumptuous home at the time. There are no battlements at Cottage Lawn; it is simply a large, gabled "rural Gothic" house—not a mansion and, certainly when compared with Glen Ellen, quite unpretentious. The villa, of which Cottage Lawn is representative, was, according to Downing,

> . . . the most refined home of America—the home of its most leisurely and educated class of citizens. Nature and art both lend it their happiest influence. Amid the serenity and peace of sylvan scenes, surrounded by the perennial freshness of nature, enriched without and within by objects of universal beauty and interest—objects that touch the heart and awaken the understanding—it is in such houses that we should look for the happiest social and moral development of our people.[30]

Cottage Lawn was built in 1849 for the family of Sands Higinbotham. His profession, it should be noted, was especially American: real estate development. Originally from New York State, he had early moved to Vermont, where, according to his obituary, "He was known as an honorable and prosperous merchant, and as a wise and conscientious man, whom all esteemed." In 1829 he purchased land in the town of Lenox, N.Y., and the following year, he increased his holdings there. Three years later, a railroad was built across his land, and oddly enough, since this was a rather sparsely settled area, one of the major depots was located there. The railroad made Higinbotham's fortune. As one of his eulogists wrote,

> In July, 1839, the cars [of the railroad] commenced to run, and from that date, under the fostering care of Mr. Higinbotham, the village of Oneida has steadily grown and improved, from year to year, without drawback or change, except to a greater and more rapid improvement as time went on. Here, in the last thirty-four years, . . . the crowning work of his life was done.[31]

Between 1834 and his death in 1868, Higinbotham encouraged Oneida's growth—much to his profit. From what was virtual wilderness grew a sizable community supporting at least half a dozen lawyers, several doctors, six churches, three banks, two newspapers (three if we include one published in the nearby Oneida Community), and a fair number of hotels and business blocks.

And what did Higinbotham and his family do with their new wealth? One project was the creation of their "rural residence," Cottage Lawn, located not out in the country but rather very near the center of Higinbotham's village. The house was then surrounded by a small landscape garden. At some point, probably not long after the house was completed, a small Gothic shelter or gazebo was built on the lawn near the house. The shelter served absolutely no practical purpose except to provide a little shade, although with heavily forested environs, shade at Cottage Lawn was not at a premium. Still, one would no more lose that shelter than the Gothic villa or the landscape garden. Cottage Lawn tells us much about an America which first destroyed wilderness—when it was economically profitable to do so—and then created ideal picturesque landscapes around homes and, as in Central Park, in the public grounds of cities. This "rural residence" in up-state New York is more typical of mid-nineteenth-century America than is Thoreau's hut at Walden Pond; indeed it was against just such villas and landscaped grounds as Cottage Lawn that Thoreau rebelled. "As I preferred some things to others, and especially valued my freedom," he wrote in *Walden*, ". . . I did not wish to spend my time in earning rich carpets or other fine furniture, or delicate cookery, or a house in the Grecian or Gothic style just yet." At Walden, there was "no path to the front-yard gate in the Great Snow,—no gate, no front-yard,—and no path to the civilized world!"[32]

LANDSCAPE GARDENING provided settings and thematic materials for several eighteenth- and nineteenth-century English novels and poems. Alexander Pope was particularly interested in the landscape gardening movement, a fact evident both in his writings, notably the "Epistle to Burlington," and in the design of his own estate at Twickenham. Jane Austen made considerable use of landscape gardening in her works, especially *Mansfield Park*, which contains quite extensive comments on the work of Humphrey Repton. A knowledge of landscape gardening was essential social equipment for the ladies and gentlemen of eighteenth- and nineteenth-century England, and therefore, the subject provided good material for the novelist of manners. In America, however, there were few Mansfield Parks and even fewer novelists of manners. The nation lacked a country gentry or aristocracy with the highly developed manners and the learning of the English upper classes. There was relatively little here to interest a Jane Austen.

In the South, however, an aristocracy—closely bound by a code of manners—survived, and if this aristocracy could not match the English upper classes in wealth, titles, or complexity of traditions, it was still an aristocracy which took itself very seriously. The only pre–Civil War Southern writer of the first order was Edgar Allan Poe, and not surprisingly, he wrote more about people of privilege and rank than did any other major American writer of the time. Futhermore, Poe had lived in England when he was a child, and quite possibly his sense of social class was reinforced during his stay there. In any case, among the aristocrats in Poe's writings is Ellison in "The Domain of Arnheim"—a man worth nearly half a billion dollars and willing to devote his wealth to the "poetry" of landscape gardening. It is worth our time to examine closely both this sketch and others like it, not because they are among Poe's more interesting works, but because they can show us how thoroughly literature can be informed and shaped by contemporary, popular thought.

THE LANDSCAPE GARDEN was utilized by Poe in both "Landor's Cottage" and "The Domain of Arnheim," the first half of which appeared in 1842 as "The Landscape Garden" and, slightly revised, was republished three years later. In 1847, an expanded version, including a detailed description of a landscaped garden, was published as "The Domain of Arnheim." "Landor's Cottage" was published in 1849, four months before Poe's death, but it may have been written much earlier.

Before examining these sketches, it would be wise to examine two of Poe's other short pieces, "The Elk" (1844) and "The Island of the Fay" (1841). These are both minor works, and they are generally overlooked by Poe's critics, but since they involve discussions of natural American landscapes, they provide an interesting contrast with the discussions of landscape gardens in "The Domain of Arnheim" and "Landor's Cottage."

In "The Elk" Poe provides, in effect, his comment on travelers who made it their business to locate poetic and historical associations in natural landscapes. Restating a claim which had been made countless times by the less socially oriented among tourists, Poe wrote in this sketch that ". . . in America generally, the traveller who would behold the finest landscapes, must seek them not by the railroad, nor by the steamboat, nor by the stagecoach, nor in his private carriage, nor yet even on horseback—but on foot."[33] The "finest landscapes," he said, are those found in the true wilderness, not along those routes preordained for the tourist. "Although the Hudson, Niagara, the Catskills, Harper's Ferry, the Lakes of New York, the Ohio, the Prairies, and the Mississippi" are "the natural lions of the land," "in fact, the real Edens of the land lie far away from the track of our own most deliberate tourists."[34] By 1844, Americans had provided all the lions with appropriate associations. Irving, Cooper, Cole, Bryant, Sedgwick, and Simms, among others, had done their work well. But the "Edens" are not those which have received the attention of tourists. For the "cultivated lover of the grand and beautiful amid the works of God"—in short, the lover of wilderness—Poe suggested a visit to a river named the Wissahiccon, a tributary of the Schuylkill, near Philadelphia.

Up to this point, Poe's sketch reads very much like hundreds of others published in annuals and magazines at the time— sketches accompanied by engravings or, as they were generally called, "embellishments." Since it was the picture, not the text, which was supposed to attract prospective purchasers, authors seldom felt called on to provide more than a brief discussion of the scene, a discussion generally carried on in terms of the picturesque, historical associations, associations with God, and so forth. However, on close reading, Poe's sketch turns out finally to be a critical commentary on American worship of natural landscapes.

The associations with landscapes along the Wissahiccon are as traditional as the associations entertained by travelers along the Hudson. One scene is compared with the paintings of Salvator Rosa—and by this time, it seemed that virtually every American landscape well known to tourists had been compared either with Rosa's or with Claude Lorrain's works. The historical associations were equally traditional:

> The heat gradually overcame me, and resigning myself to the influence of the scenes and of the weather, and of the gently moving current, I sank into a half slumber, during which my imagination revelled in visions of the Wissahiccon of ancient days— . . . when the red man trod alone, with the elk, upon the ridges that now towered above.[35]

Salvator Rosa and Indians who "trod alone"—one might well be reading a sketch by N. P. Willis. But then an elk, like the one which presumably accompanied the red man, appears on the cliff above.* Rather than be an embodiment of Poe's "vision," however, the elk is discovered to be "a *pet* of great age and very domestic habits, and belonged to an English family occupying a villa in the vicinity."[36]

Poe initially promised a landscape for the "cultivated lover of the grand and beautiful amid the works of God," then offered

---

* In *Edgar Allan Poe: A Critical Biography* (1941), Arthur Hobson Quinn reported that the episode with the elk may very well have occurred. An elk may seem a strange choice for a pet, but Poe may have encountered the one which was kept domesticated at "Spring Bank," a villa near the Wissahiccon.

associations with the "red man" and the works of Salvator Rosa. It is only in the imagination that the Wissahiccon provides an escape to "the 'good old days' when the Demon of the Engine was not, when pic-nics were undreamed of, when 'water privileges' were neither bought nor sold."³⁷ In fact the wilderness of the Wissahiccon borders on the grounds of a villa, where, of all incredible possibilities, a wild elk has become a pet. The American wilderness had indeed been domesticated, and with quiet irony, Poe provided the tourists among his readers with an easily traveled route into this Edenic region and told them of its choice sites for landscape gardens and cottages.

"THE ISLAND OF THE FAY," like "The Elk," originally served as the text for an "embellishment" in a popular magazine, and as one might expect of something written under these conditions, the sketch on first reading seems to be as gentle, casual, and minor as anything by Willis; but Poe's sketch, like "The Elk," has a serious purpose—in this case, to criticize the pervasive worship of the American wilderness.

The narrator of "The Island of the Fay" states that "In truth, the man who would behold the glory of God upon Earth must in solitude behold that glory"—a belief which can be found in many American writings of the time and which received its classical expression many years later in Thoreau's *Walden*.³⁸ Other passages also clearly echo the thinking and belief of Poe's contemporaries; the narrator sounds very Emersonian, for example, when he asks, "may we not . . . suppose . . . life within life, the less within the greater, and all within the Spirit Divine?"³⁹

In *Poe: A Critical Study*, Edward H. Davidson concludes that "It seems unlikely that Poe was in any way aware of Emerson's [*Nature*] . . .," and yet Poe, who was exceptionally well read in the literature of his day, must have been aware of what his literary brethren in Concord and Boston were writing and publishing.⁴⁰ "The Island of the Fay" is really "about" transcendentalism. In his sketch, Poe places his narrator in the midst of American wilderness and tests the true nature of the transcendental experience. As it happens, the narrator, rather than obtain the spiritual knowledge promised by such thinkers as Emerson, ends his solitary revery in a vision of death.

In form, "The Island of the Fay" is like "The Elk": an initial section, consisting of discursive material, followed by narrative example. In the second half of "The Island of the Fay," the narrator describes one of his solitary journeys into the wilderness: "a far-distant region of mountain locked within mountain, and sad rivers and melancholy tarns writhing or sleeping within all." In this primitive landscape, he rested, he says, on the bank of a stream where he saw, or imagined he saw, one of "the few gentle Fays who remain from the wreck of [their] race." In the stream is a small island, and he says, "While thus I mused, it appeared to me that the form of one of those very Fays about whom I had been pondering, made its way slowly into the darkness from out the light at the western end of the island." The Fay, standing "erect, in a singularly fragile canoe," traveled around the island several times, and the narrator speculates that each trip around the island represented a year in her life. With each revolution she seemed "feebler," "fainter," "more indistinct" until finally, with the coming of night, she was destroyed, absorbed into the darkness.[41] The narrator, in short, encounters death, "not the glory of God upon earth," in his excursion into nature and solitude.*

---

* Ishmael in *Moby-Dick* recognizes a truth similar to that which is at the center of "The Island of the Fay." In Melville's novel, as in Poe's sketch, the pantheist-narrator is offered in his solitary musings not pleasant psychic renewal but a vision of death. Says Ishmael:

> lulled into such an opium-like listlessness of vacant, unconscious reverie is this absent minded youth by the blending cadence of waves with thoughts, that at last he loses his identity; takes the mystic ocean at his feet for the visible image of that deep, blue, bottomless soul, pervading mankind and nature; and every strange, half-seen, gliding, beautiful thing that eludes him; every dimly-discovered, uprising fin of some undiscernible form, seems to him the embodiment of those elusive thoughts that only people the soul by continually flitting through it. In this enchanted mood, thy spirit ebbs away to whence it come; becomes diffused through time and space; like Cranmer's Pantheistic ashes, forming at last a part of every shore the round world over.
>
> There is no life in thee, now, except that rocking life imparted by a gently rolling ship; by her, borrowed from the sea; by the sea, from the inscrutable tides of God. But while this sleep, this dream is on ye, move your foot or hand an inch; slip your hold at all; and your identity comes back in horror. Over Descartian vortices you hover. And perhaps, at mid-day, in the fairest weather, with one half-throttled shriek you drop through the transparent air into the summer sea, no more to rise for ever. Heed it well, ye Pantheists! [Herman Melville, *Moby-Dick* (Indianapolis: The Bobbs-Merrill Company, 1964), pp. 214–215.]

"The Elk" and "The Island of the Fay" are so deceptively journalistic that they have long been ranked among Poe's lesser works. But they are essential to any analysis of Poe's attitude toward landscape—his rejection of the attitudes toward landscape entertained generally by tourists as well as those entertained by transcendentalists, pantheists, and others seeking divine significance in natural landscapes.

THE CENTRAL FIGURE of "The Domain of Arnheim" is referred to simply as Ellison, a man who "comprehended . . . the true character, the august aims, the supreme majesty and dignity of the poetic sentiment." Ellison has at his disposal a fortune worthy of Astor's envy—no less than $450 million. Rather than gratifying "the poetic sentiment" in literature, music, or art—which would surely not strain his finances—Ellison devotes his abilities and wealth to the creation of a more than regal estate, a landscape garden, for this is supposed to offer "to the proper Muse the most magnificent of opportunities."

> Here, indeed was the fairest field for the display of imagination in the endless combining of forms of novel beauty; the elements to enter into combination being by a vast superiority, the most glorious which the earth could afford. In the multiform and multicolor of the flower and the trees, he recognized the most direct and the most energetic efforts of Nature at physical loveliness. And in the direction or combination of this effort—or, still more properly, in its adaptation to the eyes which were to behold it upon earth—he perceived that he should be employing the best means—laboring to the greatest advantage—in the fulfillment, not only of his own destiny as poet, but of the august purposes for which the Deity had implanted the poetic sentiment in man.

Poe was absolutely earnest in advocating landscape gardening as poetic expression and in asserting that Ellison was "in the widest and noblest sense . . . a poet."[42] In fact, "The Domain of Arnheim" and its "pendant," "Landor's Cottage," take us to the heart of Poe's thinking on the nature of the poet and the function of his art.

It was not chance which led Poe to make his ideal poet a landscape gardener, for the best-known American landscape gardener held theories on poetry—at least the poetry of landscape gardening—which were strikingly similar to Poe's. Both

Downing and Poe considered the prime objective of this art to be the fullest possible realization of beauty in landscape, and both identified that beauty with a divine origin.

In his *Treatise,* Downing wrote that

> Beauty, in all natural objects, as we conceive, arises from their expression of those attributes of the Creator—infinity, unity, symmetry, proportion, etc.—which he has stamped more or less visibly on all his works; and a beautiful living form is one in which the individual is a harmonious and well balanced development of a fine type. Thus, taking the most perfect specimins of beauty in the human figure, we see in them symmetry, proportion, unity, and grace—the presence of everything that could add to the idea of perfect existence. In a beautiful tree, such as a fine American elm, we see also the most perfect balance of all its parts, resulting from its growth under the most favorable influences. It realizes, then, perfectly, the finest form of a fine type or species of tree.[43]

As previously noted, Downing wrote that "the Beautiful is nature or art obeying the universal laws of perfect existence (i.e., Beauty), easily, freely, harmoniously, and without the *display* of power." (On the other hand, it may be remembered, "the Picturesque," he believed, "is nature or art obeying the same laws rudely, violently, irregularly, and often displaying power only.") Downing, however, was no pantheist: like Bryant and Cole, he did not believe that nature was divine per se but that it emblematically expressed certain divine qualities.

Since Downing considered "the development of the Beautiful"—including here, apparently, the picturesque—to be "the end and aim of Landscape Gardening," the creation of a garden became essentially a religious act, for in the garden the spectator was offered a complex of images to be interpreted as expressions of divine attributes. The difference between the gardener's landscape and the natural landscape lay in the fact that in the former the expressions of divine attributes were more evident, extraneous factors having been removed. It was the artist's business to heighten the religious expression of the material world.

In the essay "The Poetic Principle," Poe stated that "The Poetic Sentiment . . . may develope itself in various modes—in Painting, in Sculpture, in Architecture, in the Dance—very especially in Music—and very peculiarly, and with a wide field, in the composition of the Landscape Garden." This "Poetic Sentiment" involves "no mere appreciation of the Beauty before us," Poe wrote, "—but a wild effort to reach the Beauty above. Inspired by an ecstatic prescience of the glories beyond the grave, we struggle by multiform combinations among the things and thoughts of Time, to attain a portion of that Loveliness whose very elements, perhaps, appertain to eternity alone." For Poe, the great end in art, guided by the "Poetic Sentiment," was "the creation of supernal Beauty." Poe's objective here suggests Downing's. Like Poe, Downing would reach, by means of the garden, "the Beauty above," not merely an "appreciation of the Beauty before us."[44]*

ELLISON quotes a landscape theorist on the distinction between natural and artificial styles in landscape gardening and condemns the former in which " 'one seeks to recall the original beauty of the country,' " for, he claims, "the original beauty is never so great as that which may be introduced." If by the artificial style, we are to understand solely Versailles and other landscape creations in which geometry places landscape entirely under regimented human control, then indeed Ellison is at odds with everything Downing advocated in landscape gardening. But it is not a thoroughly human order which Ellison wishes in the garden: "A poet, having very unusual pecuniary resources," he says, "might, while retaining the necessary idea of *art* or *culture,* or . . . *interest,* so imbue his designs at once with the extent and novelty of Beauty, as to convey the sentiment of *spiritual* interference."[45] Ellison reaches imaginatively for a landscape garden of grand and large proportions; the concept of sublimity is basic here—a fact even more evident in the sheer size of his Arnheim. Downing believed that "except . . . in very rare instances," sublimity and grandeur were "wholly beyond the powers of the landscape gardener, at least in the comparatively

---

* Similar though Poe's ideas seem to Downing's at many points, there are equally distinct differences; certainly Downing's Protestant God, for example, was not Poe's, and the attainment of Poe's objectives in landscape gardening was almost without exception elusive, while for Downing that attainment, granting the ability of any good landscape gardener, was virtually certain.

limited scale of his operations in this country." The landscape
gardener could simply respect sublimity and grandeur "where
they exist in natural landscape which forms part of his work of
art" and try somehow to incorporate them into that part of his
design over which he had greater control—a solution which
clearly would have had no appeal for a theorist like Ellison.[46]
He (and Poe) have challenged Downing. With $450 million at
his disposal, Ellison is in a position not merely to discover sublime and grand landscapes but, much as Downing would perfect
picturesque and beautiful landscapes, to perfect—perhaps even
to create—landscapes which are sublime. Ellison realizes that it
would require someone more than human to create his ideal
garden. In the end, he makes clear his break with Downing:
the "nature" which Ellison envisions for his ideal garden is "a
nature which is not God, nor an emanation from God, but which
is still nature, in the sense that it is the handiwork of the angels
that hover between man and God." Downing's gardener essentially interprets and clarifies the divine expression of landscape,
but Ellison—no humble gardener, he!—claims for himself as
poet a spiritual identification and the ability to imbue or create
landscapes of, to use Poe's words, "supernal Beauty." Like Poe
himself, Ellison sees the poet as the source of that divine beauty
which informs the poetic work. One is reminded of Poe's wish
that he could be Israfel, the angel-poet with "the sweetest voice
of all God's creatures."[47]

"The Landscape Garden" abruptly ended with the statement
that Ellison had in fact created his Paradise, and it was not
until 1847, five years after the first version of the sketch appeared, that Poe published his extended version, "The Domain
of Arnheim," in which Ellison's creation is described. In the
extended version, incidentally, the form of the sketch parallels
that of "The Elk" and "The Island of the Fay"—as well as
several of Poe's works—in which image or narrative follows and
illuminates theories provided in an initial section.

Oddly, Poe's description of Arnheim evokes no emotion of the
sublime. Possibly grandeur and sublimity were what Poe wished
to imply in the vastness and exceedingly baroque intricacy of
the domain. The following passage, which closes the revised
version of the sketch, suggests this intricacy and vastness.

There is a gush of entracing melody; there is an oppressive sense of strange sweet odor;—there is a dream-like intermingling to the eye of tall slender Eastern trees—bosky shrubberies—flocks of golden and crimson birds—lily-fringed lakes—meadows of violets, tulips, poppies, hyacinths and tuberoses—long intertangled lines of silver streamlets—and, upspringing confusedly from amid all, a mass of semi-Gothic, semi-Saracenic architecture, sustaining itself as if by miracle in mid-air, glittering in the red sunlight with a hundred oriels, minarets, and pinnacles; and seeming the phantom handiwork, conjointly, of the Sylphs, of the Fairies, of the Genii, and of the Gnomes.[48]

There is surely no "sentiment of spiritual interference" in Ellison's gaudy carnival of sounds, odors, and sights—much as Poe himself may have thought otherwise. The description of Arnheim is one of Poe's most ambitious but least successful efforts. There is no question that he intended the sketch, its descriptive passages as well as its theories, to be taken absolutely seriously.* Today the sketch seems an all too accurate foreshadowing of William Randolph Hearst's "San Simeon," George Washington Vanderbilt's "Biltmore," James Deering's "Vizcaya," and other vast American Arnheims created, so it has sometimes been claimed, in the name of art, although it would be more accurate to claim that they were created in the name of wealth. I suspect, too, that mid-nineteenth-century readers were themselves less interested in the "supernal Beauty" of Arnheim than in how much it would cost to realize in brick and stone.

Scholars have suggested various sources for Poe's conception of Arnheim: the *Arabian Nights,* Coleridge's "Kubla Khan," Downing's Hudson River estates, and so forth. One of the most interesting of these sources is suggested by Jeffery A. Hess in an article "Sources and Aesthetics of Poe's Landscape Fiction," published in *American Quarterly* (1970).[49] Hess believes—and he has considerable documentation to support his belief—that Poe drew heavily on a series of paintings entitled "The Voyage of Life" by Thomas Cole for the description of Arnheim. The pas-

---

* On October 18, 1848, Poe sent a copy of the expanded sketch to Sarah Helen Whitman with the words that it "expresses *much of my soul.*" [Edgar Allan Poe, *Letters* (Cambridge, Mass.: Harvard University Press, 1948), vol. II, p. 397.]

sage quoted above, for example, describes a scene similar in some respects to that in "Youth," the second painting in Cole's series. It is especially interesting that Poe, if in fact he did employ these paintings in his description, selected from them ideas which present largely imaginary landscapes, rather than from Cole's paintings of natural, unlandscaped scenery. Since Ellison wished not merely to improve natural scenery but to create original landscapes, it is worth noting that Poe's model for the final work should be imaginative works—works, that is, which emphasize the primacy of the artist's vision.

Another possible source for Arnheim is worth mentioning. The geography of Ellison's estate roughly parallels that of the Hudson River from New York City up through the Highlands. There are clear differences between the river route through Arnheim and the route up the Hudson—but there are also distinct similarities. A visitor enters Arnheim from a city (New York), passes a pastoral landscape (the shores of the Tappan Zee), goes through a narrow gorge in the river (entrance to the Highlands), enters suddenly a lake-like or bay-like expanse of water (that part of the Hudson near Highland Falls), passes on the left a natural terrace bounded by a cliff on its near side (West Point). (The last segment of the journey has few resemblances to Hudson geography.) Perhaps by suggesting parallels between the Hudson and the river of Arnheim, Poe was predicting a future for the American river, long worshipped for natural scenery, in which landscapes along the shore would be thoroughly reworked by landscape gardeners—something which very nearly happened. In fact, by 1860 vast stretches of the river's banks, particularly in Westchester, Putnam, Dutchess, and Columbia Counties, were lined by estates, virtually all of which had been landscaped according to the suggestions of Andrew Jackson Downing and his followers. Whether or not these gardeners obeyed the lead of nature, they left an extensive series of landscapes which, in part, survives and which continues to suggest that the artist has been at work.

SIMPLY BECAUSE "LANDOR'S COTTAGE" offers no initial theory to focus a reader's expectations, it is a far more successful sketch than "The Domain of Arnheim," where the "sentiment of spiritual interference" promised in the first half is never realized in the second. In "Landor's Cottage," there are no large expectations to fulfill. The sketch emphasizes the role of the artist in landscape gardening; there is no attempt to suggest a "sentiment of spiritual interference" either in the sense that these words would have been interpreted by Poe or in the sense that they would have been interpreted by Downing. What attracts the attention of the visitor to Landor's estate are the compositional techniques which the gardener has employed. In Downing's landscape gardens, ideally art was blended so well with nature that a visitor could not have determined where one ended and the other began: the artist's improvements and natural scenery were worked into a perfect and pictorially indissoluble unit. However, at Landor's cottage it is entirely the art—indeed, as in the plan of the road, the *"excess* of art"—which invites the visitor's approval. As the visitor-narrator, entering the estate, notes, "One thing became more and more evident the longer I gazed: an artist, and one with a most scrupulous eye for form, had superintended all these arrangements." The landscapes, furthermore, are generally commended by the narrator for their similarities to artworks: thus he says of one view, "I could scarcely help fancying that the whole was one of the ingenious illusions sometimes exhibited under the name of 'vanishing pictures,'" and of another he remarks, "The greatest care had been taken to preserve a due medium between the neat and graceful on the one hand, and the *pittoresco* . . . on the other." Furthermore, as the visitor-narrator proceeds through the grounds of the estate, he notes that the trees become "less and less lofty and Salvatorish in character." Each of the landscapes he encounters is described as a composition complete in itself, much like a painted landscape within a frame. Finally, of the cottage itself he says, "Its marvellous effect lay altogether in its artistic arrangement *as a picture.* I could have fancied, while I looked at it, that some eminent landscape-painter had built it with his brush."[50]

Hess points out that much in the arrangement and details of Landor's estate have origins in Downing's theories, and yet by emphasizing the artificial aspects, Poe created a landscape garden in a manner opposite to the kind that Downing would have preferred. For Downing, we should remember, the garden had ultimately a spiritual significance. Poe's narrator sees—or at least calls attention to—none of this. In effect the primacy of the artist's vision has been emphasized again, although the poet's spiritual nature has been ignored, and Poe has dispensed entirely with Downing's emblematically spiritual garden. In short, Poe is saying that if the garden (or, for that matter, any work of art) possesses beauty, the responsibility for that beauty belongs to the artist.

CHARLES FEIDELSON in *Symbolism and American Literature* remarked that "aesthetic sensibility" is the subject of Poe's "Fall of the House of Usher."[51] Indeed it can be argued that the works of art within the story—Roderick's paintings, for example—have much the same relation to their creator that Arnheim has to Ellison. Roderick's "aesthetic sensibility" and in turn his ability to create are directly linked to the nature of his environment and family, both of which are caught by "an influence" suggestive of corruption, decay. Roderick's creations—a poem about a madwoman unable to communicate with the world around her, a painting of a subterranean tunnel with no exit—suggest the insulated dominion of the Ushers, a dominion with no exits to or communication with either the world or a higher spiritual realm. Roderick's "aesthetic sensibility" is the product of "that silent, yet importunate and terrible influence which for centuries had moulded the destinies of his family, and which made *him* . . . what he was." Unlike Ellison, who can claim for himself the spiritual identification of a poet, Roderick, his "aesthetic sensibility," and, therefore, his creations are limited entirely by "that silent, yet importunate and terrible influence."[52]

Ideally, the man who creates has that spiritual identification which Ellison believes that he himself has; more often, however, Poe's creators and poets are as distant from that spiritual source as is Roderick. An obvious example here is Prince Prospero in "The Masque of the Red Death." His macabre creation invites by its nature, of course, that very terror, the Red Death, which it is intended to exclude. It is often Prospero and Roderick rather than Ellison who receive attention from Poe's most enthusiastic readers. But Prospero and Roderick are ultimately the exceptions in Poe's scheme, and the full nature of their spiritual imperfection as artists cannot be fully understood until they are measured against Poe's ideal poetic system in which the artist's aesthetic sensibility and his creations result from a higher, spiritual origin.

Notes

1. Andrew Jackson Downing, *The Architecture of Country Houses* (New York: D. Appleton and Company, 1850), p. iii.
2. Nathaniel Hawthorne, *The House of the Seven Gables* (Columbus, Ohio: Ohio State University Press, 1965), p. 261.
3. Samuel H. Hammond and Lewis W. Mansfield, *Country Margins and Rambles of a Journalist* (New York: J. C. Derby, 1855), pp. 237–238.
4. Nathaniel Parker Willis, *Letters from Watering-Places*, in *Rural Letters* (New York: Baker and Scribner, 1849), p. 322. Willis, *The Convalescent* (New York: Charles Scribner, 1859), p. 362. Willis, *Health Trip to the Tropics* (New York: Charles Scribner, 1854), p. 219.
5. Nathaniel Parker Willis, *Out-Doors at Idlewild* (New York: Charles Scribner, 1855), p. 19. Willis, *Hurry-Graphs* (New York: Charles Scribner, 1851), p. 74.
6. Henry David Thoreau, "Walking," in *Excursions* (New York: Corinth Books, Inc., 1962), p. 185. Thoreau, *The Maine Woods* (Princeton, N.J.: Princeton University Press, 1972), p. 155.
7. Roderick Nash, *Wilderness and the American Mind* (New Haven, Conn.: Yale University Press, 1967), p. 81.
8. Elizabeth Wheeler Manwaring, *Italian Landscape in Eighteenth-Century England* (New York: Oxford University Press, 1925), p. 95.
9. Andrew Jackson Downing, *A Treatise on the Theory and Practice of Landscape Gardening*, 6th ed. (New York: A. O. Moore and Co., 1859), p. 49.
10. Laurence Whistler, Michael Gibbon, and George Clark, *Stowe*, rev. ed. (1968), p. 17.
11. Horace Walpole, *On Modern Gardening* (New York: Young Books, Inc., 1931), pp. 43–44.
12. William Shenston, "Unconnected Thoughts on Gardening," *Works* (London: R. and J. Dodsley, 1764), p. 129.
13. Kenneth Clark, *The Gothic Revival* (Middlesex, England: Penguin Books, 1962), p. 55.

14. Frederika Bremer, *The Homes of the New World* (New York: Harper and Brothers, 1853), vol. I, p. 46.

15. John A. Kowenhoven, *Made in America* (Garden City, N.Y.: Doubleday and Company, Inc., 1948), p. 122.

16. Russell Lynes, *The Tastemakers* (New York: Grosset and Dunlap, n.d.), p. 21.

17. Joel E. Spingarn, "Henry Winthrop Sargent and the Early History of Landscape Gardening and Ornamental Horticulture in Dutchess County, N.Y.," *Year Book of the Dutchess County Historical Society*, XXII (1937), 46.

18. Andrew Jackson Downing, *Rural Essays* (New York: Geo. A. Leavitt, 1869), p. 15.

19. Downing, *The Architecture of Country Houses*, p. iii.

20. Downing, *A Treatise on the Theory and Practice of Landscape Gardening*, pp. 59, 58, 52, 53.

21. *Ibid.*, pp. 68, 60, 62.

22. Downing, *The Architecture of Country Houses*, p. 267.

23. Quoted in Barbara Novak, *American Painting of the Nineteenth Century* (New York: Praeger Publishers, 1969).

24. Louis Legrand Noble, *The Life and Works of Thomas Cole* (Cambridge, Mass.: Harvard University Press, 1964), p. 63.

25. [John Banvard], *Description of Banvard's Panorama of the Mississippi River* (Boston: John Putnam, 1847), pp. 7, 14.

26. *Ibid.*, pp. 1, 5.

27. Samuel Longfellow, *Life of Henry Wadsworth Longfellow* (Boston: Ticknor and Company, 1886), vol. II, pp. 67–68.

28. [Banvard], *op. cit.*, pp. 7–8.

29. *Ibid.*, p. 14.

30. Downing, *The Architecture of Country Houses, op. cit.*, pp. 257–258.

31. James Hadden Smith, *History of Chenango and Madison Counties, New York* (Syracuse, N.Y.: D. Mason, 1880), pp. 532, 534.

32. Henry David Thoreau, *Walden* (Princeton, N.J.: Princeton University Press, 1971), pp. 70, 128.

33. Edgar Allan Poe, "The Elk," *Complete Works* (New York: Crowell, 1902), vol. V, p. 158.

34. *Ibid.*, pp. 156–157.

35. *Ibid.*, p. 161.

36. *Ibid.*, p. 162.

37. *Ibid.*, p. 161.

38. Poe, "The Island of the Fay," *Complete Works*, vol. IV, p. 194.

39. *Ibid.*, p. 195.

40. Edward H. Davidson, *Poe* (Cambridge, Mass.: Harvard University Press, 1957), p. 283.

41. Poe, "The Island of the Fay," pp. 196, 198, 199.

42. Poe, "The Domain of Arnheim," *Complete Works*, vol. VI, pp. 180, 181–182.

43. Downing, *A Treatise on the Theory and Practice of Landscape Gardening*, pp. 52–53.

44. Poe, "The Poetic Principle," *Complete Works*, vol. XIV, pp. 274, 273–274, 274–275.

45. Poe, "The Domain of Arnheim," pp. 185, 186, 187.

46. Downing, *A Treatise on the Theory and Practice of Landscape Gardening*, p. 57.

47. Poe, "The Domain of Arnheim," p. 188. Poe, "Israfel," *Complete Works*, vol. VII, p. 47 (footnote).

48. Poe, "The Domain of Arnheim," p. 196.

49. Jeffrey A. Hess, "Sources and Aesthetics of Poe's Landscape Fiction," *American Quarterly*, XXII (1970), 177–189.

50. Poe, "Landor's Cottage," *Complete Works*, vol. VI, pp. 257, 258, 260, 264.

51. Charles Feidelson, Jr., *Symbolism and American Literature* (Chicago: University of Chicago Press, 1953), p. 39.

52. Poe, "The Fall of the House of Usher," *Complete Works*, vol. III, pp. 286–287.

Chapter Four

Tasteful Cottages

Architecture is comprehensive in the same sense as nature. Indeed, it is to man the material expression of his mind, as nature is that of the mind of God.

James Jackson Jarves, *The Art-Idea* (1864).[1]

I have frequently seen a poet withdraw, having enjoyed the most valuable part of a farm, while the crusty farmer supposed that he had got a few wild apples only. Why, the owner does not know it for many years when a poet has put his farm in rhyme, the most admirable kind of invisible fence, has fairly impounded it, milked it, skimmed it, and got all the cream, and left the farmer only the skimmed milk.

Henry David Thoreau, *Walden* (1854).[2]

There are those who rejoice in our Anglo-Saxon inheritance of the love of conquest, and the desire for boundless territory, —who exult in the "manifest destiny" of the race, to plant the standard of the eagle or the lion in every soil, and every zone of the earth's surface. We rejoice much more in the love of country life, the enjoyment of nature, and the taste for rural beauty, which we also inherit from our Anglo-Saxon forefathers, and to which, more than all else, they owe so many of the peculiar virtues of the race.

Andrew Jackson Downing, *Rural Essays* (1853).[3]

ANDREW JACKSON DOWNING was among the harshest critics of
the Greek Revival, but even if this most respected of American
architectural theorists had never attacked the "false taste" involved in making houses look like temples, it is certain that the
Greek Revival would not have lasted much longer than the
1840s. At its height in the 1830s, American mania for the Greek
was virtually nationwide, but there were simply too many arguments against porticos and peristyles for the revival to continue
much longer as a major force in domestic architecture. Columns
and pediments were costly, too costly for most Americans, and
impressive though a Doric portico might be, it served absolutely
no practical function. Associations with democratic Athens were
not overlooked in evaluations of the Greek style, and yet the
great expense involved in building the temple-house made such
homes available to very few people. A man might well have been
excused if, upon seeing those American porticos for the first
time, he was reminded less of democratic Athens than of imperial Rome. Long before Downing's objections to the Greek
style were first published, various Americans, Cooper and Irving
among others, had suggested that the Gothic and other picturesque styles were more appropriate for American homes.⁴ Downing's comments simply hastened the demise of the Greek.°

° There was at least one American architect who continued to
argue, contrary to all evidence, that the Greek Revival retained a
large measure of popularity as late as the 1850s. "In this country, as
in England," wrote Minard Lafever in 1856, "no style of architecture
may be considered as peculiar to the present age, but examples or
features of the styles of almost all times have been followed. Though
for the last few years there has been a growing taste for the Gothic
or pointed, and many fine churches, libraries, and other buildings
have been erected in this style, yet, as a general thing, the Greek and
Roman orders have been in the ascendant." Although the classical era
continued to provide ideas for much public architecture, the Greek
Revival had long been forgotten by 1856 as a suitable influence for
domestic architecture. Lafever never lost his great affection for the
Greek style, and it must have been rather annoying when he found
it economically essential to design homes in the Gothic and Italian
styles. However, he had little choice, since after 1840 there were
increasingly fewer clients who wished to erect porticos as statements
of their wealth. [Minard Lafever, *The Architectural Instructor* (New
York: Putnam, 1856), p. 342.]

It is true that throughout the century classicism continued to provide the major architectural vocabulary for some public buildings, but from roughly 1840 and continuing until long after the Civil War, the Gothic and other picturesque styles provided the dominant architectural themes for private homes. There were more than practical reasons for the shift from classicism to the picturesque in domestic architecture. In fact the picturesque in architecture was justified from so many points—moral, economic, and social, among others—that it simply could not have failed to be as thoroughly accepted as it was. And in the end the picturesque cottage or villa, surrounded by an equally picturesque landscape garden, became in fact virtually an emblem or symbol of American life, or at least of an idealized version of American life.

This emblem was of extraordinary value for American literature in the age of Emerson and Melville. If none of the greatest writers of the American Renaissance idealized this symbol as other Americans did, yet it was still of eminent value in defining their own objectives. Thoreau, for example, employed it as the counterpoint in defining his own ideal, the world of *Walden,* and Emerson used it similarly in his essays. Furthermore, the ambiguities of Melville's *Pierre* are largely those which are suggested in the idealization of garden and villa. In what follows, I will sketch out the thinking which lay behind the building of nineteenth-century villas, and then, turning to the literature of the period, suggest the effect of this thinking on American literature.

PERHAPS NO ASPECT of mid-nineteenth-century American architecture has been so entirely—and unfairly—condemned as its dependence on European styles. In a country which gave heavy emphasis to the need for picturesqueness and historical associations in architecture as well as in landscapes, it was inevitable that "pointed Gothic," for example, would find a wide acceptance. After all, there was no native tradition of picturesque architecture to draw on, and even if there had been, it could not have offered the richness of historical associations that "pointed Gothic" did. Many architectural theorists in the past century have argued that "style" in architecture must follow from structural expression—which is one way to interpret the dictum "form follows function"—but this is hardly an original observation: many mid-nineteenth-century architects, after all, said much the same thing. As Gervase Wheeler wrote in *Rural Homes* (1851),

> A Gothic house is a building, the character of whose architecture is distinguished by the upward direction of its leading lines, and by such curves as may be introduced meeting, or having a tendency to meet, in a point. It might be highly ornamental, or left perfectly simple; but true taste will be outraged if ornament, beautiful as it may be in itself, is introduced where it does not serve some purpose of construction.[5]

Although there were many architects who, like Alexander Jackson Davis, burdened their designs with picturesque details serving absolutely no practical function, there were many more who, like Wheeler, insisted in their writings that style must be linked to structural matters. Downing, the period's most influential architectural theorist, had nothing but scorn for those who, placing "style" above all, made their houses appear to be something which, structurally, they were not. Referring to "imitations of Gothic castles, with towers and battlements built of wood," he wrote in *The Architecture of Country Houses* (1850) that "nothing can well be more paltry and contemptible. The sugar castles of confectioners and pastry-cooks are far more admirable as works of art."[6]

It is also worth noting that, in matters of historical associations, most architects were less interested in medieval castles than in Gothic cottages and villas, which were supposed to express a more civilized era in English history. For those who wished to make themselves imperially known to the surrounding countryside, castles were as suitable as Greek temples, of course. Designed to keep strangers out, however, many of the castles constructed in America kept out sunlight and fresh air as well. Unlike the castles of England with their generous courtyards, many of the castles in America must have been rather dark and cavernous in the days before electric lighting. One of the most famous of these was Fonthill, the somewhat forbidding country home of the actor Edwin Forrest in the Bronx, N.Y. Windows were at a premium here, but Forrest, whose roles included Hamlet and Macbeth, no doubt found the interior gloom an appropriate setting for his histrionics. Castles like Fonthill were attacked by Gervase Wheeler in *Rural Homes:*

In the complicated Gothic contrivances sometimes seen, every-one knows that the quaint and grotesque details have no mean-ing away from their own places, that the imitation "portcullis" (such as has been seen and may be seen) never descends, nor do anything more warlike than nursery-maids and children with drums ever march across the "drawbridge." The "battlemented turrets" have no ordnance or bold archer behind, and the carved and crocketted chimney-shafts are only good, honest smoke-vents for a patent warming apparatus within.[7]

Davis designed more than one American castle, complete with portcullis, yet unlike the English, most Americans remained in-different to battlements and Barbicon towers. "It is . . . a little inconsistent," said Calvert Vaux in *Villas and Cottages* (1857), "for any true lover of freedom to take much pleasure in con-templating old castles for the sake of their associations." This most famous of all Downing's proteges, went on to add that "Dark dungeons, spiky, picturesque portcullises, and artistic machicolations for pouring down hot pitch on uninvited visitors, may, undoubtedly, have a somewhat mysterious and romantic air about them; but the sentiment they express is not, in reality, either touching or true."[8]

Second only to historical styles and structural considerations in determining the forms of mid-nineteenth-century houses was the belief that a building, at least a building in the country, should visually complement the landscape which surrounded it. One of Davis's most significant achievements at Glen Ellen, it should be remembered, was the visual union of architecture and landscape, both adhering to the dictums of the picturesque. Ac-cording to later architects, however, it could not be assumed that simply because both a house and a landscape were pic-turesque, they would visually belong together. Offering an ex-planation that is found throughout the architectural literature of the time, Wheeler noted in *Rural Homes:*

> Not merely the style and general character of a house are in-fluenced by the contour and aspect of features in the landscape around, but its outlines on the ground, its arrangement in masses, equally are subject to the same laws that would direct the form of the exterior. So that it is almost impossible to find a design which perfectly suited to one spot, shall, in every respect, be entirely appropriate in another.[9]

Although many architects published books illustrating picturesque villas and cottages, these illustrations, many of which showed houses which had already been erected, were intended only as suggestions of the types of houses one might build. A finished design could be made only after the architect had examined the location where the cottage or villa was to stand. It seems likely that then, as now, most houses were constructed from standardized plans supplied by builders. Nonetheless, the belief that houses should be designed as visual complements to their settings seems to have found wide acceptance (at least among those who could afford the architectural fees). Certainly this belief did much to promote the profession of architecture, which in fact had never prospered as well in this country as it did in the 1840s and 1850s.

FAR MORE THAN QUESTIONS of structure, aesthetics, and historical styles were involved in the designing of mid-nineteenth-century homes. Downing in fact believed that

> Every thing in architecture that can suggest or be made a symbol of social and domestic virtues, adds to its beauty, and exalts its character. Every material object that becomes the type of the spiritual, moral, or intellectual nature of man, becomes at once beautiful, because it is suggestive of the beautiful in human nature.[10]

A house should express or at least suggest "the beautiful in human nature"—the architectural correspondent to the spiritual aspect of landscape gardening. The gardener, improving a landscape, clarified a divine Beauty inherent in Nature: the architect designed a house so that it would at least suggest "the beautiful in human nature." Moreover, Downing claimed that a man's home, "in its most complete form, may be regarded as the type of his whole private life." Expanding on this, he noted that if a house

> . . . has various marked features, indicating intelligent and cultivated life in its inhabitants; if it plainly shows by its various apartments, that it is intended not only for the physical wants of man, but for his moral, social, and intellectual existence; if hospitality smiles in ample parlors; if home virtues dwell in cosy, fireside family-rooms; if the love of the beautiful is seen in picture or statue galleries; intellectuality, in well-stocked libraries;

and even a dignified love of leisure and repose, in cool and spacious verandas; we feel, at a glance, that we have reached the highest beauty of which Domestic Architecture is capable—that of individual expression.[11]

Clearly Downing's moral, intellectual, and social ideals had little in common with Thoreau's. Downing was the spokesman for, predominantly, the middle class, identifying hospitality with "ample parlors," "home virtues" with "cozy, fireside family-rooms," "intellectuality" with "well-stocked libraries," and so forth. The difficulty is that this equipment—rooms, furniture, books, etc.—which a man used to symbolize his "moral, social, and intellectual existence," included nothing which could not be bought. Indeed, given the proper architect and the proper finances, a man could have a house expressing whatever character he chose. If we consider the thousands of books with uncut, and therefore unread, pages which have come down to us from the last century, we have reason enough to question Downing's key to a man's "intellectuality." And if we consider those insipidly moral statues which adorned middle-class homes in nineteenth-century America, we have good reason to wonder whether the middle class possessed even a hint of Downing's "love of the beautiful." Remembering that Hiram Power's blandly virginal "Greek Slave" was by far the most widely praised statue in America at this time, it is not difficult to imagine the sort of sculpture found in a Downing villa. A man bought what was in fashion, and surviving pictures of home interiors of the time suggest that the difference in "individual expression" from one villa to the next was emphatically small. Villas after all were constructed for members of a class which has been traditionally identified with conformity, not individuality. However, the idea that a house might really become "the type of [a man's] whole private life" did find especially enthusiastic support from Thoreau. Interpreting the idea with an emphasis quite unlike Downing's, it became, as we will discover, a central component in his organic theory of architecture.

Although mid-nineteenth-century villas seldom express much individuality, they do tell us much about social, economic, and moral distinctions between classes at this time, or to be more precise, they tell us what the affluent middle class thought those distinctions were. Clearly the size of a man's house could be taken as a sign of his economic status—a factor which, unfortunately, has yet to be bred out of American life. Downing's *Architecture of Country Houses* provided designs for both cottages and villas, each adapted to a particular income. Many of the cottages were specifically intended for laborers who, in these pre-union days, survived on incredibly low incomes. Other house pattern books, including Lewis F. Allen's *Rural Architecture* (1852) and Henry W. Cleaveland's *Villa and Farm Cottages* (1855), also provided the public with designs for cottages which, while amply picturesque, could be erected at very little cost. Nonetheless, as the Irish shanty towns of the 1840s and 1850s indicate, there were some people who would have found even these cottages much beyond their means; the Americans who could afford only the simplest of cottages was better off financially than were many of his compatriots.

If owning a house was itself an economic distinction, an even greater distinction existed between owning a cottage and owning a villa. The former could cost anywhere from a few hundred to a few thousand dollars, and while some villas cost no more than the most expensive cottages, many required an outlay of between $10,000 and $20,000—cheap enough by today's standards but forbiddingly high in 1850. It was financially impractical, Downing warned, for a man to spend more than this on building a home, since then, having invested a fortune in architectural show, he might leave his family without sufficient income to maintain the property. In any case, $14,000 was enough to build a house with seven bedrooms, two dressing rooms, a boudoir, a drawing room, a library, an office, a dining hall, kitchens, and sundry other rooms, the whole meticulously rendered in the Romanesque style.[12] By contrast, the laborer with four rather plain rooms had good reason to be content; many workers had much less than this.

The economics of homebuilding tended to reinforce social distinctions of two varieties. The first set the fashionable off from the rest of the population, a distinction pointedly underscored in the text from one of the designs in Samuel Sloan's *Homestead Architecture* (1866):

The occupants of such a residence [as that illustrated] are not only supposed to be wealthy, but fashionable people, and to possess, in common with all the real aristocracy of every section, a character for hospitality, exhibited in the frequent entertainments of numerous guests, and a liberal allowance of time and money for the purposes of social and convivial enjoyment.[13]

Sloan, according to his *Model Architect* (1852), believed, like Downing, that "A man's dwelling at the present day, is not only an index of his wealth, but also of his character." Also like Downing and, for that matter, like most of his contemporary architects, he gave most of his attention to designing homes which suggested the character of "not only . . . wealthy, but fashionable people."[14]

A second social distinction reinforced by the economics of building a house involved *the idealization of domestic life*. The private house, as Downing made clear in *The Architecture of Country Houses,* was a symbol of family life, and this fact was of the largest significance in an age which idealized domesticity as thoroughly as the nineteenth century did. The author of *Villa and Farm Cottages* (1855) claimed:

> Every enlightened plan for the advancement of family influences and society in general will include among its earliest efforts the improvement of dwellings; and this, not only in respect of physical comfort, but of that aid which they can be made to render in the suggestion of salutary associations and the formation of desirable habits. When Architecture contributes to such an object, she may justly claim the highest praise.[15]

Houses, it is certain, were in effect symbols of the moral, domestic lives which their owners had chosen. To quote Downing once more,

> ["The true home" was] not, indeed, the feudal castle, not the baronial hall, but the home of the individual man—the home of that family of equal rights, which continually separates and continually reforms itself in the new world—the republican home, built by no robbery of the property of another class, maintained by no infringement of a brother's rights; the beautiful, rural unostentatious, moderate home of the country gentleman, large enough to minister to all the wants, necessities, and luxuries of a republican, and not too large or too luxurious to warp the life or manners of his children.[16]

Since so much importance was claimed for domestic architecture, it surely should not surprise anyone to find the author of

Villa and Farm Architecture concluding that ". . . he who improves the dwelling-houses of people in relation to their comforts, habits, and morals, makes a benignant and lasting reform at the very foundation of society."[17]

The social ideal of family life had a moral justification as its premise. Among Downing's defenses of country houses was his assertion that ". . . there is a moral influence in a country home —when, among an educated, truthful, and refined people, it is an echo of their character—which is more powerful than any mere oral teachings of virtue and morality." Domestic life provided moral examples from which all members of the family, but especially children, could benefit. Indeed family life was viewed as the moral center of civilization. Concluded Downing, ". . . the condition of the country home—in this country where every man may have a home—should be raised, till it shall symbolize the best character and pursuits, and the dearest affections and enjoyments of social life."[18] And in the works of Downing, his fellow architects, genre painters, scores of popular writers, and a few major writers as well, the country house became a fully realized symbol of domestic life or at least of a highly idealized version of domestic life. The country house, in particular the villa, stood as a visual representation of ideal social and moral patterns of living, patterns which, together with their chosen symbol, rapidly sent Thoreau packing off to Walden Pond.

THE SETTING OF THE VILLA as well as the villa itself could be used to distinguish one class of Americans from another. Landscape, it has been noted, was seen as the expression of certain divine qualities, and if so, shouldn't all good Christians, at least Protestant Americans, situate themselves somewhere in the country? But, of course, here again lay an economic problem: for many, country life was finacially out of the question. Although it is true that the countryside could be reached more easily from the city than is possible now, it was nevertheless more expensive for a laborer to buy country property and build a house than to accept company housing. Some company housing, like that at Graniteville, S.C., was built according to the Downing plan, cottages surrounded by landscape gardens, but more often factory workers were housed in plain, severe brick or wooden buildings. Not trees and fields but company buildings, especially the mills themselves, formed the dominant motifs in the landscapes in which these factory workers lived. Even if the factory worker saved enough to buy land and build a cottage near the city or town in which he worked, he had little time to benefit from his holdings. It was not uncommon for a man to work in a factory eleven or twelve hours a day, six days a week, nor for that matter was it uncommon for his wife and children to work as well.

The country home in general and the villa in particular provided a means of categorizing men economically, socially, and morally. Furthermore, the success with which a house was visually integrated with its landscape could be taken as a mark of the owner's aesthetic taste—or perhaps of his good fortune in his choice of architect. The historical style selected for the house might be taken as an expression of the owner's learning. Such at least were some of the "meanings" involved in the design of a mid-nineteenth-century American house. Furthermore, as we have seen, the setting of the house could be "read" or interpreted for its spiritual meaning. Either separately or in combination with its setting, the house was a ready-made symbol, invaluable, as it turned out, to the literature of American Romanticism.

MONCKTON MILNES, the English poet and critic, asked Hawthorne in 1854 to recommend a half-dozen American books which were, in Hawthorne's phrasing, "not merely good, but . . . original, with American characteristics, and not generally known in England." Although he included Anna Mowatt's *Autobiography of an Actress,* Thoreau's *Week on the Concord and Merrimack Rivers,* and James Russell Lowell's *Biglow Papers* among his suggestions, Hawthorne believed that there were "only three which would be likely to come under [Milnes's] description—viz., 'Walden,' 'Passion Flowers,' and 'Up-Country Letters.' "[19] Of the three which met all the criteria, only *Walden* is well known today, and even scholars who claim American literature as their field may be forgiven if they fail to recognize *Passion-Flowers* and *Up-Country Letters.* The first of these was a volume of stilted verse by the Boston bluestocking Julia Ward Howe, an acquaintance of Hawthorne's. The future author of

"The Battle Hymn of the Republic" included in this, her maiden effort, several poems on Italy, and perhaps Hawthorne saw in the American's interpretation of European civilization something which might be of interest to Milnes. *Up-Country Letters* was written by Lewis Mansfield, who lived within riding distance of Hawthorne's home in the Berkshires. The book is of particular interest to us, for it is representative of a certain type of book which was moderately popular in mid-nineteenth-century America. *Walden* should also be included among books of this type, which can be designated simply the "country book."*

Walden is the only survivor of the country books, first-person narratives of rural life defined by nature and, generally, by architecture as well. Books of this type or genre treated disparagingly such contemporary problems as immigration and the rise of cities, when indeed the authors deigned to discuss such matters at all. The centermost interest was nature, and here the writers acted both as naturalists and as moralists. For many of the writers of these books, a secondary interest, intimately related to the first, was rural architecture, and although not all the writers agreed with Downing's conclusions on the subject, most, including Thoreau, seemed quite aware of his theories. A third interest for many writers of country books was the idealized family life of rural homes.

With the exception of *Walden,* none of the country books had a serious literary purpose. Like the travel narratives and other

---

* Hawthorne's expressed enthusiasm for Mansfield's book extended, incidentally, far beyond his recommendation to Milnes. In a letter to another English acquaintance, Hawthorne asked that he "talk about [*Up-Country Letters*] or write about it, and get it into some degree of notice [in England]. England, within two or three years past, has read and praised a hundred American books that do not deserve it half so well; but I somewhat question whether the English mind is not rather too bluff and beefy to appreciate the peculiar charm of these letters. Yet we have produced nothing more original nor more genuine." The book does not deserve such unqualified praise, but it does deserve better than the literary oblivion to which scholars and historians have consigned it either because of their ignorance or because of hasty and poor judgment. [Julian Hawthorne, *Nathaniel Hawthorne and His Wife* (Boston: Houghton, Mifflin and Company, 1884), vol. II, p. 36.]

summer books, they were intended for casual reading—and God forbid the intrusion of a startling idea! The authors of these books could generally expect sympathetic readers who had, when finances permitted, rural residences of their own. All the country books occasionally preached the virtues of country life, but only *Walden* was a gospel to the heathen. While all the authors explicitly condemned fashion, all except Thoreau knew that they were not alone in their experiments in rural living. In fact, for all the condemnation of fashion, it was equally clear that country homes were among the most fashionable things in America. Only Thoreau had to assume the robes of a missionary and convince his readers that his rural experiment was worth his effort. On the other hand, N. P. Willis, the author of no fewer than three country books, took delight in the ever-increasing number of country homes in the vicinity of his own villa at Cornwall-on-the-Hudson, New York.

The casual nature of the country books, their lack of serious literary purpose, has ensured a neglect which, as documents of American life, they do not deserve. Their images and discussions of picturesque landscapes interpreted morally and spiritually and their use of the rural residence or country home as a symbol of an ideal life offer an important index to American life in the times of Emerson and Melville. Originating in some cases as columns for popular journals and in one instance as the diary of a most circumspect lady, virtually all the country books sympathetically recorded their America in ways not to be found in the best known of their type, Thoreau's iconoclastic masterpiece. Further, at least two things are achieved by discussing *Up-Country Letters* and its kind next to *Walden*. First, a discussion of this sort clarifies the America against which Thoreau reacted, and second, it places his book within its particularly American "literary" tradition. This is not to argue that *Walden* was necessarily either an outgrowth of or an influence on that tradition; rather, Thoreau's book deals with materials and assumed a form which were of equal centrality to other and significantly more popular books of its time.

THE AUTHORS OF COUNTRY BOOKS included Henry Ward Beecher, Susan Fenimore Cooper, Lewis Mansfield, Donald Grant Mitchell, Frederick William Shelton, Henry Carmer Wetmore, and Nathaniel Parker Willis—no list of names to conjure with today, but a list in which the 1850s would have found many of its best-known literati.

Susan Fenimore Cooper published her journal of life in Cooperstown, *Rural Hours* (1850), as the work of, revealingly, "A Lady," and it was truly as a lady that this daughter of James Fenimore Cooper determined to spend her days in the country. Civilized and refined, Miss Cooper was almost the cultured Englishwoman (as might well be expected of one descended from the aristocratic Delancys of New York). She approached her rural surroundings appreciatively, noting the beautiful and the picturesque in landscape and architecture and recording for all posterity not only her most enjoyable rides and walks but also the agreeable changes in scenery during the passage of a year. She was a naturalist and also a moralist and transcendentalist, and she gave attention equally to the migration of birds and the presence of God in nature. The architect Gervase Wheeler, who seldom praised anyone but himself, considered her "observations upon rural architecture, so terse and pertinent, that, but for its length, I would like to quote the entire chapter."[20] Frederick William Shelton was perfectly rhapsodic over her treatment of nature. *Rural Hours*, he said, "is . . . a complete compend, omitting nothing. Indeed it would be difficult to think of any thing in the whole range of Nature which attracts your immediate attention in the few seasons of the year of which a mention is not made in this ample volume."[21]

There was nothing discordant in her view of nature; everything was suffused with a sentimental and genteel coloring—the appropriate setting, to be sure, for the lady which Miss Cooper considered herself to be. The following passage, the conclusion of *Rural Hours*, serves as an example of her descriptions.

These calm sunsets are much less fleeting than others: from the moment when the clouds flush into color at the approach of the sun, one may watch them, perhaps, for more than an hour, growing brighter and warmer, as he passes slowly on his way through their midst; still varying in ever-changing beauty, while he sinks slowly to rest; and at last, long after he has dropped beyond the farthest hills, fading sweetly and imperceptibly, as the shadows of night gather upon the snow.[22]

Susan Fenimore Cooper seems more an Americanized version of the English rural gentry than a resident of an area which, less than a century before her book was published, was the wilderness her father described in *The Deerslayer*.

LEWIS MANSFIELD, as noted above, was the author of *Up-Country Letters* (1852), one of the volumes Hawthorne thought worthy of Monckton Milnes's attention. Mansfield was a journalist and poet with a modest reputation in the 1850s, but his name has been so thoroughly forgotten that it is not to be found in even the most comprehensive of recent guides to American literature. Mansfield's book is a series of letters describing his life at his country home, Punison House. Here he claimed to live a life of domestic but otherwise solitary bliss, untroubled by the world at large. At Punison House,

> Our feeling to the great world is that of an ever-lasting good-bye, —that we say with the lotos-eaters, now that we have floated aside into this quiet up-country home,—let us alone—let us alone, we have had somewhat to do with each other and with sufficiently happy results; now let us part in peace; we will stop here, if you please, while you go on. Some day we may meet again, but let us make no promises. People upon the outer borders—outsiders all, addio, addio.[23]

In the up-country (geographically, upstate New York) the Wordsworthian Mansfield liked to believe that nature kept him in contact with the spiritual world. For Mansfield, like other Romantics, dawn had special emblematic value: "Just over the mountains—so near; the morning, the day so near! and will it be under this firmament, or in another and higher one 'eternal in the heavens?' Ah, my child, all our mornings are with God."[24] There is much in Mansfield's work to remind one of *Walden* and its spiritual reading of nature. If Thoreau's book had not followed *Up-Country Letters* by several years, it would be tempting to consider the latter a gloss or complement to the former. Whether or not Thoreau learned anything from Mansfield remains an unanswered question. Similar as these books seem, however, Mansfield clearly lacked Thoreau's ability with words, and his country villa and domestic life defined a personal existence quite different from Thoreau's.

Few American writers have done as well financially with their works as did Donald Grant Mitchell. *Reveries of a Bachelor* (1850) sold at least a million copies, probably much more. In any age, the book would be called a financial success, and in the 1850s it was, with *Uncle Tom's Cabin, The Lamplighter,* and a few others, one of the publishing triumphs of the decade. Mitchell, who used the singularly unpleasant pseudonym "Ik Marvel," was also the author of *My Farm of Edgewood: A Country Book* (1863) and other works on rural life. Strictly speaking, these works should not be classified with the other country books we have been considering. Mitchell was more interested in his reveries and daydreams than in nature, and he spent much of his time reading—a subject discussed in *Wet Days at Edgewood* (1865)—and tending his livestock and crops. Nonetheless, he was one of the nation's best-known evangelists of country life, and the Edgewood books, published during and shortly after the Civil War, may be considered a valediction for pastoral, Romantic America.

FREDERICK WILLIAM SHELTON, the author of *Up the River* (1853), was a member of New York literary circles, a contributor to the *Knickerbocker Magazine,* and the author of *The Trollopiad* (1837), a satire on Mrs. Francis Trollope and other critics of American life. In 1847 he became an Episcopal clergyman, and until his death in 1881, he was the minister of churches in Hudson River communities and in Vermont. The first of his parishes on the Hudson was located in Fishkill, and his life there was the subject of *Up the River.*

Shelton was well acquainted with America writings on country life. His comments on Susan Fenimore Cooper's *Rural Hours* have already been noted. Mansfield's *Up-Country Letters,* he believed, "does great credit to its amiable author, abounding in much delicate limning, and many sketches of character." Willis's *Letters from Under a Bridge,* also known as *A l'Abri,* was "a book marked by all the peculiarities of a cunning and felicitous writer." Shelton was also aware of Willis's "Idlewild Papers," then being published in a journal and later to be collected in another country-book, *Out-Doors at Idlewild.* Shelton had high praise for Downing's writings and for the writings of the American naturalists John James Audubon, William Bartram, and Alexander Wilson. *A Journal of Summer Time in the Country* by the English minister Robert Aris Wilmott was another of the books on country life which received Shelton's particular approbation.[25]

In *Up the River* Shelton argued that "The prosperity of the country is marked, not so much by the growth of its cities, as by the enlarging boundaries of its cultivated lands."[26] Shelton favored a pastoral region; it was particularly the beautiful—the type of Virgillian landscape evident in the paintings of Claude Lorrain—and less the picturesque which attracted him. At one point, he noted that "In the fields the clover is knee deep, and the cattle dispose themselves in easy attitudes, and, as they remain dreamy and almost motionless on the top of some shady knoll, in relief against the blue sky, afford a picture of grace to the eye of the Claude-like painter."[27] Elsewhere in the book, he recorded that "The effect of light and shade upon the mountains, and the transformation of the golden-tinted clouds, . . . , in the transparent atmosphere of our clime, almost rival the glories of an Italian sunset."[28]—and, one could add, the golden coloring of Claude's Italian landscapes. Shelton's view of rural life was one tempered by Claudian pastoralism, not the American wilderness. His was essentially an agricultural paradise, although, unlike Mitchell, he was more interested in "Claude-like" effects than in the actual business of farming.

Shelton was an amateur naturalist, as were most of the writers of country books, and took additional pleasure in the aesthetic appreciation of nature, but it would be a mistake to label him strictly a pantheist or transcendentalist. Although there were moral benefits to be derived from country life, the author of *Up the River* was after all, doctrinally an Episcopalian, and as a minister of that church he was not likely to share the metaphysics of Mansfield or Thoreau. His country home, his paradise, was one where there was ample time for reading and reflection and for seeing relationships between art and nature: "What multitudes of pictures and images may be jotted down by the lover of Nature, let him direct his steps whither he will, but especially in those favorite and secluded spots which are peculiarly his own."[29]

HENRY CARMER WETMORE was the author of *Hermit's Dell* (1854), republished in 1856 as *Rural Life in America*. Hermit's Dell was the author's family home, a cottage on the east bank of the Hudson, and it was reminiscent, in its ideal landscape and picturesque architecture, of Landor's cottage in the sketch by Poe. Wetmore's landscapes were as paradisial as Shelton's and Mansfield's, and his attention to picturesque architecture was as thorough as Miss Cooper's. Hermit's Dell was a cottage which would have pleased Downing. As Wetmore wrote,

> Though unpretending in architecture, the high peaked roof and bracketed gables of our country dwelling may be seen from points, miles away in the adjacent country. A low piazza, whose chief beauty is in the vines which clammer up its pillars, and all the long summer festoon its lattices with their odorous wreaths, completely surrounds it. The situation is not often surpassed for rare and varied beauty. A wide expanse of water, bound within view by verdure covered shores, fills up the foreground; to the north are ranges of hills with white farmhouses glistening on their sides, and behind them in the distance "Rise the blue mountains, shapes which seem/ Like wrecks of childhood's sunny dreams."[30]

Hermit's Dell is not the only private paradise in this pastoral region.

> Here and there, where the high ground commands a fine river or mountain view, or both combined, the forest has been long since cleared away, and tasteful dwellings with velvety lawns and well kept enclosures, mark the hand of wealth and taste.[31]

Of the various country books examined so far, *Hermit's Dell* comes closest to realizing the ideal America portrayed in Downing's books. The Wetmore family escaped from the city to find, ironically, a culture and civilization of "tasteful dwellings," "velvety lawns," "wealth and taste"—all properties of Downing's ideal pastoral realm. The country, it seemed, had become more civilized than the city. As in the worlds of Miss Cooper, Mansfield, Mitchell, and Shelton, all the presumably objectionable aspects of cities—industry, mechanization, and, one suspects, the unwashed multitudes—had been replaced by a morally, socially, and economically ideal rural life. The Wetmore family attended to nature and family needs and, when they thought of the city at all, wondered only how anyone could endure living there.

THE GILDED AGE did not invent the American businessman. He is at least as old as Benjamin Franklin and can trace his lineage back to those Puritans who used their New Jerusalem for material as well as spiritual profit. In *The Americans: The National Experience* Daniel J. Boorstin suggests that it may have been Jacksonian America which gave the word "businessman" its present connotations. Boorstin offers an example of the midcentury businessman in the character of the Chicago entrepreneur William B. Ogden, who is reputed to have said,

> I was born close by a saw-mill, was early left an orphan, was cradled in a sugar-trough, christened in a mill-pond, graduated at a log-schoolhouse, and at fourteen fancied I could do anything I turned my hand to, and that nothing was impossible, and ever since, madame, I have been trying to prove it, and with some success.[32]

The antebellum businessmen did their work well, and by 1865 the groundwork had been laid for much of the nation's economic development in the last third of the century. But that which factory owners, real-estate developers, railroad tycoons, and just plain merchants did not do was create a viable culture to occupy their time when the stores and offices were closed. In order to find culture, they had to turn to those whom Russell Lynes has labeled the "tastemakers," men who, like Andrew Jackson Downing, showed Americans how to spend, tastefully, their newly acquired wealth. Among the most famous mid-nineteenth-century tastemakers were two prolific authors of country books, N. P. Willis and the Reverend Henry Ward Beecher.

Beecher was the only author of country books, aside from Thoreau, whom a present-day reader can be expected to recognize—not because of Beecher's abilities as an author, however, but rather because of the alleged goings-on in his choirloft. In the 1850s Beecher was probably America's best-known preacher, better known than even Horace Bushnell or the revivalist Charles Grandison Finney. He was also a respected journalist, a frequent contributor to the *New York Independent* and the *New York Ledger*. His contributions to these papers were collected in several volumes, including *Star Papers; or, Experiences of Art and Nature* (1855) and *Eyes and Ears* (1862), in which he detailed life at his country homes in the Berkshires and up the Hudson River.

Beecher was the minister of Brooklyn's Plymouth Congregational Church, happily endowed with a prosperous and socially prominent membership. The members of this social and financial elite owed their successes to the city, its factories, its businesses —not to the rural areas where a goodly proportion of the congregation, including Beecher, had their origins. But while Beecher, and presumably his devoted congregation, recognized that the city had given them much, they continued to believe that the country offered much which was necessary to the good life and which could be obtained nowhere else. Beecher was no Thoreau, preaching a total commitment to rural life, but he did outline a method through which his congregation and others like them could obtain the best of both worlds. He centered on Downing's scheme for a paradise defined both architecturally and naturally—the linking of civilization and nature in an America of suburbs and summer homes.

As we know, Downing wished his rural cottages, if not his villas, to be available to all people, but for reasons already sketched out, cottages were simple impossibilities for many Americans. Not surprisingly, suburbs and summer homes were early the property of the middle and upper classes. By the 1860s Henry Hudson Holly was noting that suburban life had its greatest popularity "among the business community," and another architect, George E. Woodward, saw the appeal of summer homes primarily among "prosperous merchants, bankers, professional men, and wealthy citizens.[33] Beecher was a spokesman for this sort of people and for their cultural and moral pretensions, evidenced in their tastefully designed and impressively large rural residences and landscape gardens.

There is much in Beecher's writings that reminds one of Downing's. Beecher wanted men to design their own homes but recognized that this would not be possible "until men are educated and good taste is far more common than it is. Downing, of course, was acutely aware of the need for architectural training among Americans; the country, it seemed, had many builders but few architects. Like Downing, Beecher had no love for Greek Revival homes, which he collectively called "cheerless, pretentious, frigid," and he enthusiastically advocated picturesque houses which sympathetically reflected the visual com-

The ultimate destination of travelers in search of the sublime and the picturesque was Niagara Falls, shown here in an engraving of Thomas Cole's "A Distant View of the Falls of Niagara."

Lake George, shown here in an engraving based on a drawing by William Henry Bartlett, was an especially popular place for travelers in search of the picturesque.

Gelston Castle (1832), near Richfield Springs, New York, is supplied with some medieval details and artifacts—including a moat—but it lacks the picturesque complexity of later Gothic revival buildings in America.

Roseland, designed by Joseph C. Wells and built about 1850 in West Woodstock, Connecticut, is an especially elaborate example of the picturesque villas which were considered to be in excellent taste by mid-nineteenth-century Americans.

This Tudor villa, designed by John McMurtry, was built in Lexington, Kentucky, around 1850. It is loosely based on a design in one of Andrew Jackson Downing's architectural books.

Alexander Jackson Davis designed this castle for John J. Herrick. It was built near Tarrytown, New York, on the banks of the Hudson —one of many castles which once lined the river from Albany to New York.

Those who could not afford a castle like Herrick's might build one of the smaller Italian and Gothic villas and cottages recommended in Downing's books. This cottage or small villa, erected in Lexington, Virginia, is reminiscent of a design in Downing's *Cottage Residences*.

Cottage Lawn (1849), the Sands Higinbotham house in Oneida, New York, was designed by Davis. Homes like this, said Downing, are "the most refined home[s] of America."

American magazines of the Romantic period frequently published engravings which suggested ideal, moral, and happy domestic life.

In the 1830s, when Bartlett made the drawing on which this engraving is based, New York City, seen on the left, covered all of lower Manhattan. To escape the city's heat and congestion, New Yorkers fled to the woods and fields of Hoboken, shown on the right.

    Hoboken's Elysian Fields were visited each day by thousands of
New Yorkers who wished to escape from the city. By the 1860s, however, Central Park was under construction, and since it was more
convenient, it replaced Hoboken as the city's favorite retreat. In turn,
the Elysian Fields were turned into a real estate development.

Llewellyn Park, New Jersey, was one of the earliest landscaped suburbs—a place which combined a private community with picturesque landscapes. Developed in the 1850s, Llewellyn Park was a forerunner of similar suburban developments throughout the country.

plexities of natural scenery, and he praised "that mazy diversity, that most unlooked for intricacy in a dwelling, and that utter variation of lines in the exterior, which pleases the eye, or ought to please it, if it be trained in the absolute school of Nature. . . ."[34] Again in line with Downing's architectural program, he believed that although "In fact, in the greatest number of instances, a house may be regarded as simply the measure of [its owner's] purse,"

> A house is [or rather should be] the shape which a man's thoughts take when he imagines how he should like to live. Its interior is the measure of his social and domestic nature; its exterior, of his esthetic and artistic nature. It interprets, in its material forms, his ideas of home, of friendship, and of comfort.[35]

In short, the house was understood as far more than shelter; it had acquired value as an emblem of the owner's artistic, aesthetic, domestic, and social nature.

Beecher was also an amateur naturalist, and he took delight in categorizing the physical aspects of nature. He also had an interest in horticulture—a fact which would have pleased Downing, had he lived long enough to read Beecher' s work, for Downing was, among his other achievements, the country's leading horticulturist. On the other hand, Beecher seems to have been much less interested in landscape gardening that Downing was. Downing believed, as we have noted, that the gardener's art was necessary to accent or clarify whatever spiritual meaning nature revealed. But while Beecher preferred landscaping to such geometric or artificial methods of garden design as that at Versailles, he clearly preferred natural landscapes.

William G. McLaughlin in *The Meaning of Henry Ward Beecher* argues that while Beecher was no Emersonian, he was clearly a transcendentalist, one who saw the fabric of nature as an object through which divine meaning could be perceived.[36] However, Beecher was doctrinally a Christian, and if he had been aware of Emerson's writings—and McLaughlin finds no evidence that he was—he would have found much to dispute among the Concord philosopher's ideas. Beecher certainly sounded Emersonian in *Star Papers*, when he described nature as "an interpreter of God, a symbol of invisible spiritual truths, the ritual of a higher life, the highway upon which our thoughts are to travel toward immortality, and toward the realm of just men made perfect that do inherit it."[37] On the other hand, unlike Emerson, Beecher retained his Christian identification; in an especially telling passage, noted by McLaughlin, he wrote that "Then when Christ is most with us, do we find nature the most loving, the most inspired; and it evolves a deeper significance, in all its phases, and chants, with its innumerable voices, solemn but jubilant hymns of praise to God!"[38]

Beecher's transcendentalism, indeed his whole program of country life, was directed at his congregation and, through newspaper columns, at American Protestants in general—or at least those with the time, money, and desire to escape to private domains in the country.

N. P. WILLIS's writings on country life deserve extended attention. They were best sellers at a time when Thoreau's writings, which dealt with similar subjects, were virtually ignored. Willis, not Thoreau, sympathetically reached the interests of Americans, particularly Americans of the middle class. His territory was the suburb and the summer resort, and his Hudson River estate, Idlewild, was virtually an exemplar of Downing's "smiling lawns and tasteful cottages." Willis was an apostle of good taste, and his homes—the earlier Glenmary as well as Idlewild —were looked upon, as one of his contemporaries phrased it, as "missionary station[s] of social progress."[39] It is not to be wondered at that Idlewild and Glenmary bacame as famous as they did, for their owner acquired an enormous reputation through his books and his columns in various newspapers. According to Henry Beers, Willis's biographer, Willis was "a recognized *arbiter elegantiarum,* and his correspondence columns were crowded with appeals on knotty points of etiquette or costume."[40]

In 1837, following a lengthy sojourn in Europe, Willis moved to Glenmary, an estate near the Susquehanna River and the farming community of Owego, N.Y. A series of letters in which he described life at this rural retreat began appearing in the *New-York Mirror* with the issue of July 7, 1838. Further "Letters from under a Bridge," as he called them, appeared in *Graham's, Godey's Lady's Book,* and other periodicals. The letters published through 1839 were collected and issued in book form as

A l'Abri, or the Tent Pitched (1839). With additional letters
and their original title, the *Letters from under a Bridge* went
through numerous reprintings during the following twenty years,
and as late as 1856, a new edition was offered to the public. Not
only was the book a publishing success; Glenmary itself became
a Mecca for tourists. In 1858, two decades after the first Glenmary essay was published and long after Willis had moved elsewhere, a visitor to the estate noted that "Not a pleasant day
then passed that we did not count numerous carriages waiting
at the little gate, while gay groups eagerly explored the meadows, the glens, and creek."[41]

At Glenmary, Willis preferred to spend his days fishing and
sitting under a bridge, while passing judgment on various issues
of the day. He wrote that the country provided ample opportunity for leisure and reflection as well as for "driving, fishing,
shooting, strolling, and reading, (to say nothing of less selfish
pleasures)"—surely an impressive list. "What surprises me in the
past," wrote Willis, whose social reputation in New York was
substantial, "is, that I ever should have confined my free soul
and body, in the very narrow places and usages I have known in
towns."[42] Willis was not, however, the naturalist or lover of
wilderness that Thoreau was. The leisure and reflection which
Willis desired were the leisure and reflection of a gentleman.
Nor was the countryside Willis's only recourse during the Glenmary years; there were visits both to and from his New York
friends, and from May 1839 until April 1840 he was in England.

His biographer was surely understating the case when he
wrote that ". . . Willis was something of a cockney in the
presence of great Nature."[43] The metaphors which Willis used
to describe natural landscapes—"mob of mountains," "delicious"
scenery, and so forth—clearly reflect a superficial interest in
nature. The passage of the Susquehanna River through the
mountains reminded him of Lady Blessington's calm progress
through a mob of irate citizens. His attitude toward nature and
country life is evident in Letter XX, concerned with landscape
gardening.

> The most intense and sincere lovers of the country are citizens
> who have fled to rural life in middle age, and old travellers who
> are weary, heart and foot, and long for shelter and rest. Both

these classes of men are ornamental in their tastes—the first, because the country is his passion, heightened by abstinence; and the latter, because he remembers the secluded and sweet spots he has crossed in travels, and yearns for something that resembles them, of his own.[44]

The curious assumption that "the most intense and sincere lovers of the country" are "ornamental in their tastes" does much to explain Willis's attitude toward nature and country life; in his world, landscapes and nature were virtually never of interest on their own terms. On the other hand, Willis was willing to advocate "no 'improvement' which requires more attention than the making"—but this was not because a man should be as free as possible to enjoy his rural surroundings. Important as landscape gardening might be, it was even more important to be free "to take your wife to the Springs" or "join a coterie at Niagara at a letter's warning" or "spend a winter in Italy without leaving half your income to servants who keep house at home."[45]

Willis's comments on landscape gardening were prompted by the publication of an "elegant and tempting book on Rural Architecture," Downing's *Cottage Residences,* and although Downing advocated more attention to landscaping than did this "Letter from under a Bridge," he was sufficiently pleased with it to reprint it in his journal, *The Horticulturist.* In turn Willis held Downing in inestimably high regard. Downing, he wrote, was "the ever-reminding, ever-diffusing prophet" of the "World of Taste and Refinement," and his "genius" was nothing less than "our country's one solitary promise of a supply for this lack of common currency—this scarcity of beauty coin in our every-day pockets."[46]

Willis left Glenmary in 1842 and eight year later, with money from his wife's inheritance, purchased what he called "a rocky wilderness," "a little seventy-acre world of rocks, foam-rapids, and pathless woods" near Cornwall on the western bank of the Hudson River, four miles south of Newburgh and four miles north of West Point. The land was located on the Highland Terrace, a shelf which extends along the bank of the river just north of the mountains of the Highlands. The setting was already picturesque, and Willis determined on "seeing how far a place can be improved by originating nothing—taking advantage only of what Nature has already done."[47] This attitude toward landscaping had been advanced by Downing.

Willis retained Calvert Vaux, Downing's best-known disciple, to design his house, and the result was essentially a Gothic villa, replete with bracketed gables, vergeboard, finials, oriel windows, and a main entrance and verandas with Gothic detailing. Idlewild offered a union of picturesque landscape and picturesque architecture such as Downing liked, and in fact the architect later wrote that Willis "seemed to take more interest in accommodating the house to the fancies of the genius of the place than in any other part of the arrangement."[48]

Downing's friend Henry Winthrop Sargent described Idlewild as "a piece of Nature's Landscape Gardening, where the hand of man should not, and, for the good taste of the owner, has not been allowed to appear, except in the necessary buildings."[49] The description is not quite accurate. Willis by no means left his property as he found it. Initially he did little but cut away underbrush, thin out trees, lay out paths, and build an entrance drive. Later, however, he reported that he had "been trimming the trees into frames for the scenery-pictures around," and one of the resulting views seemed like "a Salvator Rosa of great price."[50]

In the northern part of his estate was a ravine through which flowed "the Brook of Idlewild." Willis could not conceive of anything "wilder or more lawlessly picturesque" than this stream.[51] Content to leave neither stream nor ravine as he found them, he laid out more of Idlewild's ubiquitous paths, and over the ravine, he constructed bridges. Below, in the ravine itself, he constructed a dam and a waterfall. The setting might still be picturesque, but it was picturesqueness owing more than a little to artifice. To the journalist and artist T. Addison Richards, the ravine seemed "a grand gallery of wonderful pictures, which Mr. Willis's magic art—his vistas, his bridges, and his woodpaths—has restored, and framed, and hung up for the delight of the public eye."[52] Visitors, who were always welcome at Idlewild, were directed not only where to walk but also, especially with the creation of "frames," what to see, and in some respects, the "wild," confined to a series of recommended views, owed as much to art as to nature.

In early April 1853, nearly four months before the estate became his permanent home, Willis began contributing a series of letters about Idlewild to the *Home Journal,* a New York-based publication of which he was an editor. Together with an essay that had previously appeared in the *Home Book of the Picturesque,* those letters which had been published before November 1854 were collected and published as *Out-Doors at Idlewild; or, the Shaping of a Home on the Banks of the Hudson* (1855). A second series of these "Idlewild Papers," as Willis called them, were collected four years later in *The Convalescent,* but the second volume added little about the estate which had not been already detailed in the first.

Described by its author as "a simple weaving into language of the every-day circumstances of an invalid retirement in the Highlands of the Hudson," *Out-Doors at Idlewild* is a collection of informal essays with, apparently, no pretense to serious literature.* Modest as the essays are, however, their theme is in every way a significant one within the context of mid-nineteenth-century American life and thought, for aside from Downing's writings, Willis's Idlewild essays were possibly the era's best-known propaganda for domestic life in the country. It had been his aim, wrote Willis, "TO LIVE, as variedly, as amply, and as *worthily,*" as he could. In *Out-Doors at Idlewild,* he wrote that "Nature has her sad but needed lessons, which she gives us . . . incidentally and unsought, in a life not too crowded and artificial. You hear them in the country, always—in the city, almost never." The country was morally preferable to the city. In town, a family could be bound together by money, but in the country "high principles and careful statesmanship" were required. Furthermore, the country, unlike the city, could provide "the *space and liberty to be an individual.*"[53] Idlewild suggested a union of the moral and the aesthetic, country life and the picturesque.

BY 1853 WHEN WILLIS and his family moved to Idlewild, the countryside around it had already acquired a favorable reputation among tourists. Three of the country's most popular resort

---

* Willis had initially gone to the Terrace on doctor's orders—hence "an invalid retirement." However, his work as a writer and an editor remained very nearly undiminished during the Idlewild years.

hotels were situated within a short drive, and for those who desired simpler accommodations, farmhouses throughout the Terrace welcomed paying guests. (The Willises themselves had summered at the farm of a Mrs. Sutherland before Idlewild was ready for occupancy.) Nor were farmers and tourists the only people in the vicinity. Within a radius of four or five miles from Cornwall were the homes of Calvert Vaux, the poet and critic Clarence Cooke, the artist Robert Weir, and the historian Joel Tyler Headley, whose home, like Willis's, had been designed by Vaux. The neighbor immediately to the north of Idlewild was Philip Verplanck, descended from an old New York family, and among the other nearby residents were "fifteen or twenty 'old families' . . . [living] very conservatively on their estates, within calling distance. . . ."[54]

Between the local residents and the tourists, Willis should have had, one imagines, enough people to keep him company, but through the "Idlewild Papers," he actively sought out other people interested in establishing their homes on the Terrace and in the area around. For example, he promoted this region as ideal for writers, for the region would someday become "the teeming Switzerland of our country's Poetry pencil." For workers and immigrants, of whom he had read "harrowing descriptions of hunger and lack of employment," Willis noted that in his area there were many jobs available clearing fields, working the mines, and so forth.* He claimed that here the working man could earn as much as "a dollar a day—an easy opening for an industrious man to lay up money."[55] Although Willis thought that a dollar a day was a most satisfactory income for laborers, he might have remembered that on the Terrace it cost $400 to build a simple four-room cottage, the cheapest offering in Downing's *Architecture of Country Homes*. Downing believed that $400 was a "very trifling cost" but it was surely enough to discourage many industrious laborers, especially those with families to support.[56] Company housing had its real value.

* No Irish need apply, however, since the area would simply prove "too lonely" for them. Perhaps Willis was really more concerned about what he called "the increasing cost and trouble of Paddy-power." [Nathaniel Parker Willis, *Out-Doors at Idlewild* (New York: Charles Scribner, 1855), pp. 258, 164.]

Although Willis made gestures in the direction of laborers, it was pointedly not laborers for whom the future of the Hudson was intended. "*A class who can afford to let the trees grow* is getting possession of the Hudson," he remarked, and although at first the replacement of farmers with "the luxurious idler" might seem disagreeable, the presence of money would mean—instead of fields and farmhouses—"waving forests," "wooded lawns," "groves," and "shaded villas," a change which Willis decidedly welcomed. The Terrace was advertised as desirable for those with "rural tastes and metropolitan refinements rationally blended," for that class defined by "Leisure, Refinement, and Luxury." For many, "the neighborhood would be too luxurious," and the Terrace was too far from the city to serve merely as a suburb. Furthermore, "what may be understood as 'Cockney annoyances' [would] not reach it."[57]

The west bank of the Hudson was offered for the particular attention of the newly rich, and the area south of West Point was suggested as especially suitable for suburban residences. The east bank was still the social domain of the old Dutch aristocracy—the "Knickerbocracy," Willis termed it—whereas "for the first fifty miles from New York," the west bank was "as much a wilderness at the present moment, as many a river-bank of equal length in the far West." However, a proposed railroad extending north from Hoboken would prove "*a continuation, as it soon will be,* of Chamber [sic] street to West Point." Villas and gardens would follow, and "The *social contrast* of the two banks of the Hudson," Willis concluded, "will be without a precedent in the world's progress—'old-fogeyism' on one side of a river exclusively, and start-fair-dom on the other."[58] With a suburb extending from Hoboken to West Point, and with the Terrace carved up for gentleman's estates, the future of much of the Hudson's west bank would be determined, evidently enough, by the presence of wealth.

It was, finally, for those with "metropolitan refinements," "rural tastes," and, not least, wealth that Idlewild might serve as an ideal. Certainly, accounts of the problems encountered in landscape gardening could have held only detached interest for laborers at a dollar a day, and the creation of new estates must have been of little concern for the Dutch aristocracy with homes which in some cases dated back to the seventeenth century. But Willis, who was amply supplied with income from his wife's inheritance as well as from his own writings, could and did find an eager audience among the fashionable or, at least, among those with pretenses to fashion.

The real estate promoter was indeed successful in his work. "The new movement—business in the city, home in the country—" brought many requests for information on home sites on the Terrace and in the area around it, and Willis showed himself especially eager to oblige those of "the wealthier class, in search of a villa-site rather than a farm." He reported having found about a dozen outstanding villa sites—he called them "Paradises" in the area and, considering the great number of inquiries he had received, thought that within a couple of years he would have directed "tasteful appreciators and possessors" to them.[59]

There were, however, far more than a dozen potential "tasteful appreciators," if not possessors, who decided to visit the Terrace. Through the *Home Journal,* the "Idlewild Papers" reached more than 50,000 readers weekly, and more readers were certainly acquired with the publication of *Out-Doors at Idlewild* and *The Convalescent.* One immediate result was a popular interest in Idlewild itself. Tourists were welcome at the Willis estate, and the invitation was liberally accepted. According to T. Addison Richards, writing in 1858, ". . . not a summer day passes without bringing scores of pilgrims to its welcoming gates, and filling the otherwise quiet glens with happy faces."[60] In early September 1853, five months after the first of the "Idlewild Papers" had been published, Willis estimated that as many as "fifty strangers a day" visited his estate, an estimate which, if correct, would mean that in three months Willis could expect more than four thousand visits from "strangers."[61] As late as 1885, nearly twenty years after Willis's death, his biographer reported that like Sunnyside, Idlewild remained "one of the historic points of the scenery of the Hudson."[62]

In the end, Willis had reason to know how fully his idea of "the good life" was directly dependent on wealth. He was forced to sell Glenmary when he discovered that a journalist in Owego, could not earn enough to keep such a home in repair, and in late 1861, finding his income sharply reduced, he was forced to rent out Idlewild and move his family to the home of his father-in-law. Two years later, there was enough money for his family to return to Cornwall, and yet it was still necessary for Willis himself to spend the next few years working in New York. Although he occasionally returned to his home for a week or two, he did not permanently return to Idlewild until November 1866 —less than three months before his death.

BY ISOLATING EMERSON'S WORKS from those of all but a few of his contemporaries, critics and scholars of American literature have implied, intentionally or not, that Emerson's thinking was, for this country at least, largely unique. Indeed the sense that he was for some reason intellectually isolated in his native land receives support from the fact that *Nature* was read by few when it was first published. Although Emerson was popular as a lecturer, James Russell Lowell wrote, "We do not go so much to hear what Emerson says, so much as to hear Emerson."[63] Contemporary accounts of his lectures show that he sometimes left his audience less informed than confused. Yet Emerson also believed that ". . . the artist must employ the symbols in use in his day and nation, to convey his enlarged sense to his fellow-men," and he also grounded much of his work in the conventionalities of American language and experience.[64] However difficult or obscure his contemporaries may have considered his writings and lectures, Emerson attempted to express his thinking through language and symbols current in his time. Thoreau, of course, attempted a similar program.

Emerson was no Jacksonian; he placed his trust squarely in the middle class, and from this class he adpoted the idealization of domestic life and the symbol of this ideal life, the country home or villa. Emerson believed that "all great men" have their origins in the middle class, and in *The Conduct of Life*—his paean to Adam Smith, laissez faire, and wealth—he postulated that "masses" were "rude, lame, unmade, pernicious in their demands and influence, and [needed] not to be flattered but to be schooled." At the same time he insisted that "Wealth brings with it its own checks and balances. The basis of political economy is non-interference."[65] It was, of course, the economic system supported by Emerson which permitted a substantial

American middle class and in turn an American landscape of villas and landscape gardens.

Emerson's architectural theories have been compared with those of Samuel Gray Ward, James Cabot Elliot, and particularly Horatio Greenough, early advocates of functionalism in American architecture.[66] All three were among Emerson's friends and shared with him a desire to dislodge revivalist architecture and replace it with an architectural system based on structural honesty. Pure ornament would be abolished. Of the three, Greenough has received the largest share of attention from architectural historians, for in this century, he has seemed to some people, according to Vincent Scully, "a kind of light shining in an aesthetic wilderness."* In fact, Greenough's writings on architecture, like Emerson's, were much less revolutionary than some twentieth-century writers have implied. It is essential, when tracing the history of functionalism in American architecture, to note, in Scully's words, Downing's "latent tendencies toward a 'functional' approach."[67] Downing's influence was immense, but Greenough's writings were little noticed when they first appeared, and they remained fairly obscure until architectural historians—and F. O. Matthiessen in *American Renaissance* —latched onto them.[68]

There are many points on which Greenough and Downing reached similar or identical conclusions: the need to adapt a building to its site, for example, and the necessity of allowing materials to express their own natures rather than, say, painting wood in imitation of stone. Both men wished the exterior aspect of a building to be expressive of its interior function, and both had a thorough dislike of the otherwise simple cottage half-hidden by an excrescence of gingerbread. But Downing and his disciples would have parted from Greenough's uncompromising definition of beauty in architecture as "the promise of function."[69] Downing believed "that the Beautiful is, intrinsically, something quite distinct from the Useful." He thought that "The Beautiful is an original instinct of our nature. It is a worship, by

---

* Important as Greenough's writings have seemed to some architectural historians, he is perhaps remembered more often because of his neoclassical sculpture, which has been cited by many critics as an apt example of what was worst in nineteenth-century American art.

the heart, of a higher perfection manifested in material forms."
This manifestation would not invariably have been evident in a
building which offered "the promise of function." Downing considered it essential that the functional aspect of the building be
organized in such a way that the resulting visual, architectural
pattern, while continuing to demonstrate the functional aspect,
would also express that "higher perfection," physically evident
in such qualities as "proportion, symmetry, variety, harmony,
and unity."[70] Downing's system of aesthetics in architecture
would have been no more acceptable to Emerson than to
Greenough.

Part of Emerson's architectural program was given in "Self-
Reliance," where he argued that Americans should not merely
imitate the Greek or the Gothic in their buildings. (It is fitting
that Emerson, who wrote that "With consistency a great soul has
simply nothing to do," purchased and lived in a house which
had stylistic origins in the classical revivals.) He wrote:

> Beauty, convenience, grandeur of thought, and quaint expression
> are as near to us as to any; and if the American artist will study
> with hope and love the precise thing to be done by him, con-
> sidering the climate, the soil, the length of the day, the wants
> of the people, the habit and form of the government, he will
> create a house in which all of these will find themselves fitted,
> and taste and sentiment will be satisfied also.[71]

On the surface, this is not much different from Downing, who
rejected the pointless imitation of foreign styles and who, unlike
the pure architectural revivalist Davis, advocated an architecture suited to practical matters and to American circumstances
and needs. Yet Downing was not willing to sacrifice altogether
the imitation of foreign modes, such as asymmetrical Gothic
massing, if he felt that these would contribute to his ends. "Our
own soil is the right platform," he said, "upon which a genuine
national architecture must grow, though it will be aided in its
growth by all foreign thoughts that mingle harmoniously with
its simple and free spirit."[72] Unlike Emerson, Downing was
willing to employ foreign styles until indigenous styles had been
developed in America, and it was toward just such an indigenous style that Emerson was heading in his organic theory of
architecture. He sought an architecture based not on examples

from the past but on natural law: "It is only within narrow limits that the discretion of the architect may range," he reminded his readers. "Gravity, wind, sun, rain, the size of men and animals, and such like, have more to say than he." Once the function of the proposed building had been determined and the natural boundaries of architecture were understood, the building's form would develop as naturally and inevitably as a plant would grow from a seed: "You cannot build your house or pagoda as you will, but as you must."[73]

Emerson was entirely in accord with his era when he insisted that externality could be taken as a guide to moral concerns. As interpreted by Emerson—and Americans in general—a house ideally might be understood as an emblem of moral, domestic life. According to his essay "Domestic Life,"

A house should bear witness in all its economy that human culture is the end to which it is built and garnished. It stands there under the sun and moon to ends analogous and not less noble than theirs. It is not for festivity, it is not for sleep: but the pine and the oak shall gladly descend from the mountains to uphold the roof of men as faithful and necessary as themselves; to be the shelter always open to the Good and the True; a hall which shines with sincerity, brows ever tranquil, and a demeanor impossible to disconcert; whose inmates know what they want; who do not ask your house how theirs should be kept. They have aims: they cannot pause for trifles.[74]

In "The Young American" Emerson with the enthusiasm of an evangelist envisioned an America characterized by both country and city. As important as Emerson believed cities to be—in *Conduct of Life* he called them "the centres where the best things are found"—he also placed great emphasis on the rural world and looked forward to a time when the wilderness would be cultivated and subdued. Emerson's program for the future seems less agreeable today, when there is little wilderness to be found, than it did a century ago. Emerson in fact was entirely in accord with his time when he wished the wilderness to be subdued by a civilized world marked by human enterprise and imagination, and once he went so far as to claim that landscape gardening—"the bringing out by art the native but hidden graces of the landscape"—was "the most poetic of all the occupations of real life."[75] It was a claim which would have had little opposition. Downing's doctrines had conquered, it seems, even the sage of Concord.

Whatever other (and more frequently examined) aspects of Emerson's work may be, his concerns for organic architecture, country life, domesticity, the middle class, laissez faire, and wealth lead to a world quite like Downing's "smiling lawns and tasteful cottages." In *Walden*, Thoreau offered an experience which owed much to Emerson's world and to Downing's, but it was a very personalized experience which Thoreau offered— and an experience which must finally be understood as a criticism of such ideal rural worlds as Emerson's and Downing's. *Walden* provides both an indoctrination into and a criticism of the country life sought by the mid-nineteenth-century American.

THOREAU'S LANDSCAPE at Walden belongs with Glen Ellen and Idlewild as an imaginative resolution of tensions between civilization and nature, between human activity and natural law. Like Davis and Willis, Thoreau was able to obtain a resolution only through specialized definitions of these apparent opposites. It is necessary to understand what Thoreau meant by "nature" —and he surely did not mean the same thing as, for example, Davis—if the success of this resolution in *Walden* is to be understood.

Jefferson, as we have seen, made of the tensions between civilization and nature, a perpetual visual statement, Monticello at one side, the wilderness at the other. The cultivated garden in which the influence of both nature and man was evident stood between them. In Thomas Cole's "The Course of Empire," the balance was tipped in the favor of wilderness, which was shown to be ultimately triumphant over civilization. As noted above, however, Roderick Nash concluded that in "The Ox-Bow" Cole implies that "man's optimum environment is a blend of wildness and civilization."[76] At Glen Ellen, Davis applied the British aesthetics of the picturesque to suggest a visual harmony between architecture and landscape, and in the works of Downing and his architectural disciples as well as in the various country books, nature or wilderness often seemed morally or spiritually as well as visually in harmony with human life. Emerson suggested a close relationship between nature and man's work

when he insisted that architecture obey natural law. No longer
did wilderness and civilization stand eternally opposed to each
other, but they were in effect parts of the same continuum.

Leo Marx has drawn attention to the fact that the Walden
experiment no more involved a withdrawal to the wilderness
than it involved an acceptance of Concord and the civilized
ideals for which it stood in Thoreau's mind; rather Thoreau
"keeps our attention focused upon the middle ground," located
between the town and "a vast reach of unmodified nature."[77]
The intermediate position leaves Thoreau—like Willis, Downing, and others we have been examining—free to choose for his
environment those elements of civilization and nature which
most accord with his purposes.

It was necessary, he wrote in *The Maine Woods,* for the poet
"to drink at some new and more bracing fountain of the Muses,
far into the recesses of the wilderness," and he believed that the
wilderness provided "the raw material of all our civilization."
"For a permanent residence," however, he sought "the partially
cultivated country," "humanized Nature," or the civilized wilderness.[78]

There is, of course, a great difference between, for example,
Downing's conception of civilized wilderness and Thoreau's.
The former simply chose from the two worlds those aspects that
had particular significance for him and then, applying the borrowed aesthetics of the picturesque and the beautiful, welded
these aspects into a unit. Thoreau began from the other end.
The binding element or catalyst was not applied to things already chosen; instead he began with his sense of natural law,
then admitted to his ideal realm all which obeyed that law. In
effect, of course, this made all wilderness available to him, and
yet in Thoreau's scheme, wilderness, while not destroyed, was
necessarily modified to suit human needs. Wilderness remained
"the raw material of . . . civilization."

"THE SCENERY OF WALDEN," Thoreau wrote, "is on a humble
scale, and though very beautiful, does not approach to grandeur,
nor can it much concern one who has not long frequented it or
lived by its shore; yet this pond is so remarkable for its depth
and purity as to merit a particular description."[79] This passage
from *Walden* is a parody of fashionable landscape descriptions

in which the landscape is viewed objectively and the sole problem for the writer is one of supplying the right adjectives. It is as "scientific" an approach to nature as was the work of Thoreau's contemporary naturalists who spent their time endlessly classifying. In the adjective game, Walden—which could not "much concern one who has not long frequented it or lived by its shore"—was no match for the Catskills or Trenton Falls. Nor was Thoreau willing to do what Downing or George William Curtis might have wished—namely, "embellish" Walden's landscapes. Yet while he was no friend of landscape gardening, he was certain that someday his pond would be ringed, whether he wished it or not, with gardens and villas.

On the other hand, he knew that the pond provided a means for transcending materiality; the physical world, he thought, could express spiritual truth to the few who were able to apprehend it. Walden was for Thoreau the physical element which expressed this higher truth. Thus he wrote, "though the view from my door was still more contracted, I did not feel confined in the least. There was pasture enough for my imagination"— the imagination being the faculty which could apprehend spiritual truth. Situated "between the earth and the heavens," Walden simultaneously offered the spectator both spiritual and material reality, and it was a spiritual reality which was immediately available and which did not need the work of the landscape gardeners praised by Downing and Poe.[80]

The hut at Walden had "no gate—no front yard,—and no path to the civilized world." Instead of a neatly trimmed yard fronting on the public road, there was "but unfenced Nature reaching up to [the] very sills." Like the most welcome of his visitors, Thoreau had come "out to the woods for freedom's sake, and really left the village behind." Civilization, typified by Concord, identified itself in the restrictions of schedules and time, through an emotionally and spiritual barren life alleviated only by vicarious experience in gossip—although gossip, the news, might only produce "numbness and insensibility to pain . . . without affecting the consciousness." Civilized life, or at least what passed for civilized life in Concord, was little more than a narcotic. By nature "no hermit," he wished, as any attentive reader of *Walden* knows, not a "civilization" in which all people withdrew from collective experience into their personal Waldens, but instead a civilization in which the individual was accorded a fair hearing, not coerced into patterns of living which were endorsed by the majority. The individual must attend to laws "more sacred" than those of common society, and with all individuals obeying the higher laws, it would then be possible to construct "noble villages of men." The objective for the individual, as Thoreau spelled it out, must be "to maintain himself in whatever attitude he find himself through obedience to the laws of his being which will never be one of opposition to a just government, if he should chance to meet with such."[81]

"I have a great deal of company," wrote Thoreau, "especially in the morning when nobody calls"—"I am no more lonely than a single mullein or dandelion in a pasture, or a bean leaf, or sorrel, or a horse-fly, or a humble-bee."[82] The life at Walden was a life of solitude only if "solitude" is considered a withdrawal from men. There was as much "society" at Walden as one could want, but it was a society composed more of nature than of human friendship. Solitude in nature implied the affirmation of a greater community than any village supplied. The life of the village was selective, embracing little of the possibilities for human imagination and enterprise, while at the same time the life of nature embraced all of spiritual truth. For Thoreau, nature was absolute, while the institutions of men were insubstantial, transitory. The landscape at Walden had nothing to do with Concord, its citizens, and their domesticated Edens.

THE "PRIVATE BUSINESS" which Thoreau transacted at Walden involved first piercing through externality and entering the "continent and seas in the moral world, to which every man is an isthmus or an inlet."[83] But he also wished to discover whether the moral world could determine the nature of a man's work, including his house. In turn, the house, like Walden and other parts of the physical world, might be expressive of this spiritual, moral world.

In the chapter entitled "The Ponds," Thoreau predicted that the shores of Walden would someday provide the sites for villas and landscape gardens. If Thoreau had been given his way, these villas (which, as it turned out, were never built) would surely have been constructed with no regard for the imported architectural styles which Thoreau had learned to expect from his neighbors in Concord. Furthermore, just as nature provided nothing which was merely decorative, the villas would certainly have lacked all the fashionable but inessential architectural encumbrances such as porticos and gingerbread which were largely expressive of fashion and wealth. Gathering together Thoreau's various comments in *Walden* about houses and architecture, it is possible to sense what Thoreau's villas would have looked like. For one thing, they would not have been cut up into rooms, the effect of which is to divide life into compartments. The villas would have contained nothing that was not necessary to life; each would have contained "all the essentials of a house, and nothing for house-keeping." Practicality would have determined the way in which each house was designed and the ways in which it was used; there would have been no formal dining rooms or parlors. But, of course, this ideal villa implied an owner who was ignorant of or unconcerned with fashion and whose life was organized as practically as his home. Thoreau's ideal villa, like Downing's and Emerson's, could have been used as an index to the character of the man who inhabited it.[84]

The architectural beauty which Thoreau had encountered in the past had "gradually grown from within outward, out of the necessities and character of the indweller . . . , —out of some unconscious truthfulness, and nobleness, without even a thought for the appearance. . . ." This is a statement which, by itself, might have been made by Beecher or Willis or Downing or Wetmore. But Thoreau's "life ideally lived" had nothing to do with middle-class experience, nothing to do with artificially ornamented life or, correspondingly, with "architectural ornaments," the paraphernalia of architectural gingerbread which "a September gale would strip . . . off, like borrowed plumes, without injury to the essentials." True picturesqueness did not result from visual ornament but from the character of the occupant of the house:

> The most interesting dwellings in this country, as the painter knows, are the most unpretending, humble log huts and cottages of the poor commonly; it is the life of the inhabitants

whose shells they are, and not any peculiarity in their surface merely, which makes them *picturesque;* and equally interesting will be the citizen's suburban box, when his life shall be as simple and as agreeable to the imagination, and there is as little straining after effect in the *style* of his dwelling.[85]

The landscape at Walden contained two central and complementary symbols. There was first the natural landscape, through which it was possible to perceive spiritual truth. The other symbol was the house, a physical statement of life ideally lived—lived, in fact, "as deliberately as Nature."[86] The ideal life involved, further, an imagination which could pierce through materiality and could discover and benefit from the spiritual truth beyond. Therefore, both symbols were linked to the spiritual world. At Walden the emblems of civilization and nature were not worked into a unit through the application of aesthetic doctrine; they were fused together and held there by their common origins in the spiritual world and by their common abilities to express spiritual truth symbolically.

BEFORE LEAVING the nineteenth-century world of rural retreats and "smiling lawns and tasteful cottages," it would be profitable to look into those cottages and discover what life in them was ideally—and actually—like. It was, of course, far different from life preached by Thoreau and, as the following chapter suggests, ideal domesticity was not always as morally and psychologically satisfying as Downing and his followers claimed.

Notes

1. James Jackson Jarves, *The Art-Idea* (Cambridge, Mass.: Harvard University Press, 1960), p. 92.

2. Henry David Thoreau, *Walden* (Princeton, N.J.: Princeton University Press, 1971), pp. 82–83.

3. Andrew Jackson Downing, *Rural Essays* (New York: Geo. A. Leavitt, 1869), p. 123.

4. James Fenimore Cooper, *Home as Found* (Boston: Houghton, Mifflin and Company, n.d.), pp. 112–114, 117. Cooper remodeled his family home as a Gothic villa, and Irving turned an unpre-

tentious farmhouse into his elaborately picturesque country home, Sunnyside.

5. Gervase Wheeler, *Rural Homes* (Auburn, N.Y.: Alden and Beardsley, 1855), p. 32.

6. Andrew Jackson Downing, *The Architecture of Country Houses* (New York: D. Appleton and Company, 1850), p. 37.

7. Wheeler, *op. cit.*, pp. 286–287.

8. Calvert Vaux, *Villas and Cottages*, 2d ed. (New York: Harper and Brothers, Publishers, 1864), p. 261.

9. Wheeler, *op. cit.*, p. 20.

10. Downing, *The Architecture of Country Houses*, pp. 22.

11. *Ibid.*, p. 23.

12. *Ibid.*, pp. 352–363.

13. Samuel Sloan, *Homestead Architecture* (Philadelphia: J. P. Lippincott and Company, 1866), p. 57.

14. Samuel Sloan, *Model Architect* (Philadelphia: E. S. Jones and Company, 1852), vol. I, p. 10.

15. Henry W. Cleaveland, William Backus, and Samuel D. Backus, *Villa and Farm Cottages* (New York: D. Appleton and Company, 1855), p. 4.

16. Downing, *The Architecture of Country Houses*, p. 269.

17. Cleaveland et al., *op. cit.*, p. 4.

18. Downing, *The Architecture of Country Houses*, pp. v–vi.

19. Quoted by Jay B. Hubbell, *Who Are the Major American Writers?* (Durham, N.C.: Duke University Press, 1972), p. 19.

20. Wheeler, *op. cit.*, p. 145.

21. Frederick William Shelton, *Up the River* (New York: Charles Scribner, 1853), p. 14.

22. [Susan Fenimore Cooper], *Rural Hours* (New York: George P. Putnam, 1850), pp. 520–521.

23. [Lewis W. Mansfield], *Up-Country Letters* (New York: D. Appleton and Company, 1852), p. 24.

24. *Ibid.*, p. 26.

25. Shelton, *op. cit.*, pp. xiii–xviii.

26. *Ibid.*, p. xx.

27. *Ibid.*, pp. 197–198.

28. *Ibid.*, p. 221.

29. *Ibid.*, p. xix.

30. [Henry Carmer Wetmore], *Hermit's Dell* (New York: J. C. Derby, 1854), p. 5.

31. *Ibid.*, p. 27.

32. Daniel J. Boorstin, *The Americans: The National Experience* (New York: Random House, 1965), pp. 115, 116.

33. Henry Hudson Holly, *Country Seats* (New York: D. Appleton and Company, 1863), p. 21. George E. Woodward, *Country Homes* (New York: Geo. E. Woodward, 1865), p. 8.

34. Henry Ward Beecher, *Star Papers* (New York: J. C. Derby, 1855), p. 290.

35. *Ibid.*, pp. 291, 285–286.

36. William G. McLaughlin, *The Meaning of Henry Ward Beecher* (New York. Alfred A. Knopf, 1970), p. 61.

37. Beecher, *op. cit.*, p. 310.

38. *Ibid.*, p. 307. (Quoted in McLaughlin, *op. cit.*, p. 58.)

39. T. Addison Richards, "Idlewild: The Home of N. P. Willis," *Harper's New Monthly Magazine*, XVI (1858), 146.

40. Henry A. Beers, *Nathaniel Parker Wills* (Boston: Houghton, Mifflin and Company, 1885), p. 289.

41. Richards, *op. cit.*, p. 155.

42. Nathaniel Parker Willis, *Letters from under a Bridge,* in *Rural Letters* (New York: Baker and Scribner, 1849), pp. 187, 21.

43. Beers, *op. cit.*, p. 225.

44. Willis, *op. cit.*, pp. 62, 73, 176.

45. *Ibid.*, p. 187.

46. *Ibid.*, p. 175. Willis's comments are reprinted in *Horticulturist,* I (1847), 551–557. Willis, *The Rag-Bag* (New York: Charles Scribner, 1855), p. 122. Willis, *Out-Doors at Idlewild* (New York: Charles Scribner, 1855), p. 213.

47. *Ibid.*, pp. 91, 51, 53.

48. Vaux, *op. cit.*, p. 260.

49. Henry Winthrop Sargent, "Supplement," in Andrew Jackson Downing, *A Treatise on the Theory and Practice of Landscape Gardening*, 6th ed. (New York: A. O. Moore, 1859), p. 554.

50. Nathaniel Parker Willis, *The Convalescent* (New York: Charles Scribner, 1859), p. 95.

51. Willis, *Out-Doors at Idlewild,* p. 110.

52. Richards, *op. cit.*, p. 159.

53. Willis, *Out-Doors at Idlewild,* pp. v, vii, 362, 447, 409.

54. *Ibid.*, p. 200.

55. *Ibid.*, pp. 18, 257–258.

56. Downing, *The Architecture of Country Houses*, p. 73.

57. Willis, *Out-Doors at Idlewild*, pp. 47, 25, 22.

58. *Ibid.*, pp. 374, 377.

59. *Ibid.*, p. 194.

60. Richards, *op. cit.*, p. 154.

61. Willis, *Out-Doors at Idlewild*, p. 155.

62. Beers, *op. cit.*, p. 328.

63. James Russell Lowell, "Emerson the Lecturer," *Complete Works* (Boston: Houghton, Mifflin and Company, 1890), vol. I, p. 353.

64. Ralph Waldo Emerson, "Art," *Complete Works* (Boston: Houghton, Mifflin and Company, 1903), vol. I, p. 7.

65. Ralph Waldo Emerson, *Conduct of Life*, in *ibid.*, vol. VI, pp. 259, 249, 105.

66. Robert B. Shaffer, "Emerson and His Circle: Advocates of Functionalism," *Journal of the Society of Architectural Historians*, VII (1948), 17–20.

67. Vincent J. Scully, Jr., *The Shingle Style and the Stick Style*, rev. ed. (New Haven, Conn.: Yale University Press, 1971), pp. xxxvii, xxxvi.

68. F. O. Mattheissen, *American Renaissance* (London: Oxford University Press, 1941), pp. 140–152.

69. Horatio Greenough, *Form and Function* (Berkeley and Los Angeles: University of California Press, 1962), p. 71.

70. Downing, *The Architecture of Country Houses*, pp. 8, 9, 10.

71. Ralph Waldo Emerson, "Self-Reliance," *Complete Works*, vol. II, pp. 57, 82–83.

72. Downing, *The Architecture of Country Houses*, p. 264.

73. Ralph Waldo Emerson, "Art," *Complete Works*, vol. VII, p. 41.

74. Ralph Waldo Emerson, "Domestic Life," in *ibid.*, vol. VII, p. 117.

75. Ralph Waldo Emerson, *Conduct of Life*, in *ibid.*, vol. VI, p. 153. Emerson, "The Young American," *ibid.*, vol. I, p. 369.

76. Roderick Nash, *Wilderness and the American Mind* (New Haven, Conn.: Yale University Press, 1967), p. 81.

77. Leo Marx, *The Machine in the Garden* (New York: Oxford University Press, 1964), p. 245.

78. Henry David Thoreau, *The Maine Woods* (Princeton, N.J.: Princeton University Press, 1972), pp. 156, 155.

79. Thoreau, *Walden, op. cit.*, p. 175.
80. *Ibid.*, pp. 87, 176.
81. *Ibid.*, pp. 128, 154, 167–168, 140, 323, 110.
82. *Ibid.*, p. 137.
83. *Ibid.*, p. 321.
84. *Ibid.*, pp. 242–243.
85. *Ibid.*, p. 47.
86. *Ibid.*, p. 97.

Chapter Five

Idealized Domesticity

[Mr. Barclay] believed that a household, governed in obedience to the Christian social law, would present as perfect an image of heaven, as the infirmity of human nature, and the imperfections in the constitutions of human affairs, would admit.

Catharine Maria Sedgwick, *Home* (1835).[1]

This, indeed was a home,—home,—a word that George had never yet known a meaning for; and a belief in God, and trust in his providence, began to encircle his heart, as, with a golden cloud of protection and confidence, dark, misanthropic, pining, atheistic doubts, and fierce despair, melted away before the light of a living Gospel, breathed in living faces, preached by a thousand unconscious acts of love and good-will, which, like the cup of cold water given in the name of a disciple, shall never lose their reward.

Harriet Beecher Stowe, *Uncle Tom's Cabin* (1851–52).[2]

AN EXTRAORDINARY ARRAY OF UTOPIAN SCHEMES was offered the public in nineteenth-century America. Religious societies as well as social and political groups set out to establish perfect communities. New Harmony, Oneida, and other communities promised ideal social or economic lives for their members, but most of these communities and schemes had little, if any, effect on traditional American life. Of all utopian schemes, the one which did have a pervasive influence on American life was idealized domesticity—rigorously moral domesticity.

In the ideal domestic situation, it was believed, the family was very nearly self-sufficient; economically, of course, it continued to be dependent on a larger community, but in other respects, the family had little cause to trespass outside its limits. Ideally the home was situated in a rural, or at least suburban, setting. Fathers were engaged in the worldly—and morally ambiguous—business of money-getting, but mothers were available to organize the home for the moral, social, intellectual, and emotional benefit of all. The mother's role as moral exemplar and instructor to her children was her most significant function—one for which she received the highest praise and respect.

HORACE BUSHNELL, pastor of the North Church in Hartford, Conn., was among those writers who idealized domesticity in their works. In *Christian Nurture* (1846), he argued that a child would be either sinful or good according to the type of family in which he was reared. Protestants at this time gave much consideration to the fine points of theology, and Bushnell's thesis was widely considered revolutionary, even perhaps heretical. An outcry against the book arose and increased, and the publisher, sensitive to criticism from conservative Protestants, finally suppressed the work. Bushnell paid to have it republished; it began to receive more favorable attention than it had received at first. Ironically, its thesis ultimately ceased to seem revolutionary, became in fact orthodox doctrine for many Protestant theologians.

In 1846 Congregationalists—which is to say the orthodox and the majority of New England Protestants—believed that a man could not become a Christian until he was fully aware of his "inner depravity," the legacy of Original Sin. Children were largely excluded from religious life until they were old enough to understand this and to recognize their personal sinfulness. Bushnell was a Congregationalist and accepted the doctrine of Original Sin, but he believed that the process of becoming a Christian was one which was life-long and which should be initiated by the family and continued by the community and the church. Through this process of Christian nurture, furthermore, the sinful aspects of a child's character could be eliminated, might in fact never emerge. Bushnell attributed the greatest importance to the family, and in effect he made the home an extension of the church.

Bushnell was no minor figure in the mid-nineteenth century: "Through him," says Sydney E. Ahlstrom, "the romantic movement made its entrance into theological seminaries and pulpits just as, in a more indirect though perhaps more pervasive way, Emerson brought it into the nation's schoolrooms and parlors."[3] Bushnell's writings are more than historical, literary, or theological curiosities; *Christian Nurture* and other books by him transformed American Protestantism and hence the way Americans think. When the Hartford divine placed his imprimatur on Christian nurture and domestic life, he legitimized for his followers what was already becoming an essential factor of American life: the idealization of domesticity. The home, at least as much as the church, was at the center of religious life—and although, to say the least, this was doctrinally unorthodox, it was the common message of domestic novels, gift books, annuals, and other publications directed primarily at the female audience. And it should not surprise us that this message became a staple of writings for women; after all, idealized domesticity, by making moral instruction the mother's duty, offered women a major, perhaps *the* major, role in the progress of civilization.

Bushnell advanced an organic view of society in which family, community, and church nurtured the Christian; a child's moral nature, he made clear, was formed at home as well as in the church, and in the home, the mother's role was in effect the role which had traditionally been assigned to the minister. As Bushnell wrote,

> All society is organic—the church, the state, the school, the family; and there is a spirit in each of these organisms, peculiar to itself, and more or less hostile, more or less favorable to religious character, and to some extent, at least, sovereign over the individual man. A very great share of the power in what is called a revival of religion, is organic power; nor is it any the less divine on that account. The child is only more within the power of organic laws than we all are. We possess only a mixed individuality all our life long. A pure, separate, individual man,

living *wholly* within, and from himself, is a mere fiction. No such person ever existed, or ever can. I need not say that this view of an organic connection of character subsisting between parent and child, lays a basis for notions of Christian education, far different from those which now prevail, under the cover of a merely fictitious and mischievous individualism.[4]

Bushnell's idealization of domesticity and his organic view of society had origins in his own experiences. He was reared in rural Connecticut during the "Age of Homespun," as he called it, an age in which church, family, and community were bound together by shared religious beliefs. Mid-nineteenth-century Hartford presented a different reality, however; there were not only Congregationalists here but Episcopalians, Catholics, and members of other denominations as well. There were, furthermore, theological differences among the Congregationalists. But if the people whom Bushnell knew—primarily members of a prosperous middle class—were not always in agreement on matters of church ritual and doctrine, they did share the American idealization of domestic life. Bushnell transferred the organic, Christian experience of the Age of Homespun to the Industrial Age in Hartford, which was rapidly becoming a fairly sophisticated city. As he described this experience, however, much emphasis was now given to the home as well as to the church, to parents as well as to ministers. By contrast, during his childhood, the central significance of the church in all religious matters had never been seriously disputed.

Bushnell was well aware of American ideals of his time, and his greatest achievement lay in bringing his own theology and beliefs into line with them. This achievement may have had very practical origins, of course. He was a Congregationalist, and as such, his ministerial future depended upon the will of his congregation rather than upon the will of a bishop or other religious superior. Since his congregation idealized domestic life, Bushnell was certainly acting in a most practical manner, as he must have known, when he devised his theology of domesticity.

THE OVERWHELMING IMPORTANCE OF DOMESTIC LIFE to nineteenth-century Americans is evident in *Uncle Tom's Cabin,* near the end of which Mrs. Stowe indicted "the mothers of the free states" for, of all things, some of the worst atrocities of slavery.

Had these women "felt as they should"—that is, had they been Abolitionists—

> . . . the sons of the free states would not have been the holders, and, proverbially, the hardest masters of slaves; the sons of the free states would not have connived at the extension of slavery, in our national body; the sons of the free states would not, as they do, trade the souls and bodies of men as an equivalent to money, in their mercantile dealings. There are multitudes of slaves temporarily owned, and sold again, by merchants in northern cities; and shall the whole guilt or obloquy of slavery fall only on the South?[5]

This is, to say the least, an extraordinary charge: Northern complicity in slavery can be traced to mothers who have not "felt as they should." In fact Mrs. Stowe accepted the belief, then widely held, that domestic life was, or at least *should be,* morally, emotionally, and socially ideal and that it was a mother's sacred duty to provide her children with moral instruction. Clearly, the mothers in the North had failed.

Idealized domesticity was expressed emblematically, as we have seen, through domestic architecture, but it was also represented in novels and in paintings, through pictures of happy family life. Thus in *Home,* which is virtually a summa of ideal domesticity, Miss Sedgwick offered the picture of a family dinner, capable of teaching children such virtues as "punctuality, order, neatness, temperance, self-denial, kindness, generosity, and hospitality."[6] Novels, paintings, and engravings in magazines offered pictures of adoring children rapturously listening to their parents' advice. Conversely, there was the "Little Eva" school of ideal domesticity in which a dying child, like Mrs. Stowe's heroine, provided moral instruction for her elders. Idealized domesticity was implied in sentimental pictures of courtship and, oddly enough, in lugubrious views of a mother or children at the grave of one who had absorbed his moral instruction and who therefore was well on his way to heaven. There were, on the other hand, various things which were never suggested in descriptions and pictures of idealized domesticity: Drink, demon rum, was never admitted to the home, of course, for this was the age that made temperance a moral law. Anything which suggested business was also excluded—financial problems remained at the office. Women were portrayed as virtuous and passive wives, pious Christians, and devoted mothers. Their moral decisions and advice possessed Delphic finality. Children were submissive and moral. Husbands were devoted to their families and ever willing to offer advice and help. Servants were occasionally included in descriptions of idealized domesticity, though generally in the background. They were, after all, morally and socially problematical; slaves in the South and Irish Catholics in the North, they were uncomfortable additions to the idealized domestic world of a predominantly white Protestant America.

For those with the money, there was a surfeit of paintings of domestic life available. Even as great a painter (and as confirmed a bachelor) as William Sidney Mount produced some of these domestic scenes. Mount painted more scenes of country life than domestic subjects, yet among his works are, for example, "Winding Up" and "The Sportsman's Last Visit," both of which deal with courtship. Domesticity also served the purposes of art through the firm of Currier and Ives. Among the artists they employed was George Henry Durrie, who was able to suggest an idealized domesticity in his winter views of Connecticut farmhouses. His paintings seldom represented the business of farming. Farmers and their families, were gathered, one could imagine, around the fires inside their homes, while the raw, cold winter outside stretched to the horizon. The family was insulated from the world and presumably self-sufficient.

Gift books, annuals, and magazines like *Godey's Lady's Book* thrived on engravings and stories of idealized domesticity. They also published songs which involved aspects of domestic life, and the words were often the work of writers who specialized in poems which idealized domesticity—Lydia Howard Huntley Sigourney ("Sweet Singer of Hartford") and Colonel George Pope Morris, among others. The most famous of these songs was "Home, Sweet Home" (1823), the work of John Howard Payne, an American dramatist who wrote the song for a play derived from a French stage production and involving an Italian girl as the heroine. The music for the song came from a Sicilian tune arranged by an English composer. "Home, Sweet Home" had formidably international origins, but it was in America that the song achieved its greatest success—so great a success indeed that Payne's home on Long Island became and remains something of a national shrine.

When Mrs. Stowe indicted Northern mothers for complicity in slavery, her charge did not seem at all absurd; if such composers, artists, and writers as Payne, Mount, and Miss Sedgwick were correct, domestic life could provide many of the brightest spots in the moral universe.

Novels dealing with domestic life enjoyed an extraordinary popularity in the 1850s; the combined sales of *Moby-Dick*, *Walden,* and *Leaves of Grass* was but a fraction of the sales of any one of the more popular of these novels: *The Wide, Wide World* by Susan Warner, *The Lamplighter* by Maria Cummins, *The Hidden Hand* by Mrs. E. D. E. N. Southworth, and *Beulah* by Augusta Jane Evans, among others. Most popular of all the domestic novels was *Uncle Tom's Cabin* in which Mrs. Stowe demonstrated the pernicious effects of slavery on the family life of both slave owners and slaves.

The first popular author of domestic novels was Catharine Maria Sedgwick, and the first popular domestic novel was her *A New-England Tale,* published in 1822. But while this novel opens and concludes with images of blissful domesticity, the rest of the book seems to question rather than to support the idea of family life. The heroine, Jane Elton, is born into an apparently model family—a prosperous father and a contented mother. However, her father fails in business, and both he and his wife die, leaving Jane at the mercy of her father's three sisters, none of whom wish to adopt her. One of the three finally agrees to take her in but then treats her abominably, and Jane spends her life in misery until a kind gentleman takes an interest in her welfare—rather like the prince in a fairy tale—and, at the end of the novel, marries her. If the novel ends with a reassertion of domestic life, most of the work suggests that domesticity could easily be threatened by economic and social forces quite beyond an individual's control. Jane is never in a position to prevent her father's economic misfortune or, given her submissive character, to avoid the harsh and unjust treatment she receives from her aunt.

Miss Sedgwick's *Redwood* (1824) similarly questions the idea of domesticity. Here a wealthy Southerner marries a woman "beneath his station," then deserts her and goes to Europe. She gives birth to his daughter and dies shortly afterwards. The daughter—Ellen Bruce, the novel's heroine—is sent to New England to be reared. Though New England provides her with a thoroughly moral education, she receives none of the social advantages that her father's wealth and aristocratic position could provide. But *Redwood,* like all Miss Sedgwick's novels, ends with the heroine's happy marriage and hence with a re-affirmation of domesticity. Indeed Miss Sedgwick's private letters and journals leave no question that although she remained single, she held the institutions of marriage and domesticity in the highest regard. Although her early novels portray domestic life at the mercy of various destructive social and economic forces, Miss Sedgwick indisputably believed that family life was at least preferable to its alternatives.*

There was, as Miss Sedgwick and other domestic novelists knew, a great difference between idealized domesticity and the

* Domestic novels of the 1850s—the decade in which this kind of fiction enjoyed its greatest popularity—had literary origins in a number of works besides Miss Sedgwick's. Dickens' portraits of children, for example, may have inspired similar portraits in domestic novels. Certainly the domestic novels, including Miss Sedgwick's, owed much to eighteenth-century sentimental fiction, particularly the *Pamela* school in which an innocent, virtuous maiden is left to the mercy of a cruel, immoral world; the only acceptable solution to her problem is, of course, a good marriage. Miss Sedgwick's novels provided domestic novelists with a moral, religious hero who would always act in the heroine's best interest. The other hero common to domestic novels has origins in Charlotte Bronte's *Jane Eyre.* This hero is the Byronic, immoral tyrant—Rochester in *Jane Eyre*—who must be transformed, often under the vigilant eye of the heroine, into a submissive and moral husband. While some novelists were content with heroes who were always docile, Mrs. E. D. E. N. Southworth and Augusta Jane Evans made full use of the Rochester-like tyrant. Susan Warner read *Jane Eyre* shortly before writing *The Wide, Wide World* and concluded that Jane's character was much like her own—a curious conceit since the unpersonable and remarkably ugly Miss Warner had little reason for the comparison. Miss Warner may have had Jane Eyre in mind when she created her own virtuous and submissive orphan, Ellen Montgomery, but it is equally possible that Ellen is patterned after Miss Sedgwick's Jane Elton.

real thing, but they ended their novels, however unsatisfactorily, by flatly reaffirming idealized domesticity. At the end of these novels, a wayward husband comes home, a long-lost and wealthy relative appears, a suitable proposal of marriage is made, or something else happens which makes it possible once again to reaffirm and idealize domesticity.

Susan Warner's *The Wide, Wide World* (1850) was among the most popular domestic novels. The public demanded fourteen editions in two years, and there were sixty-nine editions before the book finally went out of print. *The Wide, Wide World* centers on Ellen Montgomery, a Christian girl brought up according to the standards of the upper middle class. Her father, Captain Morgan Montgomery, has prospered, and her mother is descended from a wealthy, semi-aristocratic family in Scotland. Captain Montgomery suffers financial difficulties, however, and his wife learns that she is dying of consumption. For reasons of economy and health, it is imperative that the captain and his wife journey to Europe, but since he does not feel that his daughter should accompany them, she is sent to the home of his sister in a rural upstate New York town. Ellen finds that her aunt, whom she has never met previously, neither understands her nor wishes to. For understanding and comfort, Ellen turns to the daughter and the son of a local minister. Later Ellen receives word of the death of first her mother and then her father, and she is sent to Scotland to live with her mother's family, a group of generally well-intentioned people who, nonetheless, are no more able to understand Ellen or sympathize with her problems than was her father's sister. Although Ellen suffers numerous vicissitudes of domestic life, the novel ends, presumably happily, with Ellen's return to America to marry the minister's son, now a minister himself.

The Wide, Wide World obviously emulates the plot of *A New-England Tale*, published twenty-eight years before: a young girl, who has been reared in a happy home and who is morally perfect, is thrown upon the mercies of "the wide, wide world" because of her father's financial difficulties, followed soon by the death of her parents. The girl is taken into the home of an aunt who fails to understand her or sympathize with her, and redemption finally comes through marriage to a deeply religious man— a devout Quaker in Miss Sedgwick's book and a minister in Miss

Warner's. Both books provide pictures of three very different domestic worlds: (1) the home which is subject to the vagaries of economic and social forces, (2) the home lacking in human sympathy and understanding, and (3) the home which is based on the love of a virtuous woman and a religious man. (Of course, the third type of home was as subject to economic and social problems as the first, but the third type, to use the language of domestic novelists, was "sealed in heaven," and whatever problems that family might face on earth, they were assured of being together again in eternity.) Significantly the third, ideal type of home admits no mention of sexual matters; Miss Sedgwick's hero treats Jane with fatherly concern, while Miss Warner's treats Ellen explicitly as a sister.

Augusta Jane Evans's *St. Elmo,* the best seller of 1867, demonstrated the gradual transformation of a man—under the relentless care of yet another virtuous heroine—into a moral paragon as indisputably sexless as Miss Sedgwick's and Miss Warner's heroes. On the other hand, Mary Jane Holmes demonstrated in *Tempest and Sunshine* (1854) that if a woman wished a happy marriage, she must be truly moral herself; merely the outward show of morality was not enough. Tempest is a deceitful, altogether disagreeable woman, and yet she is a good actress, good enough that a kind, moral gentleman believes that she would make an ideal wife. He proposes marriage, but Tempest never achieves the promised home. First her interest in him falters, and then he dies—a just punishment for Tempest, it seems, although rather hard on him. Meanwhile, her sister, the virtuous Sunshine, obtains the ideal, a moral marriage and the promise of eternity with her spouse.

The families in domestic novels are large, complex units; indeed in Mrs. Southworth's *The Hidden Hand,* marriage makes all the villains, heroes, and heroines members of the same family. *The Wide, Wide World,* less genealogically baroque than many domestic novels, provides the heroine not only with a mother and a father but also with two grandmothers, two aunts, two uncles (one of whom demands and receives the respect due a father), one husband, and a father-in-law as well. In the world of domestic fiction, these extensive families may adversely influence the heroine's income, friendships, and well-being, but just as these novels end with a reaffirmation of domesticity, they generally end with a welcome marriage or, as in *Uncle Tom's Cabin*, the welcome discovery of a long-lost relative. In the end, families and domestic life provide the best of all possible worlds.

NATHANIEL HAWTHORNE had little regard for most of the domestic novelists; he grouped them with other popular women writers as "that damned mob of scribbling women." He found some merit, however, in Sara Payson Willis's *Ruth Hall*, a satirical domestic novel which became a best seller in 1855. Furthermore, he considered Miss Sedgwick to be "our most truthful novelist."[7] More important, *The House of the Seven Gables* has clear similarities to domestic novels; the internecine struggles of the Pyncheon family are the sort of things which Mrs. Southworth and others dealt with on less rarefied literary heights. On the whole, however, Hawthorne had little good to say about domesticity in this book. Clifford Pyncheon, victimized by his cousin Jaffrey, has good reason for an extensive indictment of domesticity; he claims that homes are "the greatest possible stumbling-blocks in the path of human happiness and improvement."[8] However, a curse which has presumably affected the lives of the Pyncheons is dispelled in the closing chapters, and the book concludes with the anticipated marriage of hero and heroine.

Melville's *Pierre* also owes much to the domestic novel. The plot involves an aristocratic hero in love with a beautiful woman whom he cannot marry because of a mysterious happening in his family. Altogether it is the sort of literary material utilized by "that damned mob of scribbling women," but Melville, of course, turned that plot to much different ends than they might have wished.

Pierre Glendinning looks very much like a hero; he is athletic and strikingly handsome and has the perfect manners and courtliness to complement his appearance. Although much of his childhood and adolescence has been spent on the Glendinning family estate of Saddle Meadows, his mother has allowed him to spend time in the city, where he has met "a large and polished society." Pierre professes to be a Christian, and although, as his mother says, he is docile in character, there is also something noble about him. He is also thought to be well read, having had the advantages of "his father's fastidiously picked and decorous library."[9] Although his father has been dead for many years,

Pierre has been reared by his mother to identify with the Glendinnings and their aristocratic heritage.

Pierre's character, manners, religion, and education have all been determined to a large degree by his mother and by traditions within the Glendinning family. It is domesticity with a vengeance: Pierre's identity is his family's identity; they have made him what he is. The world of Saddle Meadows is essentially autistic, a world of daydreams in which things which would seem perverse elsewhere have become normal. Pierre calls his mother "sister," and the intimacies of their conversations obscure their true relationship as mother and son. Pierre's proposed marriage to Lucy Tartan would in effect provide another sister for his mother's home; nothing discordant, it seems, will ever happen in the daydreams with which the Glendinnings surround themselves.

Saddle Meadows and the region around it form a rural paradise like those praised by Downing and the authors of country books, and Melville was employing dogma of his age when he said that ". . . *it had been the choice fate of Pierre to have been born and bred in the country.* For to a noble American youth . . . this is a most rare and choice lot." But the natural world that has surrounded Pierre in his youth eventually proves as ambiguous as the idealized domesticity in which he has been raised. Saddle Meadows is identified with the military victories of Pierre's grandfather; here he led his troops in a battle which ended with the slaughter of the Indians—and his own death. It was through this battle that the Glendinnings acquired Saddle Meadows; they are the only people, aside from the Indians, who have ever owned it, and to Pierre, all the "hills and swales" of the countryside "seemed as sanctified through their very long uninterrupted possession by his race." But the landscape of Saddle Meadows, a landscape of "uncommon loveliness," has been purchased at an enormous cost; Saddle Meadows has associations with death and merciless slaughter.[10] The family estate is far from being altogether the rural paradise that Pierre thinks it is. Ultimately Pierre senses this, and then the landscape appears to him neither rural nor benign. Instead he finds "profoundest forests" and "long, mysterious mountain masses; shaggy with pines and hemlocks, mystical with nameless, vapory exhalations, and in that dim air black with dread and gloom."[11] In the end, the discovery that his father committed adultery destroys simultaneously for Pierre both the pastoralism of the Glendinning estate and the ideal domestic world in which he has lived. Melville makes explicit that both Pierre's truly ideal domesticity and the seemingly benign rural realm in which it is set are at best fragile realities.

Although Pierre turns from Saddle Meadows and moves to the city, he is unable to break away from his learned moral responsibility to his family; he goes to the city because he believes it will provide opportunities for him to support and protect his half-sister. Finally, his suicide at the end of the novel is largely due to his recognition of his incestuous and immoral love for her. If he can escape from the rural world of the Glendinnings, he cannot escape from the greater traps of civilized domesticity.

Notes

1. Catharine Maria Sedgwick, *Home,* new ed. (Boston: James Munroe and Company, 1852), pp. 13–14.

2. Harriet Beecher Stowe, *Uncle Tom's Cabin* (New York: The Modern Library, 1938), pp. 174–175.

3. Sydney E. Ahlstrom, *A Religious History of the American People* (New Haven, Conn.: Yale University Press, 1972), p. 613.

4. Horace Bushnell, *Christian Nurture* (New Haven, Conn.: Yale University Press, 1967), p. 22.

5. Stowe, *op. cit.,* p. 546.

6. Sedgwick, *op. cit.,* p. 28.

7. Caroline Ticknor, *Hawthorne and His Publisher* (Boston: Houghton, Mifflin and Company, 1913), pp. 141, 143. Nathaniel Hawthorne, *A Wonder Book* (Columbus, Ohio: Ohio State University Press, 1972), 169.

8. Nathaniel Hawthorne, *The House of the Seven Gables* (Columbus, Ohio: Ohio State University Press, 1965), p. 261.

9. Herman Melville, *Pierre* (Evanston, Ill., and Chicago: Northwestern University Press and The Newberry Library, 1971), p. 6.

10. *Ibid.,* pp. 13, 8, 5.

11. *Ibid.,* pp. 109–110.

part three

Social Realities

Conflicts between Rural Ideals and Urban Realities

Chapter Six

Reaction and Reform

None more than the Americans make it a principle to desert city, and none less than Americans know how to dispense with it.

George William Curtis, *Prue and I* (1856).[1]

Friendship and association are very fine things, and a grand phalanx of the best of the human race, banded for some catholic object: yes, excellent; but remember that no society can ever be so large as one man. He in his friendship, in his natural and momentary associations, doubles or multiplies himself; but in the hour in which he mortgages himself to two or ten or twenty, he dwarfs himself below the stature of one.

Ralph Waldo Emerson, "New England Reformers" (1844).[2]

FREDERICK DOUGLASS (1817–1895) was born a slave in Maryland, and his early life was spent there on a plantation. When he was ten, he was sent to Baltimore to serve one of his master's relatives. "I shall never forget," he wrote many years later, "the ecstasy with which I received this information, three days before the time set for my departure. They were the three happiest days I had ever known." For a long time, Douglass had wished to see this city, for a cousin had richly described it, had even declared that the plantation's "Great House, with all its pictures within and pillars without," could never be ranked with the glories of

Baltimore. When the time came for Douglass's journey to the city, he traveled by boat, stopping first at Annapolis. He had never seen a place as large as this, and he later claimed that his "feelings on seeing it were excited to a pitch very little below that reached by travelers at the first view of Rome."[3]

Although he was still a slave, Douglass found in Baltimore a freedom never available on the plantation. In the city, he learned to write and read, and—what was far more important to his subsequent history—he acquired a sense of personal worth and dignity that was denied the common fieldhand. Several years after he was sent to Baltimore, he was ordered to return to the plantation; there was no choice, but as his boat carried him away from the Baltimore docks, he "formed many a plan for [his] future, beginning and ending in the same determination—to find some way yet of escape from slavery."[4]

Baltimore was a minor city beside Philadelphia or New York, and however splendid Annapolis seemed to Douglass at first, he later realized that "It was inferior to many a factory village in New England."[5] Nonetheless, he knew that Southern cities like Baltimore offered the slave much more than the rural countryside. On the plantation, after all, life was constant labor, and one met few people except masters and slaves. In the countryside around the plantations, one might encounter merchants, free Negroes, and poor whites—but never the variety of life seen in the city.

Cities provided slaves with valuable lessons in human ambition and achievement, but few plantation slaves had extensive contact with a city, and for most, the world consisted of little except plantations, farms, and perhaps a crossroads hamlet. In the first place, there were few major cities even in the older, more settled sections of the South, and even the larger communities seemed inferior to Northern settlements of comparable size. Frederick Law Olmsted, who traveled through the South in the 1850s and wrote three volumes about his experiences there, complained that in Natchez, Miss., he found "no reading-room; no recent newspapers except *The Natchez Free Trader* . . . ; no magazines but aged Harpers [sic]; and no recent publications of any sort . . . for sale or to be seen at the booksellers!" Near the city he found several impressively large homes, but they were not "remarkable," and he thought that their grounds generally exhibited "a paltry taste." The stores and houses within the city were "generally small, and always inelegant."[6]

There were, of course, Southern cities which offered far more than Natchez did, but even such major towns as New Orleans and Charleston were culturally and economically inferior to, say, Boston and New York. It was not the city but the country which defined the South. The traveler in the North on his way to one of the great landscapes—Niagara Falls, to cite the obvious example—could chart his progress from one large settlement to the next: Albany, Utica, Syracuse, and so forth. But the traveler in the South discovered an essentially pastoral landscape of plantations and farms, divided from each other, if at all, by small villages or stretches of wilderness. In effect the South was a Downingesque (or Jeffersonian) world of rural homes, and it is not surprising, therefore, that some of the wealthier and better-educated Southerners built their homes in styles sanctioned by his books. While the Greek—which Downing so despised—was found throughout the rural South, the Gothic was also to be found from the Chesapeake to the Mississippi.

During the antebellum years, much was written about this rural world. The fugitive slave narratives in particular provided important critical discussions and images of this presumably ideal realm. The authors of these books knew well that the landscape gardens, villas, and leisurely domestic lives of Southern families were possible only because of a barbarous, inhuman social and economic system. By contrast, a Northern city might seem an Eden, and some of the fugitive slave narratives in fact follow a pattern the reverse of *Walden, Moby-Dick,* and *The Adventures of Huckleberry Finn.* In the narratives, it is not the pastoral world or the wilderness but rather the city which seems the ideal alternative and destination. However, it should be said here that the slaves' attraction to Northern cities ended at times with a measure of disillusionment: Northerners—with no social institution to reinforce their sense of racial superiority—could make racial discrimination as harshly felt as did slaveholders and other whites in the South. In the North there were many places, including some churches, where blacks were made to feel considerably less than welcome.

JOHN PENDLETON KENNEDY'S SWALLOW BARN (1832), a series
of genial Irvingesque sketches about life on a Virginia plantation, was reissued in the 1850s. At that time its sympathetic portrait of plantation life must have seemed to Southerners a welcome contrast with the harsher images of slavery given in the
fugitive slave narratives and in the decade's best seller, *Uncle
Tom's Cabin. Swallow Barn* is clear-cut propaganda, a clear
misrepresentation—or, to use the kinder word, idealization—of
Southern life. Kennedy began his book in 1828 and completed it
during the crucial years which saw the Abolitionist movement
firmly established as a politically determined force. The year
before *Swallow Barn* was published, William Lloyd Garrison
founded in Boston the *Liberator*, in the first issue of which he
demanded the immediate emancipation of slaves. The first issue
of the *Liberator* is justly recognized as a cornerstone in the
formation of the Abolitionist movement, but it is worth remembering that Garrison had previously made his famous demand
in the *Genius of Universal Emancipation*, which was published
in Baltimore, where Kennedy was at work on his book.* Certainly the time was right for a Southerner to defend his treasured
institution.

Swallow Barn is narrated by one Mark Littleton, whom Kennedy offers as an exemplary Northern gentleman. Littleton lives
with his mother and sister on a country estate, Longsides, on
the banks of the "North River"—i.e., the Hudson. A cousin from
Virginia suggests that Littleton has "fallen into some unseemly
prejudices against the Old Dominion" and recommends as an
antidote a trip to Swallow Barn, the Virginia plantation owned
by the cousin's family.[7]

The recommendation is accepted. Littleton journeys to Swallow Barn by way of the James River, and this provides Kennedy
with opportunities for descriptions of picturesque Southern landscapes. In general, of course, travelers limited themselves to

---

* Fittingly, Frederick Douglass, learning the value of freedom, was
also living in Baltimore at this time. Later he became one of Garrison's close associates. Garrison encouraged Douglass to join the
Abolitionist movement and wrote a highly complimentary "Preface"
for the *Narrative of the Life of Frederick Douglass: An American
Slave* (1845).

the North, and even Southerners knew little of the landscapes
in their native region. The Hudson, not the James, was the river
which most attracted tourists, and yet Littleton, who has lived
on the banks of the Hudson, is exceedingly impressed by this
Southern river, its picturesque landscapes, and the ruins of
Jamestown along its banks. The ruins provide the romantic associations which Americans sought but seldom found in their
landscapes: ". . . there it was—the buttress of an old steeple, a
barren fallow, some melancholy heifers, a blasted pine, and, on
its top, a desolate hawk's nest. What a splendid field for the
fancy! What a carte blanche for a painter."[8] The picture might
well be by Salvator Rosa or one of his American disciples. In
effect, Kennedy was suggesting that Southern landscapes could
be as pleasingly picturesque and as historically significant as
landscapes in the North. Even before visiting the plantation,
Littleton—and perhaps Northern readers as well—was more
favorably disposed toward the South than he had been before.

At Swallow Barn, Littleton finds no merciless slaveholder but
a genial, benevolent master, Frank Meriwether—a name indicative of his character. But what would have been most startling
to Northern readers with moral and social reservations against
the plantation system is that his slaves are said to "hold him in
most affectionate reverence, and, therefore, are not only contented, but happy under his dominion." The relationship of
Master and slave seems like that of parent and child; the plantation is in effect an extended family. All happily submit themselves to Meriwether's rule, and in return they receive his protection and care. Surely Kennedy's pictures of plantation life
could have been attractive to Northerners who idealized domestic life. Not European feudalism but American domesticity is
the apparent model for the plantation system. Back at his estate
on the Hudson, Littleton reports that he has ". . . become famous,
at least with my mother and sisters, for my long stories and
rapturous commendations of Swallow Barn, and my peremptory
way of telling how things are done in the Old Dominion."[9]

Today most readers would consider Kennedy's sketches of
happily subservient slaves—characterized by traits which later
became the stock-in-trade of minstrel shows—at best shallow,
more often crude, and always morally offensive. Kennedy's book

must be measured against less sentimental portrayals of plantation life, and in particular, the propagandistic *Swallow Barn*
must be measured against the equally propagandistic fugitive
slave narratives. Kennedy's book shows a plantation marked by
domesticity, pervasive benevolence, and high morality, and in
fact many of the fugitive slave narratives admit that such plantations did exist. But these narratives, unlike *Swallow Barn*,
never admit that a plantation of this sort gave its slaves adequate
reason to be happy and content. The debts, bankruptcy, or death
of a slaveholder like Meriwether might result in the slaves' being
sold away from their families to harsh masters—like Mrs. Stowe's
Legree—in the deep South, and in fact some of the narratives
recount the stories of people who were the property of comparatively humane masters but who were sold down the river because of their masters' deaths or financial misfortunes.

GEORGE FITZHUGH, "propagandist of the old South" in Harvey
Wish's phrase, argued in the 1850s that slavery provided a slave
not only with work and the essentials of life—food, clothing,
shelter, and so forth—but also with security and economic support during sickness and old age. Fitzhugh's *Sociology for the
South* (1854) and *Cannibals All!* (1857) clearly complement
Kennedy's images of plantation life in *Swallow Barn.* "The
negro slaves of the South," he wrote, "are the happiest, and, in
some sense, the freest people in the world." Children, the infirm,
and the elderly were not required to work at all (he said), yet
they were given "all the comforts and necessaries of life."
Women had little truly demanding work, and even men and
"stout boys" worked—when the weather was good—less "than
nine hours a day." The Southern plantation, as described by
Fitzhugh, seems quite superior even to Downing's rural paradise.
Taking the plantation as an ideal political model, Fitzhugh concluded that "The world wants good government and a plenty
of it—not liberty."[10] In the South, it seemed, the laborer could
obtain all the benefits of rural and domestic life, so idealized in
the North, yet without any of the often attendant economic
worries and concerns.

It must have required considerable bravado on Fitzhugh's
part to make such sweeping, approbatory generalizations about
slavery. In 1839, many years before he undertook his defense

of slavery, a heavily documented and widely distributed publication of the American Anti-Slavery Society, *American Slavery As It Is: Testimony of a Thousand Witnesses,* had shown once and for all that there were many slaves who were poorly fed, poorly clothed, and overworked. With data gathered from thousands of issues of Southern newspapers as well as with reliable eyewitness accounts of plantation life, the editors of this book, Theodore Dwight Weld and his wife Angelina Grimké, showed just how inhuman slavery could be. The book described a few cases of extraordinary cruelty—as, for example, when a nephew of Thomas Jefferson proved the extent of his authority over his slaves by butchering one of them alive. A case like this was, of course, truly exceptional, but the whipping and branding of slaves, as the book made clear, were practiced throughout the South. Furthermore, the slaves had no direct recourse to law, since they were not allowed to testify against a white man in court—even when, as in the case of Jefferson's nephew, the charge was murder.

As the book made clear, children were at times sold away from their parents; husbands, away from their wives. In some instances, a slave and his master shared the same father—an indication that in the South marital constancy was anything but a universally practiced virtue. The Southern plantation was not invariably an Eden, a domestic paradise, and for the slave it was degrading and inhuman. As Weld concluded,

> To deny that cruelty is the spontaneous and uniform product of arbitrary power, and that the natural and controlling tendency of such power is to make its possessor cruel, oppressive, and revengeful towards those who are subjected to his control, is . . . to set at nought the combined experience of the human race, to invalidate its testimony, and to reverse its decisions from time immemorial.[11]

In the end, neither Weld nor Fitzhugh had much faith in the goodness of mankind. Slavery had driven both of them to question the ability of the individual to govern himself. Fitzhugh could not trust the black slave, and Weld could not trust the white master. If the two were in agreement on any point, it was on the need for strong government.

Like Weld and Fitzhugh, the authors of the fugitive slave narratives could not share the era's faith in the goodness of mankind. Indeed the narratives present such bleak images of humanity that, had the well-documented *American Slavery As It Is* not shown Americans how barbarous slavery could be, readers might understandably have dismissed these books as incredible, beyond belief. As it was, the Weld book provided a framework within which the narratives seemed plausible. The *Liberator* and other Abolitionist publications, it should be noted, provided further documentation to suggest that the narratives were as plausible as they were sensational. Among the best known of the narratives was Douglass's, first published in 1845 and revised and expanded three times. Other narratives—and, if we include those published in Abolitionist journals, there were literally hundreds of them*—included those of Henry Bibb (1849), Linda Brent [Harriet Jacobs] (1861), William and Ellen Craft (1860), Solomon Northrup (1853), James W. C. Pennington (1849), and Josiah Henson (1858). An earlier version of Henson's story, written by Samuel Eliot and published in 1849, was instrumental in Mrs. Stowe's characterization of Uncle Tom. Most of the narratives were autobiographical, written by the fugitive slaves themselves. A few, like Richard Hildreth's *The Slave; or, Memoirs of Archy Moore* (1836), were fictional. Several others either were "edited" by whites—Linda Brent's *Incidents in the Life of a Slave Girl*, for example, was edited by the Abolitionist writer Lydia Maria Child—or were written by whites. Solomon Northrup's *Twelve Years a Slave* was written by David Wilson on the basis of factual information which Northrup supplied. It is generally agreed by critics and literary historians that whites tended to make the diction of these narratives more "literary" and carefully emphasized moral points, while blacks emphasized the dramatic aspects of their narratives. The fugitive, in short, was more concerned with telling his story clearly and forcefully,

---

* For an extensive list of the narratives, see Charles H. Nichols, *Many Thousand Gone* (Leiden, Netherlands, 1963). Unfortunately, none of the narratives are discussed in Jay B. Hubbell's otherwise comprehensive *The South in American Literature, 1607–1900* (Durham, N.C.: Duke University Press, 1954). The narratives form a large and important sector of Southern literature.

while white editors concerned themselves with clever phrasings, elaborate descriptions, and moral issues.

The narratives give primary attention, of course, to the slave-holding system but also concern themselves with many other aspects of Southern life. Many of the narratives include images of American wilderness, and these images are quite different from the usual pictures of wilderness offered in other American writings. The wilderness had the practical advantage of hiding the fugitive from his master—but this was its only advantage. After Harriet Jacobs escaped from her master, her friends hid her in a swamp near her home. (The exact location of the swamp is not given in her account, but if it was not located in Kennedy's Old Dominion, it was almost certainly in that part of the country.) The romantic wilderness of Cooper and Cole needs comparison with the following description from her book. The description is evidently the work of Jacobs, not her white editor.

> Peter landed first, and with a large knife cut a path through bamboos and briers of all descriptions. He came back, took me in his arms, and carried me to a seat among the bamboos. Before we reached it, we were covered with hundreds of mosquitos. In an hour's time they had so poisoned my flesh that I was a pitiful sight to behold. As the light increased, I saw snake after snake crawling around us. I had been accustomed to the sight of snakes all my life, but these were larger than any I had ever seen. To this day I shudder when I remember that morning. As evening approached, the number of snakes increased so much that we were continually obliged to thrash them with sticks to keep them from crawling over us. The bamboos were so high and so thick that it was impossible to see beyond a very short distance. Just before it became dark we procured a seat nearer to the entrance of the swamp, being fearful of losing our way back to the boat. It was not long before we heard the paddle of oars, and the low whistle, which had been agreed upon as a signal. We made haste to enter the boat, and were rowed back to the vessel. I passed a wretched night; for the heat of the swamp, the mosquitos, and the constant terror of snakes, had brought on a burning fever. I had just dropped asleep, when they came and told me it was time to go back to that horrid swamp. I could scarcely summon courage to rise. But even those large, venomous snakes were less dreadful to my imagination than the white

man in that community called civilized. This time Peter took a quantity of tobacco to burn, to keep off the mosquitos. It produced the desired effect on them, but gave me nausea and severe headache. At dark we returned to the vessel. I had been so sick during the day, that Peter declared I should go home that night, if the devil himself was on patrol.[12]

The conventions of landscape description obviously had no value for the authors of the fugitive slave narratives. It was necessary to give a more realistic picture of wilderness than could be found in most American books. Henry Bibbs' narrative, to cite another example, tells of his escape with his wife and daughter into the swamps of Louisiana's Red River. Here they wander in a wilderness where they are attacked by wolves and where at last the bloodhounds track them down.

I started to run with my little daughter in my arms, but stumbled and fell down and scratched the arm of little Frances with a brier, so that it bled very much; but the dear child never cried, for she seemed to know the danger to which we were exposed.

But we soon found it was no use for us to run. The dogs were soon at our heels, and we were compelled to stop, or to be torn to pieces by them. By this time, the soul drivers came charging up on their horses, commanding us to stand still or they would shoot us down.[13]

NORTHERN CITIES offered the fugitive greater freedom than he had known in the South, yet at times the North fell short of his expectations. Initially New York gave Frederick Douglass the identity of "a *free man,* one more added to the mighty throng which, like the waves of a troubled sea, surged to and fro between the lofty walls of Broadway."[14] But this seemingly secure identity was shortly threatened by the presence of Southerners searching for fugitives, and he had little choice except to flee northward again, this time to the greater safety of New England. Meanwhile, Harriet Jacobs found that "The north aped the customs of slavery," that blacks were widely considered the inferiors of whites. After the Fugitive Slave Law was passed in 1850, New York became in fact "a city of kidnappers," and "While fashionables were listening to the thrilling voice of Jenny Lind in Metropolitan Hall, the thrilling voices of poor hunted colored people went up, in an agony of supplication, to the Land, from

Zion's church."[15] William and Ellen Craft, victims of the Fugitive Slave Law, fled from slavehunters in Boston to Nova Scotia, yet even here in the town of Halifax they encountered racial persecution. Ellen Craft's skin was sufficiently fair to pass for white, and so her husband, "knowing that we were still under the influence of the low Yankee prejudice," sent her

. . . to engage a bed for herself and her husband. I stopped outside in the rain until the coach came up. If I had gone in and asked for a bed they would have been quite full. But as they thought my wife was white, she had no difficulty in securing arpartments, into which the luggage was afterwards carried. The landlady, observing that I took an interest in the baggage, became somewhat uneasy, and went into my wife's room, and said to her, "Do you know the man downstairs?" "Yes, he is my husband." "Oh! I mean the black man—the *nigger?*" "I quite understand you; he is my husband." "My God!" exclaimed the woman as she flounced out and banged to the door. On going upstairs, I heard what had taken place: but, as we were there, and did not mean to leave that night, we did not disturb ourselves. On our ordering tea, the landlady sent back word to say that we must take it in the kitchen, or in our bedroom, as she had no other room for "niggers." We replied that we were not particular, and that they could send it up to our room—which they did.

After the pro-slavery persons who were staying there heard that we were in, the whole house became agitated, and all sorts of oaths and fearful threats were heaped upon the "d——d niggers, for coming among white folks." Some of them said they would not stop there for a minute if there was another house to go to.

The mistress came up the next morning to know how long we wished to stop. We said a fortnight. "Oh! dear me, it is impossible for us to accomodate you, and I think you had better go: you must understand, I have no prejudice myself; I think a good deal of the colored people, and have always been their friend; but if you stop here we shall lose all our customers, which we can't do nohow." We said that we were glad to hear that she had "no prejudice," and was such a staunch friend to the colored people. We also informed her that we would be sorry for her "customers" to leave on our account; and as it was not our intention to interfere with anyone, it was foolish for them to be frightened away. However, if she would get us a comfortable place, we would be glad to leave. The landlady said she would go out and try. After spending the whole morning in canvassing the town, she came to our room and said, "I have been from one end of the place to the other, but everybody is full." Having a little foretaste of the vulgar prejudice of the town, we did not wonder at this result. However, the landlady gave me the address of some respectable colored families, whom she thought, "under the circumstances," might be induced to take us. And, as we were not at all comfortable—being compelled to sit, eat, and sleep, in the same small room—we were quite willing to change our quarters.[16]

The fugitive slave narratives, Arna Bontemps has written, "created a parable of the human condition. . . . Their theme was the fetters of mankind and the yearning of all living things for freedom."[17] In the end, however, many of the fugitives learned that in the North, racial persecution and particularly the Fugitive Slave Law kept true freedom far out of reach. For some of the former slaves, only a voyage to England ensured the freedom they were seeking. Josiah Henson's answer was to found a black community in Canada. Similarly, George Harris, a fugitive slave in *Uncle Tom's Cabin*, rejects America and sails for Africa. The accounts of the fugitives, fictional and real, are among the most unrelentingly harsh indictments of antebellum, domesticated America.

The disillusionment with cities which is expressed in fugitive slave narratives is common to the literature of the period. Indeed the general attraction of middle-class America to the wilderness and the countryside may be considered in part a reaction against cities in general. American cities were losing their eighteenth-century traditions and gentlemanly attitudes towards commerce and culture. A place like New York even *looked* less elegant than it had a half-century before; now the common building materials were brownstone and cast iron, and the city seemed darker, harsher than it had been when most buildings were constructed of wood or brick. Even when a cast-iron building was painted light grey or white, it seemed shoddy; a relatively inexpensive material was being disguised to resemble the more expensive granite or marble. The cities at midcentury were also marked by newly rich and unscrupulous businessmen—successful men who had made their money in real estate or who had capitalized on such technological achievements as railroads and canals like Clinton's Erie. A prominent example of the new fortunes was New York's Commodore Cornelius Vanderbilt, who, although born to a family of poor farmers, was a millionaire many times over before the Civil War began. He made a fortune with ferry lines around New York and, during the Gold Rush, founded a shipping line between the East Coast and California. Later he invested in railroads, and by the time of his death in 1877, he was worth as much as a $100 million, perhaps more. He was the richest man in America, but he had been given little formal education, and it was rumored that he had considerable difficulty spelling his name. It was also rumored that his businesses were at times run far outside the realm of moral principle. Other moneyed giants like Daniel Drew and John Jacob Astor had equally obscure origins but were able to acquire enormous fortunes. If new money did not rout the old aristocracy—which simply married into the new families—it was apparent that many whose ancestors had been prominent during the Federalist and colonial eras, had lost their social, economic, and political precedence. American cities under the rule of the new money surely seemed far less polished and genteel than they had been earlier in the century.

American cities were changing socially from below as well as from above. The Irish immigrations at midcentury brought essential labor for new industries but also brought customs and a religion that were unwelcome in much of Protestant America. The Irish laborer owed most of his daylight weekday hours to the factory or the railroad; he owed his Sundays to the church. Gentlemen like George Templeton Strong, the New York diarist, had little but scorn for the immigrants. Anglo-Saxons and Celts appeared to have as little in common in this country as they had on the other side of the ocean. The growth of Irish communities in the cities could not fail to make rural and suburban homes increasingly attractive to the older, middle-class American families.

American literature before the Civil War dealt more often with country life than with the life of the newly rich, the immigrants, or with the cities which these two groups were shaping, and there were surprisingly few works which dealt with the factory, clearly the symbol of the new social and economic order. One of the few works concerned with the factory is Melville's "The Tartarus of Maids," based on his visit to a paper mill near his Pittsfield, Mass., home. The factory in Melville's story is governed by a machine—"metallic necessity," "unbudging fatality"—and is served by unmarried women who work every day except Sundays, Fast-days, and Thanksgiving. The machine fills the narrator with "a curious emotion . . . not wholly unlike that which one might experience at the fulfillment of some mysterious prophecy." Mechanistic precision rules—at the expense of human dignity. Machinery is "menially served by human beings, who [serve] mutely and cringingly as the slave serves the Sultan."[18]

Rebecca Harding Davis's *Life in the Iron Mills*, originally published in the April 1861 issue of the *Atlantic Monthly*, contains images of the factory which are more intense and graphic than any others of their kind to be found in American literature of the period. In particular, the mills for rolling iron are described as:

> . . . a city of fires, that burned hot and fiercely in the night. Fire in every horrible form: pits of flame waving in the wind; liquid metal-flames writhing in tortuous streams through the sand; wide caldrons filled with boiling fire, over which bent ghastly wretches stirring the strange brewing; and through all, crowds of half-clad men, looking like revengeful ghosts in the red light, hurried, throwing masses of glittering fire. It was like a street in Hell.[19]

Much of Davis's novel is marred by murky symbolism, crude melodrama, and sentimentality, but its images of industrialization are exceptional among American writings of the time.

The city and its startling social contrasts offered writers much sensational material. Already cities were reputedly the homes of the vilest sins—a reputation long attached to English and European cities and no doubt encouraged by Dickens's descriptions of London. There was, of course, an enormous Dickens cult in this country. His books were hugely popular, and second-rate writers imitated him in both style and subject matter. Some midcentury descriptions of New York made the city seem substantially more British than American. Hack writers, describing the notorious Five Points district in New York, gave the region a vaguely Dickensian atmosphere. Even a good writer like Charles Frederick Briggs turned to Dickens's London for suggestions in characterizing New York in his fiction. If Briggs's portrait of New York were historically accurate, Oliver Twist would have been entirely at home on Nassau Street or Broadway.

American cities would have acquired their unsavory reputations even if Dickens had not had as many American imitators as he did. Large American cities were economic and political necessities, but even in the late eighteenth century, they were at times social and moral embarrassments. As early as 1791, New York provided the setting for a tale of seduction, desertion, and death—Susanna Rowson's *Charlotte Temple,* a novel which (understandably) was hugely popular and which continued to attract readers throughout the nineteenth century. Among later novels set in New York is Cooper's *Home as Found* (1838), which satirized the city's elite—as did Catharine Maria Sedgwick's *Clarence* (1830) and *Married or Single?* (1857). Theodore Winthrop utilized New York, bohemian artist-life, and the Gothic building at New York University in *Cecil Dreeme* (1862). George Lippard exposed the corruptions of Philadelphia in *The Quaker City* (1844), and in *The Lamplighter* (1854), Maria Cummins revealed both misery and salvation in Boston.

In the post–Civil War years, America was titillated by several book-length exposés of city life. The Reverend James D. McCabe, Jr., in *Lights and Shadows of New York Life* (1872) revealed to the nation what, of course, it already knew—that New York was rife with drunken debauchery, gambling, and prostitution. On the next-to-the-last page, a series of illustrations shows a country bumpkin leaving home for New York, then consorting with gamblers and women of questionable virtue. His new friends in the city rob and murder him, and his body is dumped into the river. In 1868, Matthew Hale Smith in *Sunshine and Shadow in New York* let the back country know that in the uncharitable city, the rich lived sumptuously, while the poor died in wretched poverty. Similar exposés were common in the pre–Civil War era, but they usually took the form of fiction. In addition to novels cited above, mention should be made of George Lippard's *New York: Its Upper Ten and Lower Million* (1853), which exposed the evils of Gotham as thoroughly as *The Quaker City* exposed the evils of Philadelphia. In *The Trippings of Tom Pepper* (1847–1850), Charles Frederick Briggs pictured prostitution and drunkenness in New York. Americans who followed the news realized that Poe's "The Mystery of Marie Rogêt" (1842–1843) was based not on the murder of a Paris girl whose body was found in the Seine—the guise assumed for the story—but on the murder of the New York salesgirl Mary Rogers, whose body was found on the west bank of the Hudson. The countryside provided writers with materials for tales of domesticity and virtue, but materials for somewhat more sensational fiction could be found in the city.

Since theater was especially popular in the cities, it might be expected that American dramas would have concerned themselves largely with urban themes, but Indians, frontiersmen, and the Revolutionary War were to be encountered as frequently on the stage as in novels. N. P. Willis set *Bianca Visconti* (1837) and *Tortesa the Usurer* (1839)in Milan and Florence, respectively—ideal locations for romantic tragedies which have nothing to do with nineteenth-century America. Edwin Forrest was best known for his role as Spartacus in Robert Montgomery Bird's *The Gladiator* (1831)—set in ancient Rome. Among playwrights more concerned with American materials, William Dunlap wrote a play about, as its title indicates, *A Trip to Niagara* (1828), which included Cooper's Leather-Stocking as a central character. Irving's "Rip Van Winkle," dramatized by Dion Boucicault and Joseph Jefferson in 1865, provided Jefferson, who played Rip, with his most famous role.

Although most American plays had little to do with the city, there were such notable exceptions as Boucicault's great melodrama *The Poor of New York* (1857) and Benjamin Baker's *A Glance at New York* (1848). The contrast between urban and rural manners was a stock-in-trade of American plays from Royall Tyler's *The Contrast* (1787) to James Kirke Paulding's *The Lion of the West* (1830) and Anna Cora Mowatt's *Fashion* (1845). Incidentally, these plays were often wholly unsympathetic to the manners of the city. *Fashion,* for example, concludes with the advice to the city merchant Mr. Tiffany that he sell his house and send his wife and daughter to the country, where they can learn the virtues of domestic life. The play is an exposure of the follies of leading a fashionable life in the city.

Occasionally popular poets like Willis and Bryant dealt with the city in their writings. Willis's "Love in a Cottage" in fact has much good to say of the city at the expense of the country, and in "Hymn of the City" (1830), Bryant made effective literary use of New York, his home for more than half a century. "Even here do I behold," he wrote,

> Thy steps, Almighty!—here amidst the crowd
>   Through the great city rolled,
> With everlasting murmur deep and loud—
>   Choking the ways that wind
> 'Mongst the proud piles, the work of human kind.

Among other poets, Whitman remains the finest celebrator and poet of the city, but originally, of course, his work received little attention. As long as poetry was supposed to deal, as readers and critics insisted, with ideals and not materiality, cities seemed to have little poetic purpose. It is commonplace to observe that Whitman's "unpoetic" materials made his poetry the horror of librarians and genteel readers.

MILES COVERDALE, the narrator of Hawthorne's *The Blithedale Romance* (1852), is a poet who knows (unlike Whitman) that poetry is supposed to find its inspiration in the countryside, not the city, and shortly after he finds that his real interest is in city life, he—quite naturally and simply—stops being a poet. Coverdale moves to Blithedale, a rural utopian community, for here, he hopes, he will be able "to produce something that shall really deserve to be called poetry,—true, strong, natural, and sweet, as is the life which we are going to lead [at Blithedale], —something that shall have the notes of wild birds twittering through it, or a strain like the wind-anthems in the woods, as the case may be." By exchanging the city (Boston, in this case) for the country, Coverdale thinks that he has exchanged a real world—"the weary tread-mill of the established system," "the rusty iron frame-work of society"—for an ideal.[20] However, at Blithedale the necessary business of farming leaves little time for poetry, and for various reasons, the community proves to be no utopia. In the end, Boston in fact seems the more agreeable alternative for Coverdale.

Coverdale claims that he has the ability "to live in other lives, and to endeavor—by generous sympathies, by delicate intuitions, by taking note of things too slight for record, and by bringing [his] human spirit into manifold accordance with the companions whom God assigned [him]—to learn the secret which was hidden even from themselves." Less generously, one member of the Blithedale community accuses him of "an insolent curiosity" and "a meddlesome temper," and in fact the novel is, for the most part, the record of his pryings into the lives of some of the people at Blithedale—the record certainly of "an insolent curiosity," "a meddlesome temper." It is not surprising, therefore, that Coverdale finally concludes, "whatever had been my taste for solitude and natural scenery, yet the thick, foggy, stifled element of cities, the entangled life of many men together, sordid as it was, and empty of the beautiful, took quite as strenuous a hold upon my mind. I felt as there could never be enough of it." The urbane and inquisitive Coverdale never had legitimate business at Blithedale; his proper sphere was the crowded city. By the end of the book, he has become, he says, "a man of the world," and fittingly, he has foresaken poetry and "the beautiful" for "the entangled life of many men together."[21]

MELVILLE'S PIERRE, like The Blithedale Romance, deals with the American city and in particular with its relationship and value or threat to a writer. Accompanied by Isabel—the illegitimate half-sister whom he feels morally obligated to protect—Pierre flees from Saddle Meadows, his rural home, to New York, where he arrives at "the obscure heart of the town" in the middle of the night. He expects to be welcomed by a relative but is not and finds himself surrounded by chaos and nightmare:

The sights and sounds which met the eye of Pierre . . . , filled him with inexpressible horror and fury. The before decent, drowsy place, now reeked with all things unseemly. Hardly possible was it to tell what conceivable cause or occasion had . . . collected such a base congregation. In indescribable disorder, frantic, diseased-looking men and women of all colors, and in all imaginable flaunting, immodest, grotesque, and shattered dresses, were leaping, yelling, and cursing around him.

The torn Madras handkerchiefs of negresses, and the red gowns of yellow girls, hanging in tatters from their naked bosoms, mixed with the rent dresses of deep-rouged white women, and the split coats, checkered vests, and protruding shirts of pale, or whiskered, or haggard, or mustached fellows of all nations, some of whom seemed scared from their beds, and others seemingly arrested in the midst of some crazy and wanton dance. On all sides, were heard drunken male and female voices, in English, French, Spanish, and Portuguese, interlarded now and then, with the foulest of all human lingoes, that dialect of sin and death, known as the Cant language, or the Flash.[22]

Pierre tries, as a writer, to make his way financially in the city. He moves to the "Apostles," inhabited by artists, teachers, philosophers, and poets—people, however, who have had little luck making their abilities and ideas pay in commercial New York. Nor is Pierre any more successful than they. Like morals and ideals, the imagination has no place in the city. Of course, if Pierre, who has lost his claims to the family fortune, had the wealth of Hawthorne's Coverdale, he might still have the option of being a "man of the world." But without money or salable talent, he is useless to New York—and he dies in prison.

Melville lived more of his life in New York than in any other place, and this city appears in much of his best work. Manhattan is where *Moby-Dick* begins—but it is, significantly, just such places as Manhattan from which Ishmael is fleeing when he ships out on the *Pequod*. The city appears in other Melville works (extensively in *Redburn*) and "Bartleby the Scrivener" is, as its subtitle indicates, "A Story of Wall Street." Like Pierre, Bartleby learns that the city has no use for people without money. Since Bartleby will not do productive work, since, that is, he "prefers not to do" what is expected of him, he is taken away to the Tombs, the city prison. There, being neglected as much as he has neglected gainful employment, he is left to die.

ERADICATING THE ALLEGED EVILS OF CITY LIFE was among the prime objectives of mid-nineteenth-century social reform. Drunkenness, prostitution, indolence, and the breakdown of family life were all associated with the city. While some people could afford suburban, rural, or summer homes, there were others—laborers, for example—who were economically tied to the city during the entire year. For such people, as reformers realized, it would be necessary to bring the country to the city—to make the city, that is, more rural. In his fiction, Cooper solved the problem easily. In *The Pioneers* (1822), he described the fictional Templeton (based on Cooperstown, N.Y.) as a future city, complete with a gridiron street plan; but in 1838, when cities were beginning to seem socially and morally less attractive, he described Templeton in *Home as Found* as more of a rural village.

At Versailles, Marie Antoinette reacted to the formalities of court life by creating a rural village near the palace; thus providing herself with the best of both worlds. The juxtaposition of the two worlds at Versailles could have inspired a reformer faced with the problem of the American city, for while it might be no more possible to eliminate the American city than it had been to eliminate Versailles, it might still have been possible to bring the city into close conjunction with the countryside. From the first, reformers—although they may have believed that life was always better in the country—were sufficiently practical to ask only that the city adopt certain aspects of rural life.

Attempts to make the city more rural—or at least to make the country more available to the city—may be traced back to the 1820s and the recommendation of Dr. Jacob Bigelow of Boston that his city's ultimate necessity, a cemetery, be located in a rural landscape. Bigelow's efforts resulted in 1831 in the creation of Mount Auburn Cemetery. Although it was situated not in Boston but across the river in Cambridge, the cemetery became, oddly enough, a fashionable destination for Bostonians on afternoon excursions. Cornelia W. Walter, editor of the *Boston Evening Transcript,* claimed that "crowds" went there "to meditate, and to wander in a field of peace,"[23] and *The Picturesque Tourist* insisted in the 1840s that "Every traveller of taste should visit this cemetery."[24] N. P. Willis, always the nation's consummate tourist, considered Mount Auburn to be both "picturesque and beautiful," and appropriately, it was here, in 1867, that he was buried.[25] H. Marion Stephens hauntingly invited her readers:

> *Come with me into the shadows!* through the warm sunlight which rolls down over the massive gate looming up there like another "bridge of sighs" at the entrance of this "garden of the

dead"! through the old cathedral's aisles, walled over with
shining leaves and clasping limbs, where the summer sunlight
creeps in through interstices, and lays in little pools of gold upon
mossy mounds! through the long, leafy arches, which darken and
darken as you pass along, until your heart grows cold with awe,
and you wonder if in all the world there is a spot where so
much of gloom and grandeur, of sunshine and shadow, of flowers
and graves commingled, as *here,* in beautiful Mount Auburn![26]

Mrs. Stephens and her lugubrious kind would have been
rewarded in some degree with a visit to any graveyard, but the
rural cemeteries like Mount Auburn were supposed to be of
particular aesthetic and spiritual value to those who spent most
of their days within the crowded, mercenary city. It should not
be wondered at, therefore, that Mount Auburn served as the
model for innumerable rural cemeteries throughout the country.
(By 1849, Philadelphia had nearly twenty.) In fact the rural
cemeteries seemed such an attractive solution to a disagreeable
problem that they were soon copied in England. Rural cemeteries were as much parks for the living as graveyards for the
dead, and one of these cemeteries reported no fewer than 30,000
visitors during a nine-month period in 1848. Andrew Jackson
Downing had good reason to conclude that rural cemeteries
were "doing a great deal to enlarge and educate the popular
taste in rural embellishment."[27]

In the 1850s, New York City was still bordered by rural scenery. New Yorkers who wanted to spend an afternoon in the
country could walk north and within a few miles find themselves
surrounded by farms, country estates, and open land. At the
present site of 84th Street and Broadway, for example, was the
farm of one Patrick Brennan, where Edgar Allan Poe had once
taken his wife to enjoy the country air and where, incidentally,
he had written "The Raven." Less than a half mile to the north
near the present intersection of 93rd Street and Broadway, was
the villa of Dr. Valentine Mott, but it was too far from the city
for more than summer occupancy, when the weather was good.
This region was known as Bloomingdale and had its own village
and stores. To the north of Bloomingdale lay more villages, farms,
woods, streams, and undeveloped land. Most of Manhattan
could still be classified as countryside.

New Yorkers in search of rural scenery could take the Hoboken ferry to the picturesque Elysian Fields and could cross to Brooklyn, where Greenwood Cemetery, New York's version of Mount Auburn, was located. Although there was little evidence of the countryside within the city, it was clearly easy to escape to nearby meadows and woods. Nonetheless, the city was rapidly extending northward, and where there had been farms a few years before, now there were brownstones. Furthermore, both the Elysian Fields and Greenwood were private enterprises—and might someday be closed to the public.

One seemingly permanent answer to the relentless growth of cities lay in the creation of public parks. Bryant and Downing argued for a major park within New York, but their initial arguments were largely ignored. It was not until 1857, five years after Downing's death, that the construction of Central Park was begun. Designed by Calvert Vaux and Frederick Law Olmsted, both of whom knew Downing's landscaping theories well, Central Park provided ideal rural landscapes to city dwellers. The park was immediately popular, and although in 1870 it was four miles from the southern gates to the center of the city, as many as 115,000 people frequented the park in a single day. Of course, the park was not really part of the city, was in fact cut off by a high wall. However, later projects designed by Olmsted either with Vaux or alone were more successful in blending rural scenery with the city. Among Olmsted's most successful projects were park systems for Brooklyn and Boston and the plan for the suburban community of Riverside, Ill.

Reformers who wished to graft aspects of the rural world onto the city turned also to literature, and in fact literature at this time was the steady companion of reform movements. In particular, novels were frequently valued for their moral import, and many of the most popular were stridently didactic. Many authors who did not make reform their first objective still instructed their readers in the virtues of domesticity and rural life. The shrillest reformers included Harriet Beecher Stowe, Timothy Shay Arthur, Maria Monk, and evangelists like William A. Hallock. Arthur was responsible for *Ten Nights in a Bar Room* (1854) and other tales of intemperance. In *Awful Disclosures* (1836), Miss Monk suggested that the

Catholic Church needed a thorough overhauling. As inquisitive Protestant ministers discovered, her accusations—which she claimed were based on her life in a Canadian convent—had no basis in truth, but hundreds of thousands read *Awful Disclosures,* and in Protestant America, it still had defenders long after its author had been arrested and imprisoned, reputedly as a thief. The most sweeping of reform movements was revivalism, notably that brand of revivalism preached by Charles Grandison Finney, for he insisted that the true convert would try to remake the world according to the dictates of his conscience and the Bible. In *The Mountain Miller* (1838), William A. Hallock was content, however, to reform his reader's spiritual life: "Cast yourself on [Christ's] mercy, and if you perish, perish at his feet. Do this, and your soul shall live."[28]

Reform movements found their adherents among Protestants and were marked by a strong Protestant morality. Calls for piety and morality were universal, and more than one heroine in domestic novels wrestled with the problem of loving her Savior more than her parents. Mrs. Stowe concluded *Uncle Tom's Cabin* by asserting her belief that if the Union were to be *saved,* it would have to be through "repentance, justice and mercy; for, not surer is the eternal law by which the millstone sinks into the ocean, than that stronger law by which injustice and cruelty shall bring on nations the wrath of Almighty God!"[29] Reform, she was saying, was inevitable; if the nation did not abolish slavery, God would. Either men would create a better society, or they would suffer the wrath of God.

If literature could serve the purposes of revivalists, Abolitionists, and temperance workers, then certainly it could also serve the purposes of those who wished to reform the cities. Domestic novels, which were usually written for women, and didactic tales, which were written generally for laborers, children, and immigrants, demonstrated repeatedly that rural virtues and urban life were not incompatible. Jacob Abbott, for example, wrote twenty-eight didactic children's books about his boy-hero Rollo, who left New England, was exposed to the great world, traveled even to Europe, but preserved his moral, industrious character. Although Rollo's world was full of temptations, his strength of character carried him through. In 1846, the American

Sunday-school Union published the anonymous *City Cousins,* which told how the country-bred Annie Sherwood, spending a winter in the city, was able, despite numerous temptations, to preserve her pure and unblemished character. Confronted with literature of questionable sentiments, she averted her eyes from the morally sullied pages and wished she were back home in the country—an improper wish, she knew, since she was a dutiful child and her parents had particularly urged her to undertake this visit to the city. She "had heard much of the intelligence and refinement of the society in the city," and yet when she met members of this elite, she was "shocked and pained" by "the freedom with which the characters and affairs of others were treated, and the judgment (she could not but think, often hasty and censorious, and certainly uncalled for) which was passed upon their actions."[30]

There were innumerable children like Annie and Rollo in the didactic literature of the time, and all of them—however insufferably priggish they seem today—were supposed to be heroes and heroines to their contemporary readers. A book like *City Cousins* was seemingly proof that country virtues could be preserved even amid the alluring evils of cities. It should not surprise us that Dickens's *Oliver Twist,* in which the boy-hero remains morally unblemished despite his constant exposure to London's world of vice and crime, was extremely popular on this side of the Atlantic.

Samuel Osgood, the author of various religious works, considered the need for domestic virtues in the city to be so great that he wrote a 300-page book about it: *The Hearth-Stone: Thoughts upon Home-Life in Our Cities* (1853). Although he felt there were clear advantages to life in the country, he was writing for those whose lives were linked with the city, and he felt that city life without domesticity was morally treacherous. "The state of things in our American cities," he said, "is now so peculiar, so marked by privilege and peril, that no earnest plea for home affections and virtues can be wholly thrown away."[31]

CATHARINE MARIA SEDGWICK made it her particular business to show that rural and domestic virtues could be grafted onto city life. Although the heroine of *Clarence* (1830) is taken to the country for her didactic education, Miss Sedgwick's *Home,* published five years later, describes a New England family living in New York and practicing all the domestic virtues common (presumably) in the country. According to *Home,* moral training can succeed, whatever the setting, as long as it is backed by a strong family life. The children in this tale are taught, for example, to make no artificial distinctions between classes, and thus they retain a sense of democracy such as their father knew in the rural village in which he was reared. Indeed "they [do] not regard their servant as a hireling, but as a member of their family, who, for her humble position in it, [is] entitled to their protection and care." If their father is to be believed, the city can have decided advantages; properly utilized, it can instruct children in social, economic, political, and moral matters:

A walk on the Battery [in New York] suggests many subjects to a thinking mind. A few of these would occur to a careless observor. The position of the city at the mouth of a noble navigable river,—a position held sacred by the Orientals; Long Island, with its inviting retreats for the citizen, and its ample garden-grounds seemingly designed by Providence to supply the wants of a great metropolis; Governor's Island, with its fortifications and military establishment,—a picture to illustrate the great topic of peace and war, on which a child's mind cannot be too soon, nor too religiously enlightened; the little island where the malefactor suffers his doom, an object to impress a lesson of his country's penal code; Staten Island with its hospitals and quarantine ground, to elicit important instruction concerning these benevolent institutions, and their abuses in ill-governed countries; the telegraph, the light-house, and the ship, the most striking illustration of man's intelligence, industry, skill, and courage; the lovely shaded walks of Hoboken, over which the sisters Health and Cheerfulness preside; and, finally, the Narrows,—the outlet to that path on the great deep, which the Almighty has formed to maintain the social relations and mutual dependence of his creatures.[32]

Home is a book of great significance in American social and cultural history. Not only is it among the era's clearest expositions of ideal domesticity; it is also underscored by a notably optimistic assertion that domestic and rural virtues can survive in the city. Furthermore, although the book ends with a return to the countryside, it suggests that there are many advantages to city life. However immoral cities may have seemed from some rural perspectives, New York and its kind were obviously here to stay, and Miss Sedgwick's narrative, by demonstrating that the best of country virtues could survive in the city, was decidedly welcome to readers and reviewers. Indeed one reviewer in the *Christian Examiner* concluded that she had "the character and fortunes of this nation more at her disposal than any of the ambitious politicians of the land"—a remark more enthusiastic than accurate but indicative of the great social and moral influence which was attributed to literature.[33] No wonder that reformers argued their case through the medium of fiction or that so many sermons on rural life and domesticity took the form of novels. City life, it seemed, could be reformed as effectively with literature and Olmsted's landscape gardens as with politics and law.

Notes

1. George William Curtis, *Prue and I* (New York: A. L. Burt, Publishers, n.d.), pp. 276–277.
2. Ralph Waldo Emerson, "New England Reformers," *Complete Works* (Boston: Houghton, Mifflin and Company, 1903), vol. III, pp. 264–265.
3. Frederick Douglass, *The Life and Times of Frederick Douglass* (New York: Collier Books, 1962), pp. 73, 74. This is a revised and expanded version, published in 1892, of Douglass's earlier autobiographical narratives.
4. *Ibid.*, p. 102.
5. *Ibid.*, p. 74.
6. Frederick Law Olmsted, *A Journey in the Back Country* (New York: Schocken Books, 1970), pp. 38–39, 35, 36.
7. John Pendleton Kennedy, *Swallow Barn* (New York: Hafner Publishing Company, 1971), p. 14.
8. *Ibid.*, p. 17.
9. *Ibid.*, pp. 34, 503.

10. George Fitzhugh, *Cannibals All!* (Cambridge, Mass.: Harvard University Press, 1960), p. 18. Fitzhugh, *Sociology for the South* (Richmond, Va.: A. Morris, Publisher, 1854), p. 30.

11. Theodore Dwight Weld, *American Slavery as It Is* (New York: Arno Press and the New York Times, 1969), p. 117.

12. Linda Brent [Harriet Brent Jacobs], *Incidents in the Life of a Slave Girl* (Harcourt Brace Jovanovich, Inc., 1973), pp. 115–116.

13. Henry Bibb, "Narrative of the Life and Adventures of Henry Bibb," in *Puttin' on Ole Massa* (New York: Harper and Row, Publishers, 1969), p. 128.

14. Douglass, *op. cit.*, p. 202.

15. Brent, *op. cit.*, pp. 168, 198, 195.

16. William Craft, "Running a Thousand Miles for Freedom," in *Great Slave Narratives* (Boston: Beacon Press, 1969), pp. 327–329.

17. Arna Bontemps, "The Slave Narratives: An American Genre," *Great Slave Narratives* (Boston: Beacon Press, 1969). p. xviii.

18. Herman Melville, "The Paradise of Bachelors and the Tartarus of Maids," *The Complete Short Stories of Herman Melville* (New York: Random House, 1849), pp. 209, 207, 202.

19. [Rebecca Harding Davis], *Life in the Iron Mills*, in *Atlantic Monthly*, VII (1861), 433.

20. Nathaniel Hawthorne, *The Blithedale Romance* (Columbus, Ohio: Ohio State University Press, 1964), pp. 14, 19.

21. *Ibid.*, pp. 160, 170, 146, 247.

22. Herman Melville, *Pierre* (Evanston, Ill., and Chicago: Northwestern University Press and The Newberry Library, 1971), pp. 229, 240.

23. Cornelia W. Walter, *Mount Auburn Illustrated* (New York: R. Martin, 1851), p. 14.

24. O. L. Holley, ed., *The Picturesque Tourist* (New York: J. Disturnell, 1844), p. 298.

25. Nathaniel Parker Willis, *American Scenery* (London: George Virtue, 1840), vol. II, p. 97.

26. H. Marion Stephens, *Home Scenes and Home Sounds* (Boston: Fetridge and Company, 1854), p. 75.

27. Andrew Jackson Downing, *Rural Essays* (New York: Geo. A. Leavitt, 1869), p. 157.

28. William A. Hallock, *The Mountain Miller* (New York: The American Tract Society, n.d.), p. 24.

29. Harriet Beecher Stowe, *Uncle Tom's Cabin* (New York: The Modern Library, 1938), p. 552.

30. Anonymous, *City Cousins* (Philadelphia: American Sunday-school Union, 1846), p. 38.

31. Samuel Osgood, *The Hearth-Stone: Thoughts upon Home-Life in Our Cities* (New York: D. Appleton and Company, 1853), p. 4.

32. Catharine Maria Sedgwick, *Home*, new ed. (Boston: James Munroe and Company, 1852), pp. 72, 56–57.

33. Anonymous, "Review of *The Poor Rich Man, and the Rich Poor Man*," *Christian Examiner*, XXI (1836), 398.

Chapter Seven

The Literati at Home and Abroad:
Taylor in New York;
Hawthorne in Lenox and Rome

*If you would be happy in Berkshire, you must carry mountains
in your brain. . . .*

Oliver Wendell Holmes, *The Autocrat
of the Breakfast-Table* (1858).[1]

*It takes so many things, as Hawthorne must have felt later in
life, when he made the acquaintance of the denser, richer,
warmer European spectacle—it takes such an accumulation of
history and custom, such a complexity of manners and types, to
form a fund of suggestion for a novelist.*

Henry James, *Hawthorne* (1879).[2]

*Eve was too fresh from the gorgeous coast of Italy to be in
ecstasies with the meagre villages and villas that more or less
lined the bay of New York. . . .*

James Fenimore Cooper, *Homeward
Bound* (1838).[3]

ALTHOUGH AMERICAN WRITINGS at midcentury claimed that cities
were either irremediably corrupt or, at best, in need of the
countryside's ameliorating influences, American writers gener-

175

ally found it advantageous to live much of the year in the same cities they freely condemned. Willis at the time he was publishing his "Idlewild Papers" was seen frequently on Nassau Street and Broadway. However corrupt the cities might be, it was there that writers could find the offices of the nation's major magazines and book publishers. A financially successful author might be able to maintain a home in the country, but like Irving, he would probably have one in the city as well—or if he did not maintain a home in the city, he would at least have friends there and visit often. After Melville, for example, had secluded himself in the Berkshires, he still made necessary trips to New York and his publisher.

BAYARD TAYLOR in 1846 published *Views A-Foot,* a light-hearted and light-headed account of travel abroad. The book was well received, especially by Willis,* and within a few months, he was—at the age of twenty-one—a celebrity, one of the nation's best-known writers. Wisely, he moved to New York, where many of the country's most successful writers, critical journals, and publishers were located. It was around this time that Poe wrote that New York was "the focus of American letters. Its authors include, perhaps, one-fourth of all those in America, and the influence they exert on their brethren, if seemingly silent, is not the less extensive and decisive." Further, as Poe realized, literary communities like New York's could improve or ruin an author's reputation. Literary criticism in pre–Civil War America often had less to do with objective analysis and evaluation than with hyperbole and invective. As Poe wrote:

> The most "popular," the most "successful" writers among us, (for a brief period, at least,) are, ninety-nine times out of a hundred, persons of mere address, perseverance, effrontery—in a word, busy-bodies, toadies, quacks. These people easily succeed in *boring* editors (whose attention is too often entirely engrossed by politics or other "business" matter) into the admission of favourable notices written or caused to be written by interested parties—or, at least, into the admission of *some* notice where, under ordinary circumstances, *no* notice would be given at all. In this way ephemeral "reputations" are manufactured which,

* Willis had good reason to praise the book, for his own accounts of travel abroad had served as Taylor's models.

for the most part, serve all the purposes designed—that is to say, the putting money into the purse of the quack and the quack's publisher; for there never was a quack who could be brought to comprehend the value of mere fame.[4]

Of course, one could also offend editors and then find one's writings either disparaged in the journals or altogether ignored.

Taylor's decision to move to New York was certainly wise— even though at the time his only immediate prospects in the city were a job translating articles for Rufus Griswold and part-time work at $5 a week for the *Literary World*. But it was clearly in the interest of his literary reputation that he make friends with the influential writers, editors, and publishers in New York. He did in fact make the right friends, and three months after his arrival in December 1847, he was offered the editorships of the *Union Magazine* (at least for the half-year its regular editor would be in Europe) and the *Christian Inquirer*. Taylor had become one of the city's literary lions. Although he later established his permanent home in Pennsylvania, he always maintained close New York friendships.

Shortly after Taylor moved to New York, he was invited to dinner at Willis's, and among the other guests that night was Anne Charlotte Lynch. Willis seems to have had Taylor's interests in mind, for Miss Lynch was the essential person for an ambitious young author to know. Were it not for Poe's rather flattering sketch of her in *The Literati of New York*, it is possible that her name would be unknown even to most historians of American literature, and yet there was a time when she was among the most important people in the literary world of New York. Poe's sketch is primarily concerned with her abilities as a poet but concludes by saying, "She goes much into literary society."[5] It would have been more accurate to say that she brought literary society into her home, for the Lynch residence at 116 Waverly Place was a center of literary life in New York. It was important for a young author to know Willis, for this prominent journalist could obtain favorable "puffs" and reviews in the right publications. But it was at least as important to be invited to Miss Lynch's *conversazioni*, since if anyone were successful or influential in the New York literary world, he would probably be found, sooner or later, at one of these gatherings.

Here, under the guise of social fun, professional and business friendships could be formed and strengthened.

As John S. Hart wrote in 1853,

> The combination of the social element with the pursuits of literature and art is a problem to which Miss Lynch has given a practical solution, and by which she has gained her chief celebrity. She has for many years opened her house on every Saturday evening to ladies and gentlemen of her acquaintance, connected with literature or the fine arts. Men and women of genius here meet on 'Change, without ceremony, and for the exchange of thought. They pass two hours together in conversation, music, song, sometimes recitation, and disperse without eating or drinking, nothing in the shape of material refreshment being ever offered. At no place of concourse, it is said, is one so sure to see the leading celebrities of the town.[6]

Like most of her guests, Miss Lynch was not a native of New York, and like them, she had grown up in the country. But while the countryside was supposed to be the ideal place for a home, few great literary reputations, as she discovered, were established outside the large cities. In the 1840s, she moved to New York. She already had established a small reputation as the editor of the *Rhode Island Book,* a collection of works by writers from Rhode Island, but it was in New York that she acquired her great influence in the world of letters. Shortly after her arrival, her mediocre verses were praised in the leading journals, and a volume of these verses was illustrated by some of the best-known American artists of the day.

On one of Taylor's visits to Miss Lynch, he found her attended by Willis, the poet and essayist Grace Greenwood, the editor and poet George Pope Morris, the poet Thomas Buchanan Read, the artist G. P. A. Healy, the editor Rufus Griswold, the poet and essayist Elizabeth F. Ellet, the editor William M. Gillespie, and Catharine Maria Sedgwick—all of whom were as famous then as they are obscure today. The guests danced, talked, read to each other—mainly from their own works—and made the young author feel entirely at home. At another of Miss Lynch's gatherings, Taylor reported to his fiancée, ". . . we formed a quadrille, and as Darley [the artist] did not know the figures, and we were only three couple [sic], there was no end to the sport we had. Anne Lynch," he concluded, "is a perfect jewel of a woman."[7]

Taylor made a point of visiting frequently at Waverly Place, and a month later, he attended a party there with, among others, Bryant, Willis, Morris, Mrs. Ellet, Miss Sedgwick, Fitz-Greene Halleck, the writer and editor Charles Fenno Hoffman, the editor Parke Godwin, the artist and essayist Charles Lanman, the essayist Henry Tuckerman, the poet Frances S. Osgood, the poet Mary E. Hewitt, the artist Asher B. Durand, Felix O. C. Darley, and—a name which seems a thunderclap in such a gathering—Herman Melville. Today it is only Melville and perhaps Bryant and Durand who attract major attention; and yet, of course, at that time (1848), Melville, like Taylor, had published only travel books and was far less famous than such writers as Halleck, Willis, and Miss Sedgwick.

Anyone who thought that Miss Lynch's friends were mediocre writers, undeserving of their fame, and who dared to say so publicly, risked being censured and ridiculed in New York's newspapers and journals. As Sidney P. Moss has shown, Poe was treated disparagingly in some of the city's best-known periodicals, precisely because he harshly criticized the Knickerbocker writers.[8] Taylor, on the other hand, did as he was supposed to do; he made the right friends, and while Poe was ridiculed, Taylor, whose writings we have long since forgotten, was praised.*

* In Taylor's favor, it should be added that several years later when his literary reputation was firmly established and after he had made his home in Pennsylvania, he published a novel, *John Godfrey's Fortunes* (1864), in which he critically examined his experiences among the New York literati. It is to Taylor's credit that here he spoke favorably of Poe, while at the same time he satirized Lynch and her gatherings. "The fact is, we had no criticism, worthy of the name. . . . ," remarks the narrator of the book, who speaks, one trusts, for Taylor. "All our gentle, languishing echoes found spellbound listeners, whom no one—with, perhaps, the single exception of Poe—had the will to disenchant." But while Poe is praised, Miss Lynch is satirically characterized as Mrs. Yorkton, known to her readers under the pseudonym Adeliza Choate. She describes what she calls her "process of composition" in the following passage.

I feel the approach of Inspiration in every nerve;—my husband often tells me that he knows beforehand when I am going to write, my eyes shine so. Then I go up-stairs to my *study*, which is next to my bedroom. It always comes on about three o'clock in the afternoon, when the wind blows from the south. I change my dress, and put on a long white gown, which I wear at no other time, take off my stays, and let

OTHER CITIES had their powerful literary elites, of course. Philadelphia had been an important literary center at the turn of the century and still maintained several publishing houses and magazines. Among Southern cities, Charleston had a small literary community, including William Gilmore Simms, Henry Timrod, and Paul Hamilton Hayne. But only Boston and the region around it provided a literary community which approached the size and influence of New York's. In Boston and Cambridge, one could find Oliver Wendell Holmes, James Russell Lowell, Henry Wadsworth Longfellow, and others as concerned as they with transmitting English and European literary values to the nation. Boston was also the home of the country's best historians, and here was published the *North American Review,* one of the most highly regarded American periodicals.

A few miles to the west of Boston lay the village of Concord, the home of Bronson Alcott, Ralph Waldo Emerson, Nathaniel Hawthorne, and Henry David Thoreau. Concord was more than an appendage of Boston, of course; it was almost certainly, as its residents well knew, the most intellectual village in the world. Hawthorne, however, was unimpressed by the village's determined intellectuality; too practical for its transcendental fog, he wrote that "Never was a poor little country village infested with such a variety of queer, strangely dressed, oddly behaved mortals, most of whom took upon themselves to be important agents of the world's destiny, yet were simply bores of a very intense water."[9]

Rebecca Harding Davis was another writer who remained unimpressed by Concord's claims to intellectual grandeur, and even Boston's intellectuality seemed to her at times as misguided as Concord's. Although Emerson and his friends "thought they were guiding the real world," she wrote many years later, "they stood quite outside of it, and never would see it as it was. . . ." She also wrote:

my hair down my back. Then I prance up and down the room as if I was possessed, and as the lines come to me I *dash* them on the blackboard, one after another, and chant them in a loud voice. Sometimes I cover all four of the boards—both sides—before the Inspiration leaves me. The frail Body is overcome by the excitement of the Soul, and at night my husband often finds me lying on the floor in the middle of the room, panting—panting! [Bayard Taylor, *John Godfrey's Fortunes* (New York: G. P. Putnam and Sons, 1871), pp. 228, 229, 274, 275.]

Whether Alcott, Emerson, and their disciples discussed pears or the [Civil] war, their views gave them the same sense of unreality, of having been taken, as Hawthorne said, at too long a range. You heard much sound philosophy and many guesses at the eternal verities; in fact, never were the eternal verities so dissected and pawed over and turned inside out as they were about that time, in Boston, by Margaret Fuller and her successors. But the discussion left you with a vague, uneasy sense that something was lacking, some back-bone of fact. Their theories were beautiful bubbles blown from a child's pipe, floating overhead, with queer reflections on them of sky and earth and human beings, all in a glow of fairy color and all a little distorted.

Mr. Alcott once showed me an arbor which he had built with great pains and skills for Mr. Emerson to "do his thinking in." It was made of unbarked saplings and boughs, a tiny round temple, two storied, with chambers in which were seats, a desk, etc., all very artistic and complete, except that he had forgotten to make any door. You could look at it and admire it, but nobody could go in or use it. It seemed to me a fitting symbol for this guild of prophets and their scheme of life.[10]

Although the transcendental villagers in Concord had much in common with their Boston cousins, the Concord community was exceptional in that most literary and intellectual communities in Romantic America were firmly tied to cities. Concord might share with Boston a felt need for social reform, and Boston might listen with interest to transcendental doctrine, but in general, the country village maintained a distinct literary and intellectual as well as geographical identity. In *Walden,* of course, Concord produced its best-known reply to Boston's mannered life and growing materialism and wealth. Although Holmes and Lowell wrote much in praise of nature and rural life, these writings, placed next to Thoreau's, seem stale and unconvincing—the work of cultivated gentlemen with little true sympathy for their subjects. One need only compare Thoreau's *The Maine Woods,* the sympathetic record of a naturalist, with Lowell's *A Moosehead Journal* (1853), full of learned and irrelevant observations, to understand the difference between Concord and Boston.

The Concord community excepted, Romantic America offered the paradox of writers living, by and large, in cities and yet idealizing, in their writings, the country. Not surprisingly, therefore, the country, as it appeared in their writings, was covered by a very civilized veneer. Downing, whose ideal rural homes showed all the marks of learning and cultivated taste, provided the images of rural life which had the widest appeal. Country life in Romantic American literature—a literature written in large part, it seems, by authors whose lives were centered in the city—owes much to such models as Irving's Sunnyside, the home of the gentleman sojourning in the country.

THE AMERICAN LAKE DISTRICT, as Richard Birdsall has labeled that literary and intellectual community which flourished in the Berkshires around the middle of the nineteenth century, had particular significance for American writers; here, after all, they could reacquaint themselves with both the rural virtues and the landscapes which they praised in their writings, and here, at the same time, they could maintain their close professional friendships.[11] Located in the Berkshire hills of western Massachusetts, the community—which had grown as much by accident as by design—was centered in the country villages of Stockbridge and Lenox, but writers and editors were to be found living or visiting in the neighboring towns as well. It was an ideal spot for the writer—complete not only with picturesque landscapes but also with literary figures of quite substantial reputations.*

In A Wonder-Book (1851), Hawthorne has the character Eustace Bright, speaking here apparently for Hawthorne himself, outline the literary geography of the region:

> For my part, I wish I had Pegasus here, at this moment. . . . I would mount him forthwith, and gallop about the country, within a circumference of a few miles, making literary calls on my brother-authors. Dr. Dewey would be within my reach, at the foot of Taconic. In Stockbridge, yonder, is Mr. [G. P. R.] James, conspicuous to all the world on his mountain-pile of history and romance. Longfellow, I believe, is not yet at the Ox-bow, else

* The Berkshires have never ceased to attract American writers, and, for that matter, composers and artists as well. Henry Adams, Mark Twain, Edith Wharton, and Henry James either visited or lived there. What rural village other than Stockbridge could simultaneously harbor both Arlo Guthrie and Norman Rockwell? After Norman Mailer signed a contract to write a novel with a million dollar advance, he settled down to write it—in Stockbridge.

the winged horse would neigh at the sight of him. But, here in Lenox, I would find [Miss Sedgwick] our most truthful novelist, who has made the scenery and life of Berkshire all her own. On the hither side of Pittsfield sits Herman Melville, shaping out the gigantic conception of his 'White Whale,' while the gigantic shape of Graylock looms upon him from his study-window. Another bound of my flying steed would bring me to the door of Holmes, whom I mention last, because Pegasus would certainly unseat me, the next minute, and claim the poet as his rider.[12]

Other residents of, or visitors to, this area included Emerson, Lowell, Irving, Simms, and many others, including Bryant, who lived for a time in the neighboring village of Great Barrington and later established his summer residence at his family homestead in the nearby settlement of Cummington. The country home which Henry Ward Beecher glorified in *Star Papers* was in fact a Lenox farm, and the pastoral settings which he praised in that book were for the most part in the Berkshires.

Another visitor, George William Curtis, wrote:

There was no sense of imprisonment in the hills, no feeling of oppression, and as [the visitor's] eye turned north to the tranquil dignity of Greylock it was only to confess that neither Bryant, nor Hawthorne, nor Miss Sedgwick, nor Hermann [sic] Melville, all of whom had made their home in Berkshire, had too warmly praised the beauty or described the character of its landscape.[13]

Curtis's statement is in part misleading, of course—as the nightmarish Berkshire landscapes in *Pierre* suggest. However, the hills continued to attract writers, who in turn used the landscapes and the hilltowns in fiction: Miss Sedgwick's *A New-England Tale* and *Home*, Longfellow's *Kavanagh* (1849), and Holmes's *Elsie Venner* (1861), among others.

The Sedgwick family was at the center of the American Lake District. There had been Sedgwicks in the Berkshires far back into the eighteenth century, and the *pater familias*, Theodore Sedgwick, Sr., had been the region's hero, when he served as Speaker of the United States House of Representatives during Washington's administration. By the 1840s and 1850s, the family was indisputably at the head of the local gentry. Most famous among the Sedgwicks as a writer was Catharine, but two of her

sisters-in-law, Elizabeth Dwight Sedgwick and Susan Anne Liv-
ingston Ridley Sedgwick, had obtained considerable reputations
as writers for children. Susan Sedgwick's didactic tales were particularly popular—at least among parents in search of moral
fiction for the young. The Sedgwick brothers, Henry, Robert,
and Theodore, were all dead by 1850 but were remembered particularly for their writings on politics and economics. Other
members of the family married literati from Boston and New
York, and so the Sedgwicks formed a rather formidable literary
clique in themselves.

According to the *Cyclopedia of American Literature*, compiled
by Evert and George Duyckinck, the "wide-spread celebrity" of
Stockbridge was "to be ascribed far more to the reputation
which Miss Sedgwick's descriptions and works have given it,
than to its great natural advantages."[14] The town, as *Home* and
various other Sedgwick works certified, was blissfully domestic
and rural, although it is true that her first novel, *A New-England
Tale*, had portrayed Stockbridge as a harbor for bigotry. But
A New-England Tale was published in 1822, and by the 1850s—
indeed, even by the 1830s, when she wrote *Home*—Miss Sedgwick's attitude toward this mountain village had mellowed considerably. Every summer she returned to Stockbridge or to the
neighboring town of Lenox and was eager to introduce visitors
and other summer residents to Berkshire townspeople and landscapes.

The American Lake District was essentially a summer literary
colony, although Melville, Hawthorne, and a few others lived
here year round. During the summer months, Miss Sedgwick
performed the duties that in New York fell to Anne Charlotte
Lynch. Her soirees and afternoon teas provided ways for the
literary lions to get together and to meet other famous writers
who were visiting the region. The Shakespearean actress Fanny
Kemble was often present at the evening gatherings, and it has
been said that none of them "was ever considered complete until
she had read a scene from *Macbeth* or had sung a Scotch or
German ballad to her own accompaniment."[15]

Kemble—together with Elizabeth, Susan, and Catharine Maria
Sedgwick—was one of the Lake District's "inner circle." Opin-
ionated woman and feminist that she was, Kemble would surely

have been unhappy in the Berkshires, or anywhere in America, were it not for the literary and intellectual society which gathered around the Sedgwicks. Even so, more than once Kemble found herself in trouble with literary visitors to the region and with local residents. Harriet Beecher Stowe was shocked by her profanity, and even as august a figure as Charles Sumner was humbled by her. "I confess to a certain awe and sense of her superiority," he wrote, "which makes me at times anxious to subside into my own inferiority and leave the conversation to be sustained by other minds."[16] Meanwhile, Berkshire's moral watchdogs were outraged when one of her guests was found drunk and naked. At another time, she joined some of her friends in a party of "eating, drinking, dancing, singing, tearing, climbing, and screaming."[17] Local residents, who had never been able to affect her by other means, pelted the famous actress and her friends with rotten eggs.

MELVILLE HAD KNOWN THE BERKSHIRES from boyhood, for as a child, he visited at the Pittsfield farm of his uncle Thomas Melville, and at one time, he returned to the Berkshires to teach at a district school. However, his purchase of a home near Lenox in September 1850 may have had less to do with his earlier connections with the region than with his new friendship with Hawthorne, whom he had met only a few weeks earlier but who seemed to him a literary master, a companion fit perhaps for the bard of Avon.

Hawthorne had moved to the Berkshires the previous spring, and as was his custom wherever he went, he set up decided social barriers. Of course, the Sedgwicks indefatigably tried to break through the social reserve. Certainly the now famous author of *The Scarlet Letter* would have been a distinguished addition to their literary gatherings. By the first of August, Sophia Hawthorne was telling her mother that "The truest friendliness is the great characteristic of the Sedgwick family in all its branches," and that "they really take the *responsibility* of my being comfortable, as if they were mother, father, brother, sister."[18] Within a few months of her arrival, Sophia had been taken to Stockbridge's Laurel Hill—a place of particular pride to the community since it was the setting of one of the major episodes in *Hope Leslie*. By December, the Sedgwicks had made numerous forays into Hawthorne country, and yet the great author remained as secluded as, under the circumstances, he could. Only once did he call at the Sedgwick home in Lenox and then only because "he was especially invited to spend the day."[19] Throughout his stay in the Berkshires, Hawthorne remained socially distant from the Sedgwicks; he met them on the streets and, rarely, at social gatherings, but their offers of friendship went largely unacknowledged.*

---

* It is worth noting again that Hawthorne in a passage quoted above referred to Miss Sedgwick as "our most truthful novelist." It was indeed as a *novelist* that she made her most significant contributions to literature. Her best novels made considerable use of New England characteristics, manners, customs, history, scenery, and so forth, and this aspect of her fiction may well have attracted Hawthorne's admiration, for he too, of course, was deeply interested in aspects of New England life, history, and setting. However, she had published no novels between 1835 and 1850, the year Hawthorne moved to the Berkshires. In the intervening fifteen years, her writings had consisted primarily of didactic tales, sentimental stories and sketches, and etiquette books for children. To call her "our most truthful novelist" was in effect to single out her early, admirable works and, at the same time, to ignore her later, less ambitious writings.

Hawthorne's comment on Miss Sedgwick in "The Hall of Fantasy" is also easily misread. In this sketch, he imagines a gathering which includes, among others, Longfellow, Irving, and Holmes—all of whom were highly regarded at the time the sketch was published (1843). Among them is Miss Sedgwick—"an honored guest," he says, but then adds that ". . . the atmosphere of the Hall of Fantasy is not precisely the light in which she appears to most advantage." On the one hand, it might seem that Hawthorne would like to exclude her from the literary gathering—not altogether an unlikely possibility, for in the preceding sentence, Hawthorne claims that "A number of ladies among the tuneful and imaginative crowd" do not possess all the credentials to be there. Their literary efforts have clearly been less successful than ambitious. But Hawthorne is not including her among these women; she does not appear "to most advantage" in the Hall of Fantasy, he implies, precisely because her realistic fiction is far from fantasy. Unlike the other writers, she was known for her realistic pictures of New England life and custom—at least, that is, until she started writing her didactic tales, sentimental fiction, and so forth. As in *A Wonder-Book*, Hawthorne here

Although Hawthorne had little to do with the Sedgwicks and other members of the American Lake District, he did agree to accompany various writers in early August on an outing among Berkshire landscapes associated with the writings of the senior members of the Lake District, Miss Sedgwick and Bryant. In the morning, before Hawthorne arrived, several in the group climbed Laurel Hill and then, with Hawthorne in attendance, Monument Mountain, the setting for Bryant's poem of that name. Later they hiked through Icy Glen, which Miss Sedgwick had described in *A New-England Tale,* then stopped at the summer home of a New York lawyer. Here they met the famous author herself, drank tea, and discussed *Hope Leslie.*

Among those whom Hawthorne joined that day were Evert Duyckinck, Cornelius Mathews, James T. Fields (Hawthorne's publisher), Oliver Wendell Holmes, Joel Tyler Headley, and Herman Melville. This was, of course, Hawthorne's first introduction to Melville and the beginning of the only close literary friendship which either of them was to maintain in the Lake District. Shortly after they met, Hawthorne invited Melville to spend a few days with him (a most uncharacteristic invitation, the Sedgwicks must have thought), and Melville began his famous review of Hawthorne's *Mosses from an Old Manse* for Duyckinck's *Literary World.* Within a few weeks, Melville decided to leave his New York home and buy a farm in the Berkshires. Most of the literati fled the hills before the first snowfall, but Melville and Hawthorne settled in for the harsh Berkshire winter.

From late fall until early spring, the two men encountered more farmers than writers in the hills, but following the spring

---

appears to have singled out her early, realistic works for attention. By 1850, Miss Sedgwick had long since forsaken the profession of novelist. (She did publish one final novel, *Married or Single?* (1857), before her death, but it was her weakest novel and received little popular or critical attention.) Preoccupied as a writer with sentimental, didactic fiction and essays and as a hostess with her literary teas and soirees, she clearly had little to offer Hawthorne, who at the time was at work on *The House of the Seven Gables* and, later, *The Blithedale Romance.* [Nathaniel Hawthorne, "The Hall of Fantasy," *The Pioneer,* I (1843), 51.]

thaw, literary representatives of Boston and New York began returning to the Berkshires. Just down the road from Melville lived Oliver Wendell Holmes. Hawthorne's neighbor and landlord, William Aspinwall Tappan, was a writer and had married Caroline Sturgis, Emerson's friend and a contributor to *The Dial*.* The Sedgwicks were, of course, within walking distance. As soon as summer arrived, the literary community must have been virtually unavoidable—its representatives were next door or just down the road. Nonetheless, despite the probable interruptions from literary neighbors, Melville and Hawthorne were able to accomplish much significant work during the summer months. Melville, as is well known, spent part of the summer in New York, where *Moby-Dick* was completed and set in type, but he also spent much time in the Berkshires, where he began work on *Pierre* and where Hawthorne began *The Blithedale Romance*.

CERTAINLY NEITHER PIERRE NOR THE BLITHEDALE ROMANCE was written to please the literary society that gathered in the Berkshires. In one novel, the hero flees from Berkshire's pastoralism, while in the other, the narrator ultimately chooses the city over the country. (Soon after Hawthorne began *The Blithedale Romance*, he deserted the Berkshires for the neighborhood of Boston; he was by that time as disenchanted with rural life as the narrator of his novel.) But both novels were concerned with far more, of course, than inadequacies of the rural world idealized in other American writings. The reformers among Berkshire's literati—and there were many reformers in that group— would have had good reason to be annoyed, indeed offended, by both Hawthorne and Melville's rather savage attacks on those

* Emerson met Tappan in New York—"a lonely beautiful brooding youth," he said, "who sits at a desk six hours of the day in some brokerage or other"—and introduced him to Caroline. They were married in 1847, three years before leasing their red cottage in the Berkshires to Hawthorne. While the Hawthornes lived in the cottage, the Tappans occupied what had been, from 1844 to 1850, the home of yet another of Emerson's friends, Samuel Gray Ward. [Ralph Waldo Emerson, *Letters* (New York: Columbia University Press, 1939), vol. III, p. 149.]

endlessly optimistic Americans, reformers in general and utopians in particular. The objects of Hawthorne's criticism, of
course, were the socialist utopians who composed much of the
Blithedale community, and as we have seen, *Pierre* is in part an
assault on that nineteenth-century utopian sensibility which
found—or presumably found—all human virtue and happiness
within the home.

In characterizing Blithedale, Hawthorne, as is well known,
drew heavily on his experiences at Brook Farm—the utopian
community which George Ripley inauspiciously founded on
April Fool's Day, 1841. Some thought that Hawthorne's copy
was a little too close to the original. F. B. Sanborn, for example,
claimed that Hawthorne "had gone beyond what strict delicacy
demanded in his treatment of former associates at Brook Farm,
some of whom I knew."[20] But it seems likely that Berkshire as
well as Brook Farm contributed to Hawthorne's characterization
of Blithedale. Hawthorne had spent a few months at Brook
Farm—not because he shared the community's social theories
but because, quite practically, he was looking for a means of
supporting himself and, eventually, his prospective wife. But the
community, he soon found, would not leave him with sufficient
time to write; it was continually impinging on his time. Nor
could he sympathize with these utopians who had blindly forsaken their cities and towns in the belief that earthly paradise
was to be found on a farm in West Roxbury, Mass. In 1851, ten
years after his experiences at Brook Farm, Hawthorne, then living in the Berkshires, had reason to remember his early life. Time
and place had changed, but once again he found himself among
utopians of a sort. Again he could hear recited the litany of rural
life, and again he was surrounded by a group altogether willing
to occupy his time. The difference lay, of course, in the fact that
in the Berkshires Hawthorne was able to keep the neighboring
intelligentsia socially at a distance, but members of, and visitors
to, the American Lake District could not be avoided entirely.
Once, in fact, Hawthorne tried to escape from a literary visitor
by hiding in the garden.

The Berkshires, like Brook Farm and Blithedale, were filled
with the spirit of reform. Among the numerous Sedgwicks, to

cite the obvious example, were highly vocal advocates of Abo-
lition and educational reform. But to discover reformers in the
Berkshires, Hawthorne needed to look no further than his neighbors; in fact Mrs. Tappan had been a member of the Brook Farm
community, and when Hawthorne wished to read Fourier's works
"with a view to my next romance"—*Blithedale*, of course—he
had only to ask her husband; they were part of his library.[21]
When Hawthorne created Zenobia, he had available for a model
not only Margaret Fuller, a visitor at Ripley's community who
was a feminist and a woman of decidedly independent opinion,
but also the Sedgwicks' friend, Fanny Kemble.* Berkshire as
well as Brook Farm could have found itself reflected—and not
to advantage—in Blithedale.

If Hawthorne's novel seemed disagreeable to some of Berkshire's literati, Melville's would have seemed the less tactful and,
therefore, the more reprehensible. In the Berkshires, of course,
it was treasonous to criticize the home, for here, as we know,
the high priestess of domesticity—herself a spinster—made her
summer home. But like Hawthorne, Melville appears to have
had little to do with the Sedgwicks and their friends and surely
did not share their utopian ideals.† Furthermore, Melville's
"Poor Man's Pudding and Rich Man's Crumbs" is certainly, as
Richard Birdsall has conjectured, "a savage satire on the com-
placent attitude of such books as Catharine Sedgwick's *The Poor*

* If the Hawthornes had not left the Berkshires, which they did in
late November 1851, they probably would have rented Kemble's
home in Lenox. She had recently left for a visit in England, and the
Hawthornes could have had for themselves, at a very modest rent, a
home far more comfortable than the Tappans' very small and crowded
cottage. Incidentally, Kemble may have served Melville's literary
purposes as well as Hawthorne's, for she is thought to be the original
for Goneril in *The Confidence Man* (1857).

† On the other hand, as a child, Melville almost certainly knew
Miss Sedgwick and other members of her family. Until the Melvilles
settled in Albany in 1830, they were, like the Sedgwicks, among
New York City's social elite. Incidentally, the house in which Melville
spent most of his early childhood, 55 Courtlandt Street in New York,
became in the mid-1820s the home of Henry Dwight Sedgwick,
Miss Sedgwick's brother.

Rich Man, and the Rich Poor Man."[22] And in turn, *Pierre* is in part a satire on such bibles of domesticity as *Home*.

In this novel and in *The Blithedale Romance*, Melville and Hawthorne placed the Sedgwicks' world, the middle-class world of nineteenth-century America, under the literary microscope and found little worth salvaging. If ever novels were written *not* to please a middle-class audience, it was these, and this may in part explain why they were both among their respective authors' least popular works. While the travel books of Bayard Taylor, domestic novels, and didactic tales for children sold in the tens of thousands, sometimes in the hundreds of thousands, *Pierre* went largely unnoticed and unread. *The Blithedale Romance* received more attention than did *Pierre*, and yet it must have seemed negligible attention beside that which was given such contemporary best sellers as *The Wide, Wide World* and *Uncle Tom's Cabin*. "What I feel most moved to write," Melville once told Hawthorne, "that is banned,—it will not pay."[23]

Catharine Maria Sedgwick's comments on *The Blithedale Romance* and *Pierre*—if indeed she ever read them—apparently do not survive, but her comments on *The House of the Seven Gables* may suggest the sorts of things she would have said about them. Not surprisingly, she found little to praise in that novel. It was like "a passage through the wards of an insane asylum, or a visit to specimens of morbid anatomy." Undoubtedly the book had "the unity and simple construction of a Greek tragedy," and yet it lacked "the relief of divine qualities of great events." Hawthorne, she said, had failed "in the essentials of a work of art; there [was] not essential dignity in the characters to make them worth the labor spent on them." When she read a novel, she wished to find not "corruption, barrenness and decay" but rather "elixirs, cordials, and all the kindliest resources of the art of fiction." (Predictably, she concluded that *Wuthering Heights*—another novel notably lacking in elixirs and cordials—was a waste of time, "a most signal waste of talent."[24]

THE HAWTHORNES LEFT THE BERKSHIRES in the midst of a November snowstorm in 1851 and settled in the eastern part of the state. The poet William Ellery Channing, who had visited in Lenox and Stockbridge while Hawthorne was living there,

congratulated him on his descent from the hills: "I am glad you
have shortened your longitude, and evacuated that devilish
institution of Spitzbergen,—that ice-plant of the Sedgwicks. . . ."[25]
Hawthorne, as one would guess, left the hills with few regrets.
Earlier he had written to a friend in Boston, "I have stayed here
too long and too constantly." His neighbors might have been
interested in the statement that followed: "To tell you a secret,
I am sick to death of Berkshire. . . ."[26]

HAWTHORNE'S EXPERIENCES IN THE BERKSHIRES were in effect
a prelude to his experiences in England and Europe. The social
optimism which characterized Americans in the Berkshires and
Boston was with them, Hawthorne found, when they traveled
abroad and was the most obvious sign of their provinciality.
Americans, as Hawthorne recorded in *The Marble Faun,* went
abroad with a fairly specific sense of what they wanted to find
and then spent their time trying to find it. In the meantime,
their optimism and their innocence prevented them from ever
honestly coming to terms with their European experiences. Confronted with moral and social problems which their cultural
background had not prepared them for, they turned their backs
on Europe and, like the hero and heroine of *The Marble Faun,*
returned home. In this novel, it is, once again, idealized domesticity which is offered, at least by the Americans in the book, as
the cure for social ills. At the end of the book, the hero and
heroine, having seen more of Europe than they wished, return
in fact to Downing's world of "smiling lawns and tasteful
cottages."

American provinciality, Hawthorne must have realized, was
especially evident in Italy; here the American travelers, while
professing a great interest in, if not always a great knowledge
of, Italian art and the classical past, showed little positive interest in the region's contemporary life. Protestants that they were,
they found little which pleased them in the rituals and doctrines of the Catholic church. Protestant America seemed to be
morally superior to Catholic Italy, and the beggars and peas-
ants—however picturesque they may have seemed in travelers'
sketchbooks—were taken as signs of the peninsula's social and
political decay. At times Italian landscapes, which had long been
praised by English and European travelers, were dismissed by

Americans as inferior to those which they had left at home.*
Cooper and Margaret Fuller came to the rescue of Italian landscapes, but few Americans were willing to admit that Italy
could equal or surpass the landscapes of the Hudson River, Lake
George, or Niagara Falls.

The provinciality of the American in Italy is illustrated by an
incident which occurred when Benjamin West visited Rome. He
was among the first Americans to go there, and when he arrived
—this exotic, this savage from across the ocean—he became, as
one would expect, a local sensation: how would this young man
from a continent where great art was virtually unknown react
to the wealth of art gathered in Rome? Whatever the Romans
expected, they were disconcerted when West, seeing the Apollo
Belvedere for the first time, said that it looked like a Mohawk
warrior. The Indian was supposed to suggest savagery; the
statue, civilized ideals; yet West implied that the dignity and
heroic stature of the ideal Mohawk paralled that of the statue.
If the Romans were at first disconcerted by West's comment,
they were pleased (or relieved) when they learned that he had
intended it as a compliment. Still, in the surety of their cultural
traditions, some of them must have continued to wonder if their
visitor weren't a little brazen—or mad.

American travelers found much to criticize in nineteenth-century Italy, but their profound respect for Italian art and the
classical past was usually strengthened. Henry Wadsworth Longfellow's description of a visit to the Coliseum suggests well the
intensity of American respect for the classical past. Longfellow
went to the Coliseum at midnight, for it was generally considered essential for the tourist to see the place by moonlight—
"the hour, the silence, and the colossal ruin have such a mastery
over the soul. . . ." From a distance, the Coliseum seemed "like
a cloud resting upon the earth," but as he approached "the
majestic ruin," now dark and silent, he thought of the Roman
throngs which had gathered there. Within, lit by moonlight,

---

* It is worth noting that Samuel Hammond, in the passage quoted
near the beginning of Chapter Three, claimed that a landscape which
he saw in upstate New York was one "which . . . no painter could
transfer to canvas, or Italy excel"—a remarkable conclusion, since
Hammond had never been to Italy.

". . . the columns [stood] majestic and unbroken, amid the ruin around them, and [seemed] to defy 'the iron tooth of time'." He looked out across the amphitheater: the past

> . . . was before me in one of its visible and most majestic forms. The arbitrary distinctions of time, years, ages, centuries were annihilated. I was a citizen of Rome! This was the amphitheatre of Flavius Vespasian!
>
> Mighty is the spirit of the past, amid the ruins of the Eternal City![27]

Achievements in Italian art were approached with as much reverence as the monuments of the past. American artists in particular looked upon a visit to Italy as an event of overwhelming significance in their careers. American reverence for Italian art was underscored by the fact that Thomas Cole, Horatio Greenough, and Robert Weir lived, at various times, in houses which were thought to have been at one time residences of Claude Lorrain, and in Rome, Robert Vanderlyn lived in what had been the home of Salvator Rosa. Like their compatriots, American painters and sculptors abroad were far less interested in the Italy of the present than the Italy of the past, and their business abroad was in effect to create an American art which would rival the art of the past. Like Americans in general, they accepted the dictum, discussed in Chapter One, that "Europe is Memory, America is Hope."

Hawthorne had considerable interest in classical mythology and the classical past, but it was clearly Sophia's interest in art which determined the nature of their stay in Italy.* Many years earlier, she had received some training as a painter, and she shared the contemporary American opinion that Italy must be the ultimate destination of any artist's pilgrimage. There were few works by the Italian masters in America, and almost all of them were in private collections. American artists, or at least those who had enough money, studied in Italy, where they could find abundant works by the masters.

* While others were insisting on the need for American themes in American literature, Hawthorne appropriated classical mythology and brought it to the Berkshire hills for *The Wonder Book* (1851). His knowledge of classical mythology is also, of course, evident throughout *The Marble Faun*.

Sophia had been recognized as an artist of some ability by Thomas Doughty and Washington Allston, both of whom demonstrated in their paintings a close sympathy for the works of the Italian masters. She was particularly interested in the paintings of Salvator Rosa and had copied some of them. Her visit to Italy must have been as overwhelmingly important to her as such visits were to Cole, Allston, and other major American artists of her time.

For his part, however, Hawthorne had little interest in painting, and despite his wife's enthusiasm, he remained unexcited by the great collections. In Rome, as he wrote, he was "continually turning away disappointed from the landscapes of the most famous among the old masters, unable to find any charm or illusion in them." When he did find a painting which he considered worthy of particular attention—Guido Reni's "Beatrice Cenci," for example—his recorded impressions were largely literary; Guido's work was "the most profoundly wrought picture in the world," but, he added, ". . . we bring all our knowledge of the Cenci tragedy to the interpretation of it."[28] In *The Marble Faun,* the painting is discussed at much length—not because of its aesthetic value, but because of the seeming ambiguities in the character it expresses.

THE MARBLE FAUN is in large measure Hawthorne's letter home, his report as a tourist in mid-nineteenth-century Italy. Its descriptions of Rome and the Italian countryside, it is well known, were in some instances lifted from his journal; they are meticulous, detailed; and they would be superfluous for a reader who had spent much time in Italy. The descriptions have the value of a guidebook, and so it should not surprise us that by 1879, Henry James could write that *The Marble Faun* was "part of the intellectual equipment of the Anglo-Saxon visitor to Rome, and [was] read by every English-speaking traveler who [arrived] there, who [had] been there, or who [expected] to go."[29] But the book was a letter home in other respects, for while its descriptions could be taken as the notes of a tourist, the narrative taught Americans that Europe could offer a rich spiritual and intellectual life—but only after the forfeit of certain American ideals. This conclusion, which is thematically central to the novel, is suggested in the dramatic confrontation of two American artists, Hilda and Kenyon, with European experiences which seem far more complex and morally ambiguous than anything they have encountered in America.

As Hawthorne understood it, art should provide an idealized representation of nature, and so he considered artists to be copyists of a sort, confined to recording reality, but eliminating nature's errors or mistakes. Hilda and Kenyon are in effect copyists of European history and art, for Kenyon's finest work is a statue of Cleopatra, and Hilda's greatest efforts go into making a copy of Guido Reni's "Beatrice Cenci." These are indeed strange subjects for artists who are descendants of the Puritans, particularly for Hilda, whose "womanhood," says Kenyon, "is of the ethereal type, and incompatible with any shadow of darkness or evil." But Hilda is an optimist and an idealist; confronted with the threat of evil, "the white shining purity of [her] nature" ultimately carries her through to an ideal, contented life.[30] She is perfectly the nineteenth-century American's virtuous woman, modest, submissive, and pure.

Hilda witnesses an incident which Hawthorne explicitly intends his reader to interpret as an allegory of the Fall of Man. Among Hilda and Kenyon's friends is Donatello, an Italian count who seems to have inherited the innocence of the Golden Age —or of Eden. But at the behest, or what he thinks is the behest, of another of Kenyon and Hilda's European friends, he commits a murder, seen by Hilda. It is her "first actual discovery that sin is in the world." "Adam falls anew, and Paradise, heretofore in unfaded bloom, is lost again, and closed forever, with the fiery swords gleaming at its gates."[31] Donatello, whose character was previously marked by innocence and gaiety, is marked now by sorrow—but also by wisdom. Somehow his sin ends not only in punishment but in moral and intellectual education as well. He has lost his innocence but acquired a profound sense of human tragedy, a sense which might never have been his without the empirical knowledge of sin.

Hilda is told that people who are like the count when he was still marked by innocence—that is, who are like Adam before the Fall—"have no longer any business on earth, or elsewhere." They were "compounded especially for happiness," but "Life has grown so sadly serious, that such men must change their nature, or else perish, like the antediluvian creatures, that required, as the condition of their existence, a more summer-like atmosphere than ours." But "hopeful and happy-natured Hilda" refuses to accept this, nor will she accept the explanation which Kenyon advances, namely that Donatello's remorse for his crime, "gnawing into his soul, has awakened it; developing a thousand high capabilities, moral and intellectual." Kenyon tells her,

> Here comes my perplexity. Sin has educated Donatello, and elevated him. Is sin, then—which we deem such a dreadful blackness in the universe—is it, like sorrow, merely an element of human education, through which we struggle to a higher and purer state than we could otherwise have attained? Did Adam fall, that we might ultimately rise to a far loftier paradise than his?

But this possibility only horrifies Hilda, backed by her orthodox morality: "This is terrible," she cries, "and I could weep for you, if you indeed believe it." In fact the possibility is no more acceptable to Kenyon than it is to her: "I never did believe it!" he exclaims. Idealists and strict orthodox moralists that they are, Hilda and Kenyon are really fit only for that American world which Hawthorne, in his Preface to the novel, described as one of "commonplace prosperity, in broad and simple daylight."[32] In Europe with its insistent history of human tragedy and sin, they could never be anything more than travelers, passing through. As artists, or copyists, and as Americans, only a select portion of the European experience is morally open to them; when confronted with anything except that portion, they turn away.

Hilda, says Hawthorne at the end of the book, "had a hopeful soul, and saw sunlight on the mountaintops." For Kenyon and her, life seems to be filled with "so much human promise," and they are returning to America, where Hilda, as Hawthorne says in the sentimental language of domestic novelists, will be "enshrined and worshipped as a household Saint, in the light of her husband's fireside."[33] Ideal domesticity will protect her from experiencing anything morally or intellectually unpleasant. An American like Hilda could remain in a state of paradisial innocence as long as it was possible to deal selectively with experience.

HAWTHORNE'S AMERICAN NOTE-BOOKS, said Henry James, offer a picture "characterized by an extraordinary blankness—a curious paleness of color and paucity of detail." American society as suggested in the *Note-Books* seemed to James "crude and simple," and Hawthorne's American experience evidently lacked the richness, density, and warmth of the "European spectacle." Had he been English or French, ". . . his personal life, his sense of the life of his fellow-mortals would have been almost infinitely more various."[34]

The Preface to *The Marble Faun* offers evidence which seems to support James's contentions. The United States, Hawthorne wrote, is a country with "no shadow, no antiquity, no mystery, no picturesque and gloomy wrong, nor anything but a commonplace prosperity, in broad and simple daylight," but as any attentive reader of Hawthorne should realize, American shadows, antiquities, mysteries, picturesque and gloomy wrongs had provided Hawthorne with subjects for nearly all his major fiction written before *The Marble Faun*. Yet there were other American points of view—Emerson's, for instance—which denied or ignored the darker half of American experience. And there were the reformers, such as those who prevailed in the Berkshires and at Brook Farm, who were certain that with time and possibly money the darker half could be eliminated, that if the country was not already a land of "commonplace prosperity, in broad and simple daylight," it eventually would be. Hawthorne's sense of American life was far more complex than his *Note-Books* suggest. As he knew, the problem was not that Americans believed they had, or someday would have, a country of "commonplace prosperity," but that they denied other, darker possibilities.[35] As *The Marble Faun* suggests, the problem with Americans was—and James should have appreciated the distinction—an impoverished point of view.

Notes

1. Oliver Wendell Holmes, *The Autocrat of the Breakfast-Table* (Boston: Houghton, Mifflin and Company, 1882), p. 265.

2. Henry James, *Hawthorne*, in *The Shock of Recognition*, Edmund Wilson, ed. (New York: Grossett and Dunlap, 1955), vol. I, p. 459.

3. James Fenimore Cooper, *Homeward Bound* (Boston: Houghton, Mifflin and Company, n.d.), p. 495.

4. Edgar Allan Poe, *The Literati of New York City, The Complete Works* (New York: Crowell, 1902), vol. XV, p. 9.

5. *Ibid.*, p. 118.

6. John S. Hart, *The Female Prose Writers of America* (Philadelphia: E. H. Butler and Company, 1852), p. 303.

7. Bayard Taylor, *Life and Letters* (Boston: Houghton, Mifflin and Company, 1885), vol. I, p. 115.

8. Sidney P. Moss, *Poe's Literary Battles* (Durham, N.C.: Duke University Press, 1963), *passim*.

9. Nathaniel Hawthorne, *Mosses from an Old Manse* (Columbus, Ohio: Ohio State University Press, 1974), pp. 31–32.

10. Rebecca Harding Davis, *Bits of Gossip* (Boston: Houghton, Mifflin and Company, 1904), pp. 32–33, 36–37.

11. Richard D. Birdsall, *Berkshire County* (New Haven, Conn.: Yale University Press, 1959), p. 323.

12. Nathaniel Hawthorne, *A Wonder-Book* (Columbus, Ohio: Ohio State University Press, 1972), p. 169.

13. [George William Curtis], "Editor's Easy Chair," *Harper's New Monthly Magazine*, XXXV (1867), 665.

14. Evert A. Duyckinck and George L. Duyckinck, *Cyclopedia of American Literature* (New York: 1856), vol. II, p. 242.

15. Birdsall, *op. cit.*, p. 335.

16. Edward L. Pierce, *Memoir and Letters of Charles Sumner* (Boston: Roberts Brothers, 1877), vol. II, p. 319.

17. Birdsall, *op. cit.*, p. 331.

18. Rose Hawthorne Lathrop, *Memories of Hawthorne* (Boston: Houghton, Mifflin and Company, 1897), pp. 130–131.

19. Statement made by Charles Sedgwick, Miss Sedgwick's brother, and quoted by Birdsall, *op. cit.*, p. 358.

20. F. B. Sanborn, *Hawthorne and His Friends* (Cedar Rapids, Iowa: The Torch Press, 1908), p. 55.

21. Julian Hawthorne, *Nathaniel Hawthorne and His Wife* (Boston: James R. Osgood and Company, 1884), vol. I, p. 416.

22. Birdsall, *op. cit.*, p. 373.

23. Julian Hawthorne, *op. cit.*, vol. I, p. 402.

24. Mary E. Dewey, *Life and Letters of Catharine M. Sedgwick* (New York: Harper and Brothers, Publishers, 1871), pp. 328–329, 307.

25. Julian Hawthorne, *op. cit.*, p. 432.

26. James T. Fields, *Yesterdays with Authors* (Boston: Houghton, Mifflin and Company, 1871), p. 62.

27. Henry Wadsworth Longfellow, *Outre-Mer* (Boston: Ticknor and Fields, 1856), pp. 337, 338, 340, 341.

28. Nathaniel Hawthorne, *Passages from the French and Italian Notebooks, Complete Works* (Boston: Houghton, Mifflin and Company, 1888), vol. X, pp. 89, 90.

29. James, *op. cit.*, vol. I, p. 552.

30. Nathaniel Hawthorne, *The Marble Faun* (Columbus, Ohio: Ohio State University Press, 1968), pp. 128, 287.

31. *Ibid.*, p. 204.

32. *Ibid.*, pp. 459–460, 3.

33. *Ibid.*, pp. 462, 461.

34. James, *op. cit.*, vol. I, p. 459.

35. Hawthorne, *The Marble Faun*, p. 3.

Selected Bibliography

I HAVE LIMITED the following bibliography, for the most part, to general works on American literature and its backgrounds between 1817 and 1860. Those who wish additional suggestions should see *Eight American Authors,* edited by James Woodress; *Fifteen American Authors before 1900,* edited by Robert A. Rees and Earl N. Harbert, and *Articles in American Literature,* edited by Lewis Leary. For titles published recently, see the recent issues of the *MLA International Bibliography* and *American Literature.* The annual issues of *MLA Abstracts* provide summaries of many of the studies listed in the *MLA International Bibliography,* and *American Literary Scholarship,* which also appears annually, is a forum in which scholars in American literature discuss and criticize (not always graciously) recent work in their field. A useful guide to American literature and its backgrounds is Clarence Gohdes' *Bibliographical Guide to the Study of the Literature of the U.S.A.* Good bibliographies can also be found, of course, in many of the works listed below.

Much of this book has benefited from various studies which have grown out of the American Studies movement, particularly Henry Nash Smith's *Virgin Land: The American West as Symbol and Myth* (Cambridge, Mass., 1950; new edition, 1970), R. W. B. Lewis's *The American Adam: Innocence, Tragedy, and Tradition in the Nineteenth Century* (Chicago, 1955), Roy Harvey

Pearce's *The Continuity of American Poetry* (Princeton, N.J., 1961), Charles L. Sanford's *The Quest for Paradise* (Urbana, Ill., 1961), Leo Marx's *The Machine in the Garden: Technology and the Pastoral Ideal in America* (New York, 1964), Quentin Anderson's *The Imperial Self: An Essay in American Literature and Cultural History* (New York, 1971), and Richard Slotkin's *Regeneration through Violence: The Mythology of the American Frontier* (Middleton, Conn., 1973). In general, these works examine American literature to see what it says about American civilization—in other words, their program is exactly the reverse of the program of this book, and yet they suggested to me, in many instances, the sort of literary-cultural correspondences with which this book is concerned.

Among the more important recent works which discuss methodology in American Studies and particularly ways in which literary-cultural relationships can be determined, are Richard Slotkin's *Regeneration through Violence* and Cecil F. Tate's *The Search for a Method in American Studies* (Minneapolis, 1973). See also Leo Marx's "American Studies—A Defense of an Unscientific Method," *New Literary History,* I (1969), 75–90; Roy Harvey Pearce's *Historicism Once More: Problems & Occasions for the American Scholar* (Princeton, N.J., 1969); and John William Ward's *Red, White, and Blue: Men, Books, and Ideas in American Culture* (New York, 1969), especially the first section, "History and Culture." A negative but unsatisfactory criticism of Smith, Marx, and others can be found in Bruce Kuklick's "Myth and Symbol in American Studies," *American Quarterly,* XXIV (1972), 435–450.

A study of American Romanticism might begin with Russel B. Nye's *Society and Culture in America: 1830–1860* (New York, 1974) and with the relevant chapters in Howard Mumford Jones's *O Strange New World: American Culture: The Formative Years* (New York, 1964) and *Revolution and Romanticism* (Cambridge, Mass., 1974). A concise introduction to American thought in the Romantic period is Irving H. Bartlett's *The American in the Mid-Nineteenth Century* (New York, 1967). Merle Curti's *The Growth of American Thought,* third edition (New York, 1964), is, of course, the standard work. Perry Miller's *The Life of the Mind in America from the Revolution to the Civil*

War (New York, 1963) was left uncompleted at his death but is still invaluable to the student of the period. Essential to any study of American Romanticism are various essays in Miller's *Errand into the Wilderness* (Cambridge, Mass., 1956) and *Nature's Nation* (Cambridge, Mass., 1967). See also, among countless other studies of American ideas and thought, Yehoshua Arieli's *Individualism and Nationalism in American Ideology* (Cambridge, Mass., 1964); D. H. Meyer's *The Instructed Conscience: The Shaping of the American National Ethic* (Philadelphia, 1972); Roy Harvey Pearce's *The Savages of America: A Study of the Indian and the Idea of Civilization* (Baltimore, Md., 1953), reissued as *Savagism and Civilization: A Study of the Indian and the American Mind* (Baltimore, Md., 1967); and Morton White's *Science and Sentiment in America: Philosophical Thought from Jonathan Edwards to John Dewey* (New York, 1972).

The most comprehensive critical survey of American literature remains the *Literary History of the United States* (New York, 1948), edited by Robert E. Spiller and others, and the best brief introduction to the field is Spiller's *The Cycle of American Literature: An Essay in Historical Criticism* (New York, 1955). For a richly suggestive history of American literature in the Romantic period, see Van Wyck Brooks's *The World of Washington Irving* (New York, 1944), *The Flowering of New England* (New York, 1936), and *The Times of Melville and Whitman* (New York, 1947). Russel B. Nye's *American Literary History: 1607–1830* (New York, 1970) provides an excellent introduction to the early phase of American literary Romanticism. Students with little knowledge of American literature and its cultural setting may find helpful *Backgrounds of American Literary Thought*, third edition (New York, 1974), by Rod W. Horton and Herbert W. Edwards. See also Russell Blankenship's *American Literature as an Expression of the National Mind* (New York, 1931). Benjamin Spencer in *The Quest for Nationality* (Syracuse, N.Y., 1957) deals with the early problem of creating a uniquely American literature, while D. H. Lawrence's *Studies in Classic American* (New York, 1923) remains the most suggestive study of factors which make American literature seem especially American. Documents concerning the problems of

American literary nationalism can be found in *The American Literary Revolution, 1783–1837* (Garden City, N.Y., 1967), edited by Robert E. Spiller.

Among critical studies of mid-nineteenth-century American literature, none has had more influence on subsequent criticism than F. O. Matthiessen's *American Renaissance: Art and Expression in the Age of Emerson and Whitman* (New York, 1941). His study of relationships between the literature and culture of the period has had much beneficial influence on the American Studies movement. Vernon L. Parrington's *Main Currents in American Thought: The Romantic Revolution in America, 1800–1860* (New York, 1927) still makes good reading, even though Parrington is not always sympathetic to his subject. Among studies of the social themes of American literature, see Marius Bewley's *The Eccentric Design: Form in the Classic American Novel* (New York, 1959), A. N. Kaul's *The American Vision: Actual and Ideal Society* (New Haven, Conn., 1963), and James W. Tuttleton's *The Novel of Manners in America* (Chapel Hill, N.C., 1972). Among the many other works which relate American literature to a larger cultural setting are Ursula Brumm's *American Thought and Religious Typology* (New Brunswick, N.J., 1970), translated by John Hoaglund; Leslie A. Fiedler's *Love and Death in the American Novel* (New York, 1960); Daniel Hoffman's *Form and Fable in American Fiction* (New York, 1961); Terence Martin's *The Instructed Vision* (Bloomington, Ind., 1961); and Constance Rourke's *American Humor: A Study of the National Character* (New York, 1931).

Anyone interested in popular American literature should know Russel B. Nye's *The Unembarrassed Muse: The Popular Arts in America* (New York, 1970). Important specialized works include Carl Bode's *The Anatomy of American Popular Culture, 1840–1861* (Berkeley and Los Angeles, 1960), reissued as *Antebellum Culture* (Carbondale, Ill., and Edwardsville, Ill., 1969); James D. Hart's *The Popular Book: A History of America's Literary Taste* (Berkeley and Los Angeles, 1950); and Frank Luther Mott's *Golden Multitudes: The Story of Best Sellers in the United States* (New York, 1947).

Studies of nineteenth-century American writers and their role within their culture include Lewis P. Simpson's *The Man of Letters in New England and the South: Essays on the History*

of the Literary Vocation in America (Baton Rouge, La., 1972)
and William Charvat's *The Profession of Authorship in America,
1800–1870* (1968), edited by Matthew J. Bruccoli. Anyone interested in the rise and fall of literary stocks will want to read Jay
B. Hubbell's *Who Are the Major American Writers? A Study of
the Changing Literary Canon* (Durham, N.C., 1972), and those
who are interested in changing fashions in academic criticism of
American literature should read Richard Ruland's *The Rediscov-
ery of American Literature: Premises of Critical Taste, 1900–
1940* (Cambridge, Mass., 1967).

Part One: The Wilderness

The Erie Canal and its importance to the development of
American civilization are the subjects of George E. Condon's
Stars in the Water (Garden City, N.Y., 1974). The significance
of wilderness landscapes to nineteenth-century American art is
examined in James Thomas Flexner's *That Wilder Image: The
Painting of America's Native School from Thomas Cole to
Winslow Homer* (Boston, 1962). The best recent work on American painting of that period is Barbara Novak's *American Painting in the Nineteenth Century* (New York, 1969). See also her
article "American Landscape: The Nationalist Garden and the
Holy Book," *Art in America,* LX (1972), 46–57. Henry H.
Glassie's "Thomas Cole and Niagara Falls," *The New-York
Historical Society Quarterly,* LVIII (1974), 89–111, is a study
of the complex reactions of one artist to what was certainly the
most famous of American landscapes.

More than a hundred years ago, Henry T. Tuckerman published what is still the best study of travel in America: *America
and Her Commentators, with a Critical Sketch of Travel in the
United States* (New York, 1864). For accounts of the Hudson's
economic and aesthetic importance to nineteenth-century America, see *The Hudson* (New York, 1939) by Carl Carmer and
Chronicles of the Hudson (New Brunswick, N.J., 1971), edited
by Roland Van Zandt. Van Zandt is also the author of a book on
the most famous of antebellum resort hotels in the Catskills:
The Catskill Mountain House (New Brunswick, N.J., 1966). See

also Alf Evers's *The Catskills from Wilderness to Woodstock* (Garden City, N.Y., 1972)—as comprehensive a history of that region as is likely to be written for many years. John K. Howat's *The Hudson River and Its Painters* (New York, 1972) provides illustrations of the Hudson and the region around it by nineteenth-century artists.

Important books on the beautiful, the sublime, and the picturesque include Walter John Hipple's *The Beautiful, the Sublime, and the Picturesque in Eighteenth-Century British Aesthetic Theory* (Carbondale, Ill., 1957), Christopher Hussey's *The Picturesque: Studies in a Point of View* (London, 1927), and Samuel H. Monk's *The Sublime: A Study of Critical Theories in XVIII-Century England* (New York, 1935). Students should also be acquainted with Paul Shepard's *Man in the Landscape: A Historic View of the Esthetics of Nature* (New York, 1967), Arthur A. Ekirch's *Man and Nature in America* (New York, 1963), Hans Huth's *Nature and the American: Three Centuries of Changing Attitudes* (Berkeley and Los Angeles, 1957), and Roderick Nash's *Wilderness and the American Mind* (New Haven, Conn., 1967).

Among books concerned at least in part with American literary responses to wilderness landscapes are those works listed above by Arthur A. Ekirch, Hans Huth, Howard Mumford Jones (*O Strange New World*), Leo Marx (*The Machine in the Garden*), Perry Miller (*Errand into the Wilderness* and *Nature's Nation*), Roderick Nash, Roy Harvey Pearce (*The Savages of America*), Charles L. Sanford, Paul Shepard, Richard Slotkin, and Henry Nash Smith. Also valuable, among many others, are Wilson O. Clough's *The Necessary Earth: Nature and Solitude in American Literature* (Austin, Tex., 1964); Marx's "American Institutions and Ecological Ideals," *Science*, CLXX (1970), 945–952; and Donald A. Ringe's *The Pictorial Mode: Space and Time in the Art of Bryant, Irving, and Cooper* (Lexington, Ky., 1971). Worth special attention is the chapter entitled "The Melvillean Setting" in Warner Berthoff's *The Example of Melville* (Princeton, N.J., 1962). James T. Callow's *Kindred Spirits: Knickerbocker Writers and American Artists, 1807–1855* (Chapel Hill, N.C., 1967) suggests parallel interests in American landscapes among various artists and writers. Edwin Fussell's *Frontier:*

American Literature and the American West (Princeton, N.J., 1965) is concerned with the frontier and the wilderness essentially as literary metaphors. Robert Edson Lee's *From East to West: Studies in the Literature and the American West* (Urbana, Ill., 1966) would have us believe that Western writings—and descriptions of Western landscapes—have long been tainted by aesthetics and sensibilities more at home in the East. Finally, for a superb collection of nineteenth-century paintings of American wilderness, see Patricia Hills's *The American Frontier: Images and Myths* (New York, 1973).

Part Two: Smiling Lawns and Tasteful Cottages

Among general introductions to landscape gardening and its history are G. B. Tobey's *A History of Landscape Architecture: The Relationship of People to Environment* (New York, 1973) and Julia S. Berrall's *The Garden: An Illustrated History* (New York, 1966). There have been many books on landscape gardening in eighteenth-century England, but the most detailed and informative is Christopher Hussey's *English Gardens and Landscapes, 1700–1750* (London, 1967). Other works which provide useful introductions to English landscape gardening include H. F. Clark's *The English Landscape Garden* (London, 1948), Peter Coat's *Great Gardens of Britain* (London, 1967), and Edward Hyams's *The English Garden* (London, 1966). Those who wish to study the subject in more detail will want to read Hyams's *Capability Brown and Humphrey Repton* (New York, 1971) and various other available studies of individual gardeners. All the great English landscape gardens have had their historians, and Stowe, as one would expect, has received the most attention. A detailed history of Stowe's development can be found in *Stowe: A Guide to the Gardens, revised edition* (1968), by Laurence Whistler, Michael Gibbon, and George Clark. A specialized study of much value is Elizabeth Manwaring's *Italian Landscape in Eighteenth-Century England: A Study Chiefly of the Influence of Claude Lorrain and Salvator Rosa on*

English Taste, 1700–1800 (New York, 1925). B. Sprague Allen surveyed the development of landscape gardening in England in his *Tides in English Taste (1619–1800): A Background for the Study of Literature* (Cambridge, Mass., 1937).

A comprehensive history of the landscape gardening movement in America has yet to be published, but brief histories of the subject can be found in such books as Tobey's and Berrall's. Downing and Olmsted, of course, have attracted much scholarly attention, but we do not yet have a full evaluation of Downing's obviously considerable impact on American landscape gardening and architecture. In the meantime, brief evaluations of his historical importance can be found in the books listed above by Carl Carmer, Arthur A. Ekirch, Hans Huth, Roderick Nash, and Paul Shepard, and in Ulysses Prentis Hedrick's *A History of Horticulture in America to 1860* (New York, 1950) and John William Ward's "The Politics of Design," available both in *Red, White, and Blue*, listed above, and in *Who Designs America?* (Garden City, N.Y., 1966), edited by Laurence B. Holland. George B. Tatum's dissertation, "Andrew Jackson Downing" (The University of Pennsylvania, 1950), is the most comprehensive study of Downing which is now available. Books on Olmsted are listed in Part Three below.

In a few quarters, it is still fashionable to dismiss most pre-twentieth-century American architecture as unworthy of more than antiquarian interest. In this century, one of the first and possibly the best defender of nineteenth-century American architecture has been Vincent J. Scully, whose *The Shingle Style and The Stick Style*, revised edition (New Haven, Conn., 1971), is required reading for anyone interested in American architecture of the last century. Scully's views on the subject can also be found in his article "American Houses: Thomas Jefferson to Frank Lloyd Wright" in *The Rise of an American Architecture* (New York, 1970), edited by Edgar Kaufmann, Jr. See also Scully's *American Architecture and Urbanism* (New York, 1969) and *The Architectural History of Newport, Rhode Island: 1640–1915* (Cambridge, Mass., 1952), which Scully co-authored with Antoinette F. Downing.

Among general histories of American architecture, Wayne Andrew's *Architecture, Ambition, and Americans* (New York,

1955) is warmly sympathetic to architecture in the Romantic period. *The Architecture of America: A Social and Cultural History* (Boston, 1961) by John Burchard and Albert Bush-Brown is another well-known historical survey, but its treatment of the nineteenth century is somewhat less sympathetic than Andrews's and is cursory and inadequate. Anyone confused by the welter of styles in American architecture during the Romantic period can find help in Marcus Whiffen's *American Architecture since 1780: A Guide to the Styles* (Cambridge, Mass., 1969). Other general treatments of American architecture include Alan Gowan's *Images of American Living* (Philadelphia, 1964)—a well-written book which can be strongly recommended—and James Marston Fitch's *American Building: The Historical Forces that Shaped It,* revised and enlarged edition (New York, 1973).

An introductory study of Romantic American architecture is James Early's *Romanticism and American Architecture* (New York, 1965). See also *The Gingerbread Age: A View of Victorian America* (New York, 1957) and *The Victorian Home in America* (New York, 1972), both by John Maass. Agnes Addison's *Romanticism and the Gothic Revival* (New York, 1938) is largely superficial and not very helpful. A good visual survey is *Victorian Houses: A Treasury of Lesser-Known Examples* (New York, 1973) by Edmund V. Gillon, Jr., and Clay Lancaster.

English origins for the Gothic Revival in America are recorded in Kenneth Clark's *The Gothic Revival: An Essay in the History of Taste* (London, 1928). Roger Stein's *John Ruskin and Aesthetic Thought in America, 1840–1900* (Cambridge, Mass., 1967) has some interesting things to say about Downing. On Alexander Jackson Davis, see Roger Hale Newton's *Town and Davis: Pioneers in American Revivalist Architecture, 1812–1870* (New York, 1942). Unfortunately Newton's book does not always distinguish between those of Davis's houses which were actually built and those which were left on the drawing board. The book is based on Davis's architectural drawings rather than the houses which were built from them. Jane B. Davies' promised study of Davis will hopefully deal with his work more comprehensively than Newton's study does. For several articles on Lyndhurst, Davis's best-known structure, see *Historic Preservation,* XVII (March–April, 1965).

The definitive study of the Greek Revival is Talbot Hamlin's *Greek Revival Architecture in America* (New York, 1944), but see also William H. Pierson's *American Buildings and Their Architects: The Colonial and Neoclassical Styles* (Garden City, N.Y., 1970), especially chapter X. A recent article which places the Greek Revival in a larger cultural context is James E. Vance's "The Classical Revival and Urban-Rural Conflict in 19th Century North America," *Canadian Review of American Studies*, IV (1973), 149–168. On Monticello, see *Mr. Jefferson: Architect* (New York, 1973) by Desmond Guinness and Julius Trousdale Sadler, Jr.

Dover Publications, Inc. (New York) has reprinted in paperback a number of nineteenth-century American books on architecture. Among those with value for students interested in Romantic American architecture are Andrew Jackson Downing's *The Architecture of Country Houses* (1969), Orson Squire Fowler's *The Octagon House: A Home for All* (1973), and Calvert Vaux's *Villas and Cottages* (1970).

Aside from my comments in Chapter Four, the country book, so far as I know, has never been given much attention as a genre, and except for *Walden,* the individual country books published in the mid-nineteenth century have been generally overlooked by recent scholars and literary historians. Beecher's *Star Papers* and his other writings about the country have been studied, however, in William G. McLoughlin's generally excellent *The Meaning of Henry Ward Beecher: An Essay on the Shifting Values of Mid-Victorian America, 1840–1870* (New York, 1970).

Charles R. Metzger has published a comparative study of *Emerson and Greenough* (Berkeley and Los Angeles, 1954). The chapter on Greenough in Fitch's *American Building* should be read, but his analysis of Greenough's aesthetics—along with similar analyses by other scholars—has been largely superseded by Sylvia Crane's chapter on Greenough's aesthetics in *White Silence: Greenough, Powers, and Crawford: American Sculptors in Nineteenth-Century Italy* (Coral Gables, Fla., 1972). Thoreau's architectural theories have been discussed numerous times, perhaps most comprehensively by Theodore M. Brown in "Thoreau's Prophetic Architectural Program," *New England Quarterly*, XXXVIII (1965), 3–20. See also Metzger's summary of Thoreau's architectural theories in *Thoreau and Whitman: A Study of Their Aesthetics* (Seattle, Wash., 1961).

Barbara Cross's *Horace Bushnell: Minister to a Changing America* (Chicago, 1958) is the definitive book on its subject, but see also Sydney E. Ahlstrom's comments on Bushnell in *A Religious History of the American People* (New Haven, Conn., 1972). E. D. Branch's *The Sentimental Years, 1836–1860* (New York, 1934) is an entertaining history. The best historian of American domesticity is Russell Lynes; see his *The Domesticated Americans* (New York, 1963). A recent specialized study which has received much favorable attention is *Catharine Beecher: A Study in American Domesticity* (New Haven, Conn., 1973) by Kathryn Kish Sklar. The house as a symbol in nineteenth-century American literature is discussed in chapter II, "Images of Value and a Sense of the Past," of Allen Guttmann's *The Conservative Tradition in America* (New York, 1967).

The best book on the domestic novel is Helen Waite Papashvily's *All the Happy Endings: A Study of the Domestic Novel in America, the Women Who Wrote It, the Women Who Read It, in the Nineteenth Century* (New York, 1956). See also Alexander Cowie's *The Rise of the American Novel* (New York, 1948), Russel B. Nye's *The Unembarrassed Muse: The Popular Arts in America* (New York, 1970); Luther Mott's *Golden Multitudes: The Story of Best Sellers in the United States* (New York, 1947); James D. Hart's *The Popular Book: A History of America's Literary Taste* (Berkeley and Los Angeles, 1950); and Carl Bode's *The Anatomy of American Popular Culture, 1840–1861* (Berkeley and Los Angeles, 1960), reissued as *Antebellum Culture* (Carbondale, Ill., and Edwardsville, Ill., 1969). Further treatments of the subject can be found in Herbert Brown's *The Sentimental Novel in America* (Durham, N.C., 1940), William R. Taylor's *Cavalier and Yankee: The Old South and American National Character* (New York, 1961), and Ann D. Wood's "The 'Scribbling Women' and Fanny Fern: Why Women Wrote," *American Quarterly,* CCIII (1971), 3–24. The relationship of *Pierre* to the domestic novel is discussed briefly by Leon Howard in his "Historical Note" to *Pierre* (Evanston, Ill., and Chicago, 1971).

Part Three: Social Realities

The fugitive slave narratives, until recently, were usually available only in large libraries and rare book collections, but several of these narratives have been reprinted in the last few years and are now available in paperback editions. Arna Bontemps included three of them in *Great Slave Narratives* (Boston, 1969), and another three have been reprinted in *Puttin' on Ole Massa* (New York, 1969), edited by Gilbert Osofsky. William Loren Katz is the editor of *Five Slave Narratives* (New York, 1969). *Father Henson's Story of His Own Life* by Josiah Henson is also available in paperback (New York, 1962), and there are several paperback editions of Frederick Douglass's narrative in its various versions. *Incidents in the Life of a Slave Girl* by Linda Brent [Harriet Brent Jacobs] is another fugitive slave narrative now available in paperback (New York, 1973). Historical and critical studies of the narratives include Charles H. Nichols' *Many Thousand Gone: The Ex-Slaves' Account of Their Bondage and Freedom* (Leiden, 1963). See also Jean Fagan Yellin's *The Intricate Knot: Black Figures in American Literature, 1776–1863* (New York, 1972). Finally, for a study of fugitive slaves and other blacks in the North, see Leon Litwak's *North of Slavery* (Chicago, 1961).

Students interested in the nature and problems of nineteenth-century American cities might begin with Kenneth T. Jackson and Stanley K. Schultz, editors, *Cities in American History* (New York, 1972). For a variety of approaches to the subject, see George F. Chadwick's *The Park and the Town: Public Landscape in the 19th and 20th Centuries* (New York, 1966), especially chapter 9, "The American Park Movement"; John W. Rep's *The Making of Urban America: A History of City Planning in the United States* (Princeton, N.J., 1965); Vincent J. Scully's *Urbanism and American Architecture;* and Albert Fein's "The American City: The Ideal and the Real" in *The Rise of an American Architecture,* edited by Edgar Kaufmann, Jr. Writings on the American city by Christopher Tunnard are worth particular attention; see, for example, *The City of Man: A New Approach to the Recovery of Beauty in American Cities* (New York, 1953) and *American Skyline* (Boston, 1953), which he co-authored with Henry Hope Reed. The decline of certain manners and customs which disinguished the old aristocracy is viewed in Stow Persons' *The Decline of American Gentility* (New York, 1973). For visual materials on the nineteenth-century American city and particularly New York, the student will find valuable John A. Kouwenhoven's *The Columbia Historical Portrait of New York: An Essay in Graphic History* (Garden City, N.Y., 1853; reissued, New York, 1972) and Mary Black's *Old New York in Early Photographs: 1853–1901* (New York, 1973).

An interesting but often superficial study of anti-urbanism among American intellectuals is Morton and Lucia White's *The Intellectual versus the City* (Cambridge, Mass., 1962). A better book but one obviously much smaller in scope is Michael H. Cowan's *City of the West: Emerson, America, and Urban Metaphor* (New Haven, Conn., 1967). On the effects of mechanization on American culture, see Siegfried Giedion's *Mechanization Takes Command* (New York, 1948); John A. Kouwenhoven's *Made in America* (Garden City, N.Y., 1948), reissued as *The Arts in Modern American Civilization* (New York, 1967); and Leo Marx's *The Machine in the Garden: Technology and the Pastoral Ideal in America* (New York, 1964).

The rural cemetery is discussed in Hans Huth's *Nature and the American: Three Centuries of Changing Attitudes* (Berkeley and Los Angeles, 1957) and in Roderick Nash's *Wilderness and the American Mind* (New Haven, Conn., 1967). See also Stanley French's "The Cemetery as a Cultural Institution: The Establishment of Mount Auburn and the 'Rural Cemetery' Movement," *American Quarterly*, XXVI (1974), 37–59.

A number of excellent works have been published recently on Frederick Law Olmsted's work and influence. In particular, see *Frederick Law Olmsted's New York* (New York, 1972) by Elizabeth Barlow; *Frederick Law Olmsted, Sr.: Founder of Landscape Architecture in America* (Amherst, Mass., 1968) by Julius Gy. Fabos et al.; *Frederick Law Olmsted and the American Environmental Tradition* (New York, 1972) by Albert Fein; and—the best book to date on the subject—*FLO: A Biography of Frederick Law Olmsted* (Baltimore, 1973) by Laura Wood Roper. An older work, still useful, is *Frederick Law Olmsted, Landscape Architect, 1822–1903* (New York, 1922), edited by Frederick Law Olmsted, Jr., and Theodora Kimball.

On New York's mid-nineteenth-century literary cliques, see Perry Miller's *The Raven and the Whale: The War of Words and Wit in the Era of Poe and Melville* (New York, 1956) and Sidney P. Moss's *Poe's Literary Battles: The Critic in the Context of His Literary Milieu* (Durham, N.C., 1963). On literary Boston, the book to read is Martin Green's *The Problem of Boston: Some Readings in Cultural History* (New York, 1966). We are still in need of a thorough treatment of the literary community in the Berkshires, but for an introduction, the student can turn to the relevant chapters in Richard D. Birdsall's *Berkshire County: A Cultural History* (New Haven, Conn., 1959). In *Catharine Maria Sedgwick* (New York, 1974), I have dealt briefly with Miss Sedgwick's significance to the American Lake District. On Hawthorne and Melville in the Berkshires and on the literary results of that friendship, see especially Leon Howard's *Herman Melville: A Biography* (Berkeley and Los Angeles, 1951); Edward G. Lueders' "The Melville-Hawthorne Relationship in *Pierre* and *The Blithedale Romance*," *Western Humanities Review*, IV (1950), 323–334; Perry Miller's *The Raven and the Whale*, mentioned above; and Charles N. Watson's "The Estrangement of Hawthorne and Melville," *New England Quarterly*, 46 (1973), 380–402. The American Lake District is discussed in Juliet Throckmorton's "In the Sweet Valley of the Housatonic River," *Yankee*, XXXVIII (1974), 78–85, 96–97, but unfortunately the article contains numerous errors of fact.

Americans abroad have been the subject of a considerable number of books, the best of which include Paul R. Baker's *The Fortunate Pilgrims: Americans in Italy, 1800–1860* (Cambridge, Mass., 1964) and Sylvia Crane's *White Silence* (Coral Gables, Fla., 1972). Other studies worth attention include Van Wyck Brooks's *The Dream of Arcadie* (New York, 1958), Ernest Earnest's *Expatriates and Patriots: American Artists, Scholars, and Writers in Europe* (Durham, N.C., 1968), Harold T. McCarthy's *The Expatriate Perspective: American Novelists and the Idea of America* (Rutherford, N.J., 1974) and Nathalia Wright's *American Novelists in Italy* (Philadelphia, 1958).

Index